THE
EDUCATION
OF
KENDRICK
PERKINS

THE EDUCATION OF KENDRICK PERKINS

KENDRICK PERKINS
WITH SETH ROGOFF

ST. MARTIN'S PRESS
NEW YORK

First published in the United States by St. Martin's Press,
an imprint of St. Martin's Publishing Group

www.stmartins.com

Library of Congress Cataloging-in-Publication Data

Names: Perkins, Kendrick, 1984- author. | Rogoff, Seth, 1976- author.
Title: The education of Kendrick Perkins / Kendrick Perkins with Seth Rogoff.
Description: First edition. | New York : St. Martin's Press, [2023]
Identifiers: LCCN 2022039369 | ISBN 9781250280343 (hardcover) |
    ISBN 9781250280350 (ebook)
Subjects: LCSH: Perkins, Kendrick, 1984-. | African American basketball
    player—Biography. | Basketball players—United States—Biography. |
    African American athletes—Political activity.
Classification: LCC GV884.P437 A3 2023 | DDC 796.323092 [B]—dc23/eng/
    20220825
LC record available at https://lccn.loc.gov/2022039369

Our books may be purchased in bulk for promotional, educational, or business use.
Please contact your local bookseller or the Macmillan Corporate and
Premium Sales Department at 1-800-221-7945, extension 5442,
or by email at MacmillanSpecialMarkets@macmillan.com.

First Edition: 2023

10 9 8 7 6 5 4 3 2 1

This book is dedicated to my wife, Vanity,
and our four amazing kids,
Ken, Kenxton, Zoey, and Karter.
To my grandmother, Mary Lewis.
To the memory of my grandfather, Raymond Lewis,
my first elder and my best friend.
To my mama, Ercell Minix.

Contents

THE
EDUCATION
OF
KENDRICK
PERKINS

Prologue

THE ROAD TO BOSTON

IT WAS THE MIDDLE OF AUGUST 2003 WHEN I LEFT BEAUMONT, TEXAS. I WAS EIGHTEEN years old. My friend George Davis and I had decided to drive cross-country to Boston for the start of my NBA career with the Celtics. At the time, I had no way of knowing just how long this journey would be. In some ways, I'm still on the road.

I'd never lived outside Beaumont. Since I was five years old, I hadn't lived anywhere but my grandparents' house—a small, run-down shack on Glenwood Avenue painted yellow with green trim. That's not to say I'd never left Beaumont. I'd traveled around the country to play ball, competing with the youth basketball elite for the attention of college and pro scouts. I'd played in the highest-level camps and tournaments. I'd banged and bruised with the biggest and most skilled players the amateur basketball world had to offer, guys like Dwight Howard and LeBron James.

But that wasn't leaving Beaumont, that was taking Beaumont with me as I went in search of a fantasy—a fantasy dangled right before my eyes. Every player in every game I played in on those trips and in those elite camps thought he was going pro. Each guy dreamed of the NBA contract floating right there. He just needed to reach out, take a pen, and stroke a signature on the bottom and he'd be rich, famous, and set for life. When he opened his eyes, when he woke up in the morning after that sweetest of dreams, what was there? No pen. No paper. No money. Nothing. Just the same grinding poverty, and a day of hard work ahead.

That's what I felt like after those tournaments. I'd be back in my grandparents' house. I'd go to the kitchen and look across the table at their faces as they ate breakfast and got ready for a day of work, my grandfather as a janitor, my grandmother cleaning houses for forty dollars a week. Those two faces, belonging to Mary and Raymond Lewis, were real—every expression, wrinkle, and mark were as real as something could be real for me. I'd sit there for a moment before heading out for a day of training and school, gazing at them, and think that when I left Beaumont, I'd know it, because I would be leaving it forever. I would be going *somewhere*.

I woke up early on the day we left. I'm not one for sentimental good-byes. I didn't tell any of my friends I was leaving on that hot summer morning. The only people who knew we were taking off were my girlfriend, Vanity; my grandparents; and my coach, Andre Boutte. I brought my gear out and packed it into the back of my new Denali, quite a change of ride from the 1993 metallic green Lincoln Town Car in which I'd been cruising my corner of Southeast Texas, "the 409," for years. I climbed into the plush driver's seat and put my hands on the wheel.

Catholic school lessons pushed their way into my mind. Over the years of Catholic school and church, I'd absorbed many stories about going places, setting off, stories about leaving things behind. They were the epic journeys of faith: Lot leaves Sodom and is told by the angels of God not to look back. Lot's wife looks back to face the destruction and is turned into a pillar of salt. Leaving meant going in one direction. Paul leaves Jerusalem on the road to Damascus—he sees Jesus and his whole life shifts; he knows there's no going back to how he lived before. Abraham leaves his home, a place of idolatry, following God's instructions to travel to the Promised Land. No return. Moses parts the sea and takes the people out of Egypt, and the sea closes behind the wanderers, swallowing Pharaoh's army, cutting off the path back into the land of affliction.

Life is full of movements, transitions, and changes large and small; some are epic, others barely visible, even to ourselves. In 2003, I was young. I was big. I was full of ambition. I was headed east to Boston.

As I pulled away from the house on Glenwood Avenue on my way to pick up George, I saw that my grandparents had come outside to the front of the house. In the rearview mirror, I could see the main building of Ozen High; in the side mirror, my grandparents were stoically watching me go. My grandfather was a strict, proud man. He worked hard. He volunteered at the church, dedicated himself to the community. We were close, spending countless days fishing for reds, waking up before dawn to be out on the Gulf's waters before daybreak in his small boat. We'd talk or just be together in silence, enjoying the calm, the time together, the unspoken closeness, the love. On most of those trips, we'd bring back a good catch, which my grandmother would fry up for dinner.

Even though my grandparents worked hard their whole lives, we were poor, and we depended on the fishing for food. We raised chickens and ducks at the house, and each day it was chicken, duck, or fish on the plate. I was, and still am, a country boy.

The yellow house framed my grandparents from the back. The house might have been a cheerful color, but inside the space was hot and cramped. The ceilings were too low for me, and I'd have to walk through with my head bent in order to avoid banging it against the ceiling and doorframes. The light bulbs were uncovered; the walls were thin, affording no privacy. The place had no hallways—we had to walk through one room to get to another. There was a single air-conditioning unit in one of the windows, but we couldn't afford the electricity to run it.

I turned the corner and the whole scene vanished: the house, the ruined sandlot basketball hoop that my grandfather had set up and repaired

countless times when I was a kid, my grandparents, Ozen High in the
background. I didn't want to think about these things and switched on
the radio, immersing myself in the booming, smooth sound that filled
the Denali's cab. A few minutes later, when I pulled up at George's place,
I saw he was already outside waiting for me, bags packed and ready to
go. George threw his two suitcases in the back, got in, unfolded his road
map of the U.S.A., and told me to head out of town on I-10 through Lake
Charles in the direction of Baton Rouge.

What was I leaving behind in Beaumont? The short answer is all I
had and all I was—everything I'd ever known. The long answer is too
long to write here, but here's some of it. I was leaving behind the ghost
of my mama, Ercell Minix, who was murdered when I was five years
old. I carried her memory out of Beaumont's Pear Orchard neighborhood with me, embodied in the small rose tattoo on my shoulder. I was
leaving behind the shadow of my father, Kenneth Perkins. It was the
shadow of a man I hardly knew. I'd heard plenty about him. He had been
a star basketball player at the local Lamar University and had moved
overseas to play when I was about three, leaving me and the rest of the
family behind. Gone. Didn't look back—a man from the tribe of Lot.

I was leaving behind in Beaumont my dominance. It was a combination of size and skill that enabled me to plow through Texas high school
basketball, reigning supreme. My Ozen High School team had been to
three straight Texas state championship games. I'd averaged around 28
points per game at Ozen, over 16 rebounds, and nearly 8 blocks, numbers that surpassed those of Shaquille O'Neal. Our Ozen team had won
over one hundred games in those years against a mere three losses, one
at the hands of future NBA star Chris Bosh's Lincoln High in the 2002
Texas state championship game, another in my final high school game
against Fort Worth Dunbar.

That was high school.

I knew enough about the NBA to know what lay ahead of me. I would be trading my three years of utter domination for a steep climb toward relevance. It would be a battle for survival. In March, some months before the draft, I'd played for the West in the McDonald's All-American Game. On our roster we had guys like Shannon Brown, Aaron Brooks, Kris Humphries, and Leon Powe, all future NBA players. And the East—they had a player named LeBron James and a point guard heading to Wake Forest University named Chris Paul.

These were the biggest high school stars, the best twenty-six players in the nation, and still, many of them didn't make the NBA. Most of the guys who made it didn't last long. The other center for the West that year was Brian Butch. He was a two-time Wisconsin Player of the Year, went to the University of Wisconsin, then wasn't drafted when he came out in 2008. On the other side, the East, the big James Lang tried, like me, to move from high school to pro. He got drafted in the second round by New Orleans but didn't make the team. Jackie Butler, another East center, went to the University of Tennessee, bounced around the NBA for a couple of years, then was gone.

Just being good didn't matter. It was no guarantee, even among the elite, the guys headed to Duke, Kansas, Kentucky, or Michigan State. They had given everything they had to the game; they'd lived and breathed basketball for their first eighteen years. They'd sacrificed more than you can imagine in pursuit of the NBA dream. And they'd made it to the court to play with or against a young LeBron James in Cleveland's Gund Arena in front of eighteen thousand fans.

Little did they know, it was not the beginning for them, but the beginning of the end.

That could have been me, too, at the end of my high school career. I couldn't let that happen.

I drove east. Though our destination was Boston, and I'd been to Boston a few times by this point, I didn't have much of an idea about specifically where I was going. I was *going*. That was enough. When a person is eighteen years old and leaving home for the first time, it doesn't really matter where. What seems to matter is the movement, the path ahead to the next bend in the road. What matters is the speed.

It wasn't long before Lake Charles came into view. I knew western Louisiana pretty well by then. My grandmother's family had come to Beaumont from across the border in 1947, when she was twelve years old, part of the Great Migration. The city had appeared on the horizon. Dozens of smokestacks from oil refineries and petrochemical plants puffed smoke into the Louisiana sky. Like most of Southeast Texas and the rest of the Gulf Coast, it is a landscape of prairie, wetlands, coastal marshes, and estuaries. When my grandfather would take me fishing, we'd see all kinds of birds: tropical birds, beautiful reds and yellows, migrating through the area, gulls, terns, egrets, and herons, all in search of the same catch we were after, surviving, like us locals, on a diet of fish and shrimp (without the Cajun spice). In this land of natural beauty and endless miles of sandy beaches, the people smacked down a nearly unbroken string of industrial plants, subdivisions, and highways and other roads. That's the Gulf Coast of Texas, like Texas in general: a combination of beauty and ugliness.

George wasn't saying much that morning, but I was happy he was there with me. He was four years older than I was, a real adult at the age of twenty-two, or so it seemed from my perspective. I had known George since I was in the seventh grade. He'd helped me through a lot over the years. When I needed something my grandparents couldn't afford, he'd be there for me. If I needed a lift to a game or tournament, George would drive me. He'd gone to college and graduated with a degree in business, then come to Ozen High to do some work. Beaumont wasn't one of those places where kids automatically went from graduating high school to a college or university. About half of Beaumont students went to college, and only half of those finished a degree. Among the Black students, those numbers were even smaller.

At the time, I didn't think about these patterns. I was too busy training, playing ball, and just doing everything I could to make the leap to the pros. I saw what was happening around me, of course, but in ways a teenager sees things without really "seeing" them. There were structures that channeled our vision, like those rules set down by parents or grandparents, church traditions with their moral lessons, the values and care of the community. It was the community that looked out for me, raised and sheltered me. Coaches, neighbors, friends—always providing me with a little extra: a meal, a dessert, or just a pat on the back. I was open to everyone, friendly with all the students in my graduating class of three hundred seniors at Ozen High. This was the universalism of the faith, and it gave me the vision, even if I didn't consciously think about it, to treat each person as an individual soul, each soul a spark of the divine light.

What I felt, but didn't have the time or space to process or dwell on, were the barriers, the obstacles, visible and invisible, and the social forces that defined much of our existence. These forces ran deeper than the neighborhood of Pear Orchard, deeper than Ozen High or even Beaumont. I loved my teachers at Ozen, people like Coach Payne, Coach Clayton, and Ms. Ladd, God rest her soul. How would I have known that Ozen's test scores put it in the category of a "failing school"? Graduates from Ozen faced brutal conditions—high unemployment, college costs that were far beyond a family's reach, jobs offering poverty-level wages for hard labor. I'd lived it.

My grandparents lived this poverty every day. It was one of the main reasons I entered the draft instead of going to college: to give back to my grandmother and grandfather, who had taken me in, adopted me after my mama was shot and killed, given me everything they had to give, material and spiritual. This background of poverty and barriers was one of the reasons I looked up to George Davis. He'd gone to college and finished. He'd earned his degree when so many others had failed. He'd accomplished something extraordinary. He had my respect.

George was asleep as we made it through Lafayette and Baton Rouge. It was good he was catching up on some rest. It had been a busy summer for both of us after George had agreed to come to Boston to help me out. He had an itch to get out of our hometown to discover something new, to see what Boston had to offer. Around Baton Rouge, the highway split, Route 10 leading down to New Orleans. I kept on Route 12, heading east, skirting by Lake Pontchartrain on its northern edge. I kept turning as we sped by the lake to see if I could catch a glimpse of New Orleans as we shot past. No luck—just an endless stream of eighteen-wheelers.

By the time we made it to Mobile, George was up, and we decided to pull off for something to eat. George and I shared a love of fast food, and there were plenty of options to choose from around the city. I can't remember where we went, but I do recall that even though we were only half a day's drive from Beaumont, home already felt far away. Training camp lay ahead in a couple of weeks, the NBA preseason directly after that. I knew, at eighteen, that Danny Ainge and the others on the Celtics didn't expect me to show up on day one with the power of Shaq and the post moves of Hakeem Olajuwon. For me, it was about trying to get on the floor, to earn some real game minutes.

We talked about what we had in front of us. George's future was open. He would be helping me out in ways I couldn't have yet imagined, making sure I stayed on the right path. On the other hand, he was young, smart, and driven. He wanted to see what else was out there for him, what a big, rich city in the fabled "North" would have to offer a young Black man from Southeast Texas.

What stood in front of me was more material. George and I were breaking it down over that first lunch out of Beaumont. There were two centers on the Celtics roster. One was a guy by the name of Tony Battie. I knew a fair bit about him, because he was a fellow Texan. He was about nine years older than me. I remember hearing about him when he played for South Oak Cliff in Dallas, then as he starred at Texas Tech for four years as a rebounding and shot-blocking powerhouse. In 1997, he was taken fifth overall in the NBA draft by the Denver Nuggets. Battie was traded to the Lakers the following year, and that same season traded again, this time to Boston.

Boston's starting center heading into the 2003–2004 season was Mark Blount. Blount was a true seven-footer, weighed a sleek two hundred and fifty pounds. He'd gone to the University of Pittsburgh and then spent a couple of years in the development league before he got his shot in Boston. Over the past couple of seasons, he'd established himself as a quality NBA center. He had decent defensive instincts and a good mid-range shot.

Patience, George was telling me—be patient, do the right things, and think about the long term. Don't go in with unrealistic year-one aims. Think about year three, year four, when the Celtics had the option to pick up an extra year of my rookie contract. Think about the second phase, he said, the second contract, the one that could set up a player and his family for life.

I listened as George spoke, fighting down the rising hubris, my desire to push back against this version of the story. I could go in and muscle Blount, I thought, overpower him. I could run the floor better than Battie. I could do this; I could do that. I'd never sat on a bench in my life. Why now?

One of the problems with the youth basketball industry is that its goal is to convince every player on the elite level (and maybe beyond) that he is already a star. On some level, the job isn't that hard: these guys are stars. They are the best players on their high school teams. They dominate their respective leagues, putting up gaudy stats night after night. They win regional and state championships. They go around the country playing AAU ball, some recruited to the famous summer camps sponsored by Nike or Adidas where every single guy has a shot at the pros. The best players have been marked from as early as junior high.

They have been recruited by high school powerhouses like Coach Steve Smith's Oak Hill Academy in Virginia, where my future teammate Rajon Rondo played, or Bob Hurley's St. Anthony's. It's not that all or even most of these guys lost the desire to compete or the work ethic to get better, it is just that every rung on the ladder from high school to the NBA is fraught with difficulty.

A guy who has been a superstar in junior high and high school goes, for example, to Michigan State, and suddenly it is a fight just to make it onto the floor. When he gets his chance, he's feeling pressure, starts making mental mistakes. He gets frustrated. His commitment flags— and he starts slacking a bit in his workouts or in practice. As a result, his body isn't getting to where it needs to be. Suddenly, others are faster and stronger. He's being pushed around. While others have improved their footwork and shot, his game has plateaued. He's done.

It is mentally, emotionally, and psychologically exhausting to try to figure out how to go from being a superstar to being a guy just fighting to make it to the floor. As I listened to George laying it out for me that day, I knew it wouldn't be easy for me. Don't get it twisted—at Ozen I had worked hard, as hard as I knew how to work. But that wasn't enough for the NBA. It would be years of excruciating work to remake my body, mind, and game to become a serious force in the league.

As we sat in that roadside joint outside of Mobile, Alabama, I had this whole process in front of me. Hills behind me, mountains left to climb.

George took the wheel after lunch. It was time to get some rest, to try to make up a few of the thousands of hours of sleep I'd given up in order to get to that point. "Time to get to work"—that's the last thing my grandfather said to me before I left that morning. His words were truer than he knew. Or maybe he knew well enough. He had a lifetime of hard work behind him, work that went unnoticed, work that earned low pay, barely enough to survive, certainly never enough to have anything extra or enough to not think about money day after day. Still, Raymond

Lewis, my grandfather, knew how to find dignity in work, even if the work itself did not provide him with a material reward in return.

As George pulled back on the road, I remember thinking about how good it would feel to finally get them out of that run-down yellow shack, to give them comfort and peace of mind, even if the only luxury they desired was another modest house in Beaumont a few blocks away from Glenwood Ave.

After Mobile, the road turned to the north and we started our slow ascent toward Boston. George had music playing. He was quiet and focused, maybe lost in his own thoughts. Out the window, the Gulf Coast landscape vanished from view. I closed my eyes and fell into deep, calm sleep.

We stopped for the night in Atlanta. George and I were both tired from the long day on the road, but we were also feeling antsy and needed to stretch our legs. After a walk and some dinner, we went back to the motel. I thought about Vanity, my high school girlfriend. I'd been with her since the tenth grade. The night before I left, we'd sat together in the front seat of the Denali for hours, hardly speaking. She was crying and so was I. Neither of us could know what was coming, whether our relationship would be strong enough to survive my leaving and everything that would come with the transition to life in the NBA. I was dying to hear her voice on the first night away from Beaumont. Many times, I flipped open my phone to call her but then shut it again. I'd never been good at talking on the phone. I couldn't think of what to say. I hated the awkward feeling of the silence.

I lay in bed that night—an uncomfortable bed in a cheap roadside motel—with a strange feeling of being in-between. In the immediate sense, I was between Beaumont and Boston, between an old house where I knew every detail, every crack in the walls, chip in the paint, creak of the floor, and a new house I'd never seen. I was between high school and the pros. I was between being a grandson, whose grandmother had done all of his cooking, laundry, and cleaning, and a man who'd have to organize his own daily life. In eighteen years, I'd never been shopping at the grocery store. I'd never picked out my own shampoo, laundry detergent—nothing. Most profoundly, I was between being poor and being well-off, and if things worked out, being rich. My rookie deal with Boston had been negotiated by the king of high school–to-pro agents, Arn Tellem. My initial connection with Boston had come through William Wesley, known as "World Wide Wes," and "Uncle" Sonny Vaccaro, who'd arranged my pre-draft workout with the Celtics. I had gotten to know Sonny when he invited me to take part in his annual ABCD basketball camp the summer after my sophomore year at Ozen. My play at the camp, among the best talent in the country and in front of the biggest college coaches and pro scouts, put me on the map. By the next summer of camp, some of the national talent evaluators had me as the second-ranked prospect in the country behind LeBron James. Because of how things had gone at the camp, I quit playing AAU ball and just focused on developing my own game with the folks in Beaumont.

By the time the McDonald's All-American Game came around in March 2003, my weight had risen to over three hundred pounds. I was too heavy for the NBA. It was affecting my speed getting up and down the floor, my explosiveness. I had to drop weight and build strength. Through the spring, I continued training with Coach Boutte. He'd open up the gym for the Ozen team at 5 A.M. I'd spend a couple of hours working out before school. At noon, I had my daily three-mile run. After school, it was another long workout, followed by playing pickup with the local guys. Three days a week, I had weight training. There was no time for hanging out, for doing nothing, for partying, for enjoying the typical senior year festivities, for getting into trouble.

The work paid off. I felt good when I went to Boston for the workout with Celtics president Danny Ainge and coach Jim O'Brien. I was paired with Brian Cook, who was four years older and coming off one of the best careers of any player in the history of the University of Illinois. But that workout belonged to me. I felt faster, stronger, more explosive than Cook. I was dunking, shouting, having fun, playing hard.

After the draft, between summer league sessions, I resumed Coach Boutte's grueling summer workouts, which I'd been doing every year since the summer before seventh grade. Coach Boutte didn't have basketball tryouts at Ozen High School. If you wanted to play for him, you showed up every day in the summer at 8 A.M. at the school's track in the hundred-degree Texas heat ready to be tortured.

My summer days in 2003 began with an hour and a half of running the track, high-kneeing, backpedaling, and sprinting. After that, I hit the weights, then the court. Ozen High's gym had three courts, and that summer after the draft the other guys would clear a half-court for me. I'd finish the morning working on my inside game: footwork, positioning, and post moves. After lunch and a short rest, I was back at the gym. Afternoons were for shooting. I'd get up at least seven hundred shots a day from five spots: top of the key, wings, right and left baseline. Then I'd finish the day of training on the stationary bike, Coach Boutte pushing me hard for forty-five minutes.

Unfortunately, this hard work was undone by a foot injury in summer league, and when I arrived in Boston for training camp I had fallen into disastrous shape. Even if I hadn't suffered the fracture, my body was not yet ready for the physicality of the league. Size, speed, explosiveness, agility, quickness, touch, instinct, knowledge of the game—this is what it takes to make it in the NBA, and that's only a foundation. The rest is built through the daily dedication to painstaking work.

Before the 2003 draft, I'd worked out with the Rockets, Mavs, Spurs, and Celtics. After my session in Boston, Ainge had called and told my people that I didn't need to meet with anyone else, that the Celtics were committed to taking me in the first round. Coach Boutte knew about the plan, but he didn't tell me, so when the day of the draft came, I was nervous. That day, Coach Boutte had arranged for my family and friends to gather in the conference room of a local bank. I sat there, all dressed up, with the most important people in my life around me.

I watched and waited as NBA commissioner David Stern announced each pick. This was one of those special drafts, a draft that would fundamentally alter the face of the league.

LeBron, as the whole world expected, went number one to Cleveland. Carmelo Anthony went third to the Nuggets, just months after dominating college basketball on his way to leading Syracuse University to the national championship as a freshman. Chris Bosh, my Texas rival, went next, to Toronto. Then came Dwyane Wade, drafted by the Miami Heat. The selections continued. T. J. Ford of UT-Austin went at number eight. Marcus Banks, who'd be traded with me that day from Memphis to Boston, was picked at thirteen. Sharp-shooting Luke Ridnour of Oregon was gone at fourteen. My former ABCD campmate Travis Outlaw, making the leap from high school to pro, went at twenty-three. Brian Cook, whom I'd handled in that Boston workout, was picked at twenty-four by the Los Angeles Lakers. Ndudi Ebi went to the Wolves at twenty-six.

I was really sweating now. There were only three more picks in the first round of the draft, and the difference between going in round one and going in round two was massive. The money, the guaranteed contract—these were round-one realities. "With pick number twenty-seven, the Memphis Grizzlies select Kendrick Perkins, Ozen High School, Beaumont, Texas!" An unreal feeling washed over me as I sat in that bank conference room. It was a flood of sensations that pulled me in every direction at once. I felt riveted to the conference room chair. The room exploded—friends, coaches, family hugging, shouting, celebrating—but I could barely hear any of it, barely feel the hands on my shoulders, the arms around my neck. The long, tightly held dream was now a reality.

Memphis and Boston had worked out a deal to exchange picks. Boston drafted and sent Troy Bell and Duke's Dahntay Jones to the Grizzlies for me and Marcus Banks. That summer, Arn had the deal done with Boston. My first-year salary was around $900,000, same for the second year. In the third year, it rose to around $1.2 million. The Celtics had the option of picking up a fourth year for around the same number. In other words, from having nothing but my 1993 Lincoln Town Car, a gift from Coach Boutte, from having to bring rolls of pennies to school to buy my lunch, I'd signed a deal worth over four million dollars. It felt crazy, totally crazy, from the sheer size of the numbers to the small but significant fact that the next morning in Atlanta I could pay for our motel room without worrying about what the fifty-dollar charge would mean for the weeks and months ahead.

I took the first shift behind the wheel again. George had his map out, refolding it to get Georgia, the Carolinas, and Virginia together on the same square. Our destination for the night was Washington, D.C., via Charlotte, Greensboro, Durham, and Richmond. As we cruised up I-85, I saw the signs for Greenville, South Carolina. I knew this was the hometown of the player who'd led the way for kids to go pro out of high school. He was the model, the ideal. He'd entered the league in 1995, drafted by the Minnesota Timberwolves.

I'm talking, of course, about Kevin Garnett. Before Garnett, it had been decades since a player had skipped college and the NCAA system. They'd called Garnett "The Kid," told him he'd fail, that he wasn't strong enough to bang with the likes of Karl Malone or Shaq. By 2003, it was impossible to move through the youth basketball scene without hearing about his legend. Garnett had shown up at Vaccaro's Nike summer camp as a complete unknown. He dominated the camp, and then repeated this domination the following year. By the end of that second summer, the previously unknown Garnett was the top prospect in the nation.

Toward the end of his junior year at Mauldin High School in Mauldin, South Carolina, a suburb of Greenville, while Garnett was in the halls of the school, some guys attacked and injured a white student. The next day, the police came and arrested Garnett. They took him directly out of class. He hadn't committed any violence, but he'd been in the halls when the attack took place, or, as the police put it, he was "part of the crowd." The police charged the seventeen-year-old Garnett with second-degree lynching. I can't think of a more ridiculous charge.

Years later, after KG came to Boston, we became tight. I can tell you that there is no part of KG that would join a mob and attack another human being. Second-degree "lynching"—the very practice of calling a schoolyard fight "lynching" is an abuse of history and language. In the summer of 2003, though I'd known about KG as a player, I hadn't thought that much about the specific struggles NBA guys faced on their way to the league, about what they had overcome, the pathways, often bent in unexpected ways, they took to make it to where they were. The white police charging a bunch of Black high school kids with "lynching" a white student in the halls of Mauldin High School . . . Come on.

In this sense, I'd been lucky. I'd lost my mama when I was five, it's true, and for years I'd cry myself to sleep over it, suffering the irreparable loss of her presence. But the community had protected me, looked out for me, nurtured me, just as the Greenville community had targeted, persecuted, and driven out KG. The poor, Black, "failing" Ozen High had proven itself far superior, on a moral and spiritual level, to the middle-class, majority-white, suburban Mauldin.

We drove through Charlotte and deep into the heart of basketball country—that corridor between Charlotte and Richmond. Jordan country. Tar Heel country. Dean Smith. Coach K and the Duke Blue Devils. Wake Forest and their star recruit, the point guard Chris Paul. I'd signed with John Calipari at the University of Memphis in case my draft prospects dropped too low, but I never seriously thought about playing college ball. This was the high school–to–pro era, not the era of the "one-and-done." Skipping college had its dangers, but so did going to college to play. There could be injury, a bad fit with a system, a team that just didn't gel. Added to that, and most important, going to college would have meant the continuation of my family's unending economic crisis. I'd take my chances, despite what Calipari and the other doubters might have thought. I was a born poker player, after all, and I was placing the wager of my life on myself. There would be no second hand dealt in this game.

There were times on the trip when these thoughts would weigh on me, turn me inward. I'd gaze at the stretch of road ahead, try to clear my mind, and just drive, just keep moving. I imagine George could sense something was going on, because he'd keep quiet, too, or turn on the radio to find a good beat, or bury his face in the map like it might contain some hidden message. If the mood in the Denali's cab got too heavy, one of us would come through with a joke, and we'd both let ourselves go and laugh.

George took over the wheel after our stop around Durham. He drove into Virginia, passed Richmond, and headed toward D.C. I closed my eyes to try to sleep, but my thoughts were racing. Maybe it was the shifting landscape, the thickening traffic; or perhaps it was the knowledge that the next day would be the end of the trip and the beginning of what came next. The Church taught me that faith that wasn't tested wasn't true faith. Isn't this what the story of Job is all about? It is about the power of doubt and the impact of uncertainty. True faith isn't a lack of doubt or the banishment of uncertainty from one's thoughts; no, true faith is the will to overcome doubt and to rise above uncertainty— finding one's faith in the fog of doubt, discovering the glimmer of certainty amid the storm of uncertainty.

I didn't think about these things directly as we moved through Virginia that day, but the ideas were there in the background. Our most important ideas, I think, are those that linger in the background. They are intuitions and feelings that connect us to our deeper selves. This is what shows us the way, what allows us to go in the right direction.

We avoided downtown D.C. and instead stayed in another shabby place near the highway. George and I both slept late the next morning and grabbed a big breakfast at the diner near the hotel. The day's route traced, fittingly, the NBA's Atlantic Division: Philadelphia, New Jersey, New York, and Boston. As we hit the road, my thoughts turned to Boston and the Celtics. I hadn't spent a lot of time in the North, and when I traveled to camps and tournaments, it was usually in the summer months. The cold, the snow, winter—it would be new to me. Boston had a totally different environment from anything I was used to. The brick buildings, the narrow, winding streets—a far cry from the wide-open feel of Texas. The fast-food chains I relied on in Beaumont didn't exist in Boston—and I remember the first time I tasted New England clam chowder. The difference between New England and the Gulf Coast could be described as no more and no less than the difference between clam chowder and gumbo. The closeness of a place like the Pear Orchard, with its Southern friendliness and hospitality, couldn't be replicated in the North. I'd grown up in a mostly Black neighborhood, and now I was going to live surrounded by white New Englanders. It was a culture shock for me, to say the least.

There had been talk of Boston around the youth basketball circuit. People had said it was a white town, a racist town. Even though I'd grown up in the 1990s after the fabled Magic-Bird era, the image of the Boston Celtics as the white rivals to Magic's Black Lakers had stuck. The media's obsession with Larry Bird's "work ethic" and "team game" as opposed to Magic's "natural abilities" and "showman style" had always irritated and insulted players in the Black community. We knew well enough, from our own experiences, that "natural ability" was not nearly enough to become a Magic Johnson. To become that good, one of the all-time greats, was a product of talent and the daily grind of getting better, both on and off the court, both physically and intellectually. Same with Bird. It's nonsense to think that someone could become Larry Bird through sheer work. Bird had massive talent, too, the same level of "natural ability" as Magic.

My youth was encompassed by the Jordan era, when the Boston Celtics were at best a footnote to the season, at worst an utter irrelevancy. Boston would finish behind Ewing's Knicks, Iverson's 76ers, the emerging Nets. I grew up as a Rockets fan and was especially a fan of one of the greatest centers ever to play the game, Hakeem Olajuwon. Hakeem "The Dream" had all of the pieces—speed, power, footwork, touch, and finesse. During the two seasons when Jordan went to play baseball, The Dream was unstoppable, leading Houston to back-to-back championships. I relished Olajuwon's performance in the 1995 NBA championship series against the young Shaq. It was a legendary display of dominance, as The Dream owned Shaq, not through force or raw power, but through the polish of his game, his fine-tuned skill. It was like watching a musical virtuoso at work.

In 2003, the image of the Boston Celtics as a "white" team or as the team of Bird, Kevin McHale, and Danny Ainge had faded. Bird had gone on to coach the Pacers and was universally respected among the league's players, white and Black. McHale was out in Minnesota and had the vision and guts to take Garnett out of high school—and I had played my high school ball in a pair of Kevin Garnett shoes.

To become a Celtic is to enter into one of the most storied of all basketball traditions. For me, as a big man, I thought immediately about the legacy of Bill Russell. Russell created the model for the modern big man, especially a big man like me who didn't have the silky touch of Kareem Abdul-Jabbar or the footwork of Olajuwon. Russell combined scoring his share of points with stout rebounding and tenacious defense. He was the heart and soul of the Celtics from the mid-1950s until around 1970, for a few of those years serving as both player and head coach.

He was the first Black head coach in NBA history. He was a true leader. The fact is that Bill Russell won more NBA championships, by far, than any other player in any era. Russell's eleven rings will probably never be matched. And his game face, that mean Russell look, was my model for a center—the enforcing big man, a look that told anyone in the world, no matter who it was, "Don't mess with me."

The vets on the 2003 Celtics team welcomed me with open arms, and I can say with all sincerity that their guidance allowed me to build the foundation of a fourteen-year NBA career. Tony Delk, Walter Mc-Carty, Tony Battie, Eric Williams, Paul Pierce—these were the guys who taught me how to be a professional basketball player, how to act responsibly, how to be accountable to my own high standards and to the team. Be in the gym first, leave last, work hard, avoid getting enticed by the inevitable allures of NBA life, the clubbing, fashion, cars, money—a lifestyle that pulls a man away from who he is at his core, creates distraction, shortens or ends careers, even ruins or ends lives. Because of the guys on my first Celtics team, because of the upbringing I'd had from my grandparents and others in Beaumont, I was prepared to hear the advice and to act on it.

Later, when I got closer with Danny Ainge, he told me that he always went into the NBA draft looking for guys with heart. Ainge built a championship team with that mentality: Garnett—you can't find a guy with more heart than KG—Rajon Rondo, Paul Pierce, Ray Allen, James Posey, Eddie House, Leon Powe, and all the others, myself included. We were brothers on and off the court, a family of warriors with a common goal: to win it all. When Doc Rivers came on as coach in 2004, everything started coming together for me, and those core principles were etched in stone.

But that was in the future. What lay ahead, as George and I passed through Philadelphia and New York City, I hardly knew. There was a city to the north, Boston, with a barely comprehensible culture, with an environment more foreign to me than Mexico or Brazil. I was heading into another country, another world.

The third day on the road passed by in a blur of thoughts or half-thoughts, a tumult of expectation and anticipation. As we neared Boston, I could feel a physical urge inside my body to get at it: to hit the gym, to pound, to punish, to work on my body and my game. Enough thinking and feeling—it was time to hoop.

Late in the day, toward sunset, George pulled the Denali into the driveway of a town house in Waltham, Massachusetts. We sat in the driveway for a minute or two staring up the house's façade. It was nothing special, but to me it looked like a luxury compound next to the little yellow shack on Glenwood Avenue where I'd spent my entire life. "Welcome home," George said with a smile. We both lost it, burst out laughing. This was no "home," and he knew it. We each grabbed some bags from the back, and George unlocked the house. At some point, he'd gotten the keys. He'd arranged all of it. I carried the bags inside and dropped them in the front hallway. I remember that the impact of those bags hitting the floor sent an echo through the space—the echo of emptiness.

While George went outside to make a couple calls, I slowly moved through the downstairs rooms—the living room with a fireplace, the kitchen with its gleaming stainless-steel appliances and granite countertops polished to a shine, a dining room with a long, dark mahogany table that seemed straight out of Puritan times. There was an upholstered sofa with a floral pattern, an armchair with a matching design. In the corner of the living room, there was a desk of the same dark stained wood as the table. Everything matched, everything was deliberately chosen and placed—chosen, I thought, to be nondescript, to reflect the standards of an average New Englander of some means. I stood in the large living room and gazed at the empty walls, the barren surfaces of the furniture, the austere neatness and soullessness of the place. Eighteen years old and cut off from everything I knew, a young Black man in a foreign land.

Years later, I started to sense that there had been another layer to our trip from Beaumont to Boston. It had been there with me and George as we moved across the country, but it had remained invisible. Or it was visible, but I didn't have the tools or perspective to see it—not yet. I had my eyes on the dark circle on the map with the word "Boston" next to it in bold black print. I was focused only on that dot and the thin lines leading to it. How could I know at eighteen years old that beneath these dots—Beaumont, Atlanta, Baltimore, New York City—there was another route leading across a totally different type of map? I'm talking about the map of history, our shared Black history, and it, too, connects my hometown of Beaumont to the city of Boston. Maybe this is what George Davis was searching for as he gazed into the maze of roads and highways. Here's some of what I've found.

Galveston, Texas: June 19, 1865. General Order No. 3 is issued not far from Beaumont, informing the people of Texas that the quarter million slaves who live there have been set free. Beaumont, Texas: June 15, 1943. Thousands of white workers, mainly from the Pennsylvania shipyards, riot after rumors spread that a white woman has been raped by a Black man. The mob, growing as it moves, marches to downtown Beaumont and starts burning and looting Black-owned property, starts beating on every Black body it can find. The Mississippi River: 1920. Seventeen-year-old Langston Hughes, on a train to see his father in Mexico, writes a poem called "The Negro Speaks of Rivers." He writes, *I heard the singing of the Mississippi when Abe Lincoln went down to New Orleans, and I've seen its muddy bosom turn all golden in the sunset.* It was in New Orleans that Lincoln witnessed the largest slave market in the United States.

Mobile, Alabama: 1902. The city starts to enforce segregation on its streetcars. The Black community of Mobile organizes a boycott. The boycott fails to change Alabama law, and the state, like the South as a whole, becomes a society ruled by white-supremacist terrorism, otherwise known as Jim Crow. Montgomery, Alabama: December 1, 1955. Rosa Parks is arrested for refusing to leave her bench to make room for a white man who has entered a city bus. Atlanta, Georgia: 1895. Booker T. Washington speaks at the Cotton States and International Exposition and implores his fellow Black Americans to resist the urge to protest racial inequality. When a young W. E. B. Du Bois hears this, he can't remain quiet. He responds to Washington: "The black men of America have a duty to perform, a duty stern and delicate—a forward movement to oppose a part of the work of their greatest leader." Charlotte, North Carolina: 1958. Bill Russell and Sam Jones, on the road with the Celtics, are denied entry to the team's hotel and have to lodge in a hotel specifically set aside for Black people. The next day, Russell tells the media he'll never play in Charlotte again. When Red Auerbach says that Russell doesn't speak for the Celtics, Russell responds to Red, "I was speaking for Russell . . . man, Negro, basketball player, American citizen."

Richmond, Virginia: May 29, 1890. The massive bronze statue of Robert E. Lee, Confederate general, is dedicated on Monument Avenue, where it would stand until September 2021 as a symbol of racial violence, injustice, and hate. Washington, D.C.: August 1933. The New Negro Alliance starts its boycott campaign against businesses in the nation's capital. Its slogan: "Don't buy where you can't work." Baltimore, Maryland: April 1968. Black residents of the city riot in reaction to the murder of Martin Luther King Jr. During the 1960s, Baltimore has become increasingly segregated. Decades of property redlining and white flight have left the city and its now Black majority in economic ruin.

New York City, New York: Summer 1919. White rioters unleash a reign of terror on Black people throughout the city as part of the nationwide Red Summer, a tsunami of violence by Northern white workers and the KKK. New York City, New York: 1934. The Harlem Renaissance painter Aaron Douglas creates his epic mural *Aspects of Negro Life* on a wall in the New York Public Library. In the panel *From Slavery Through Reconstruction*, the central figure clutches a ballot in his left hand and bravely points to the Capitol Building on the hill in the distance. To his left loom hooded figures on horses, weapons in their hands—white reaction to Black empowerment.

How far away are we today, in 2022, from this scene? Boston, Massachusetts: April 25, 1950. The Boston Celtics draft Chuck Cooper, the first Black player drafted in NBA history.

We'd made it from Beaumont to Boston. The trip was over, and I was standing in the living room of this sterile town house, alone. When the angels of God led Lot and his family out of Sodom, they told them not to look back. But who are we if we don't look back, if we don't look closely at the past? In front of us are those blank walls. Behind us, whether we are conscious of it or not, are the layers of history that have set the stage for our lives. Lot's wife looks back and is turned into a pillar of salt. The people in power don't want us to turn around, don't want us to see the past, because they are afraid if we find this truth, we will start to understand, we will start to demand change. To know anything for real requires taking a chance, facing danger: the danger of trying to find out where we came from and who we are.

I turn to face it. I am six feet ten inches, two hundred and seventy-five pounds of salt.

1

The Pear Orchard

IT'S CALLED THE GREAT MIGRATION. TENS OF THOUSANDS OF BLACK FAMILIES, MILLIONS of people, were on the move. If you're a Black man or woman in the United States and you dig down into your family tree, you'll probably discover that some of your people came from the Mississippi Delta, the Louisiana backwater, Alabama and Arkansas, rural Tennessee, the Black Belt of central Georgia and South Carolina. Their destinations were just as varied as their points of origin. Tens of thousands, including my ancestors, moved from rural life to cities not far away—from Louisiana, Texas, or Tennessee farmland to Houston, Memphis, or Nashville. Some went west to California. Millions made the journey north to America's industrial and economic centers: Detroit, Chicago, Boston, and New York City. This movement of Black folk out of the rural South reshaped the country. Its legacy still resounds through American life today in ways large and small. This is why my writing about Beaumont starts with it. The Great Migration shaped Beaumont profoundly, and through Beaumont, it shaped me.

The reasons for this incredible movement of people were many, but the roots of the migration can be found in the legacy of the slave society that remained powerful in the South after the Civil War. For a fleeting moment after the war, the prospect of the emancipated former slaves acquiring ownership of Southern farmlands was a glimmer in the national imagination. Most people know the phrase "forty acres and a mule." This was the idea of breaking the power structure of the South by raising up the former slaves, allowing them the chance at self-sufficiency. It should have happened, but it didn't. This failure to compensate the former slaves, to give to them what they deserved—and what was by any decent measure a small step toward justice—laid the foundation for the development and growth of slavery's grotesque twin: the hierarchical, exploitive, violent, segregationist society called Jim Crow. At its heart, Jim Crow society was based on the exploitation of Black workers by white planters. This is critically important, and no one should misunderstand it: wealth throughout the South, meaning white planter wealth, was not based on the value of what came out of the soil, it was extracted from the Black workers' bodies, just as it was under slavery.

After the Civil War, slavery turned into sharecropping and tenant farming. These models of labor were constructed precisely to maintain the conditions of slavery by trapping Black people on the land through a combination of debt peonage and lack of opportunity. To rebrand and continue slavery, the white South dismantled the reforms that came in the wake of the war. The war and its aftermath had provoked the federal government to guarantee Black male suffrage. With the vote, Black communities in the South during Reconstruction gained political power. In the decades after the end of Reconstruction, as the federal government turned away, the white South launched an assault on the political and legal status of Black people across the region. For Black men, voting rights were destroyed. Only hundreds out of hundreds of thousands of Black men cast a ballot. Black representation vanished throughout the South.

The loss of political power meant Black folk in the South had no protection from the abuses of law and order. The law in the South, together with the institutions of law enforcement—courts, state and local prosecutors, sheriffs, state National Guardsmen, police—became the key tool for the enforcement of white supremacy. It was through its systems of "law and order" that Jim Crow society was built and maintained. Let's make no mistake, the Jim Crow South was a violent, racially hierarchical, terrorist state.

White Southerners used every possible legal channel to exercise power over Black people, and when these "legal" operations were deemed not enough, they formed vigilante groups like the Klan to carry their violence deep into the heart of Black communities. Thousands, maybe even tens of thousands, of Black people were lynched during the decades before and during the Great Migration. Lynching—whether the actual murderous event or the threat of it—became a shadow that hung low over Black life in the South. Some Black people were targeted for economic reasons. For example, they might have dared to buy land or open a shop that threatened white interests. The majority of lynchings, though, related to white fear about racial mixing, especially Black men having or desiring sexual relations with white women. Again, as with the issue of economics and labor, white terrorism was directed at the Black body.

To the political and legal campaigns to debase Black folk, Jim Crow added economic oppression and exploitation. The impact of this oppression is still evident in our communities today—it is history as current event. Black schools went unfunded or underfunded. Universities, colleges, and professional schools remained closed to Black students. Black people were denied access to ownership of businesses in the more economically prosperous white neighborhoods of towns and cities. White businesses hired Black workers only at the very bottom levels of pay and then prevented them from rising. White residential neighborhoods were off limits, and Black ones received sparse public investment. Bank lending was deeply prejudiced. Few Black members of the community owned substantial tracts of land, and if they did, they were under constant threat from the white mob.

Beneath all of this—beneath the violence, the disenfranchisement, the enforced segregation, the miscarriage of justice in the courts—was the vast campaign by the South's white planters to bind Black workers to the land through an unending spiral of debt. In this way, the Southern planter tried to blot out the most potent site of resistance to his power: people's hope for the future.

The Great Migration is the name for millions of individual and family stories. Taken together, these interwoven stories forever changed the United States. Each act of migration was a heroic tale of struggle and survival—we shouldn't forget this. The Black people, like my family, who left the rural South had nothing, and it was a kind of nothing that might be hard for some of us to imagine these days. They had no money. They had no property to sell. They had little or no formal education and few specific skills beyond agricultural ones. They had no health insurance and no welfare programs to get them through the transitions and tough times. Added to this nothing, these migrants faced constant danger. The act of leaving itself was opposed, often violently, by the South's white power structure. White communities in the North met the new arrivals with open hostility, forced segregation, and discrimination of every type.

Throughout the country beyond the Cotton Belt, urban areas witnessed a dramatic growth in their populations of Black residents. Some of the iconic urban neighborhoods rose during this time: New York's Harlem, Chicago's South Side, Roxbury in Boston, Houston's Third Ward. Wherever—Cleveland, Detroit, St. Louis, Los Angeles, etc.—Black communities grew, violence and oppression followed. The spirit of white supremacy, nurtured at the heart of the South, followed migrants north and west like a looming shadow, permeating every corner of the American landscape. Northern cities became racially segregated, like Southern ones. Real estate agents and banks worked hand in glove to create and sustain white-only neighborhoods and suburbs. Instead of welcoming

Black workers, labor unions targeted the new arrivals as enemies of the white worker. White businesses remained stubbornly closed to Black workers beyond the level of the most menial jobs.

Violence followed these migrants out of the Deep South. Klan chapters opened nationwide, harnessing, organizing, and activating white hate. Urban police forces from New York to Los Angeles became fascistic orders largely focused on maintaining racial hierarchy. Rates of Black male incarceration began their meteoric rise, finding ghastly mature form in the U.S.'s prison-industrial complex, the largest penal system the "peacetime" world has ever seen. The South's terror state was now the size of the nation.

My story—like the stories of Black families throughout this country, like the family histories of most Black players who play or have played in the NBA—includes the Great Migration. Beaumont, Texas, is the center of my family's migration story. Around 1900, Southeast Texas and the Gulf Coast were in flux. People were moving, and not only from Georgia's Black Belt to Harlem or Newark. Tens of thousands of rural Texas Black tenant farmers were headed for the Gulf Coast's cities. Many of these people, and others from Louisiana and the Mississippi Delta, settled in Houston. Houston's Black neighborhoods—the Third Ward, Sunnyside, Frenchtown, and others—swelled with the new arrivals. Beaumont was no different.

For many readers, Beaumont, Texas, of the 1930s and 1940s might seem like ancient history, but to me it might as well be yesterday. For eighteen years, I saw this history etched into my grandparents' faces. I saw the effects of it around me. I still do. This history is felt everywhere in our society. It couldn't be more visible, if we're paying attention.

On the eve of the Civil War, Beaumont, like the rest of Texas, was slave territory. The town was built around a local sawmill and had a railroad line passing through on the way from New Orleans to Houston. Slaves worked in capacities such as domestic laborers, farmers, and railroad workers. On June 19, 1865—Juneteenth—the slaves in Beaumont gained their freedom. They started to exercise their right to vote. They held local political offices. By the last decade of the century, however, Jim Crow society was being built in Beaumont piece by piece, arresting the progress made by Black Beaumonters, who lost the ability to vote and were subjected to strict segregation, economic and political oppression, and daily threats and acts of violence.

Life changed in Beaumont in 1901, when oil was discovered on Spindletop Hill. The Lucas Gusher transformed Beaumont from a small railway town into a boomtown. The population spiked as people flocked to town in search of jobs and a better life. The oil business formed the industrial core of Beaumont and other cities on the Gulf Coast, turning the once rural area into an important industrial center. To oil drilling, the Gulf Coast added petroleum refining, shipbuilding, chemical production, and a host of related industries and businesses. By 1950, the former small town of a couple thousand people contained well over a hundred thousand inhabitants, a third of whom were Black.

Jim Crow structured life in Beaumont. Strict racial segregation barred Black people from eating in white-only restaurants, drinking in white-only bars, shopping in white-only stores. Schools, of course, were segregated, neighborhoods racially divided, and by the first years of the new century, Black people were forced by law to sit or stand at the back of Beaumont's buses and to travel by segregated railway cars. Despite the incredible profits generated by oil and related enterprises, Black workers saw none of it. Whether it was on Texas' oilfields, in its refineries, or elsewhere, white workers claimed the best jobs, leaving the most menial and lowest paying to Black employees. No Black workers were taken into management or executive positions; hardly a Black man or woman held a white-collar post.

The oilfields are a good example of the norm. Black workers were allowed on the field predominantly as diggers, whether it was slush pits, trenches for pipelines, or holes for storage tanks. Earthmoving was the worst-paid work in Texas' entire oil economy, and even this work, by the 1920s, was prohibited for Black Beaumonters by the increasingly intolerant and radicalized white culture.

To grasp the nature of Beaumont during Jim Crow, we must combine an understanding of the facts with a willingness to imagine the daily reality of both white and Black folk. For white people, this daily reality meant the constant, vigilant enforcement of the norms and practices of social domination.

The foundation of this domination was the policing of the "color line," the social boundary between the races. For white people, this meant above all the "protection" of white womanhood from the sexual "threat" posed by Black men. If Jim Crow meant any one thing for white America, it meant the control of the Black male body, which it sought to bend and break under unrelenting pressure. For Black people, Jim Crow, beyond the political and legal oppression, meant the performance of subordination and inferiority. "Performance" is a perfect word for it, because beneath the mob violence and lynching, there was a Texas-sized mountain of bows, doffed hats, sidewalks stepped off, streets crossed, back entrances used, seats vacated, faces averted, insults swallowed, undeserved apologies uttered, and unearned respect given.

The performance of Jim Crow, both the performance of domination (always backed up with very real state or vigilante violence) and its mirror image, the performance of subordination, was found on every level, from language to gesture to facial expression. Let's not be confused: the performance of Jim Crow was not separate from its structures of legal, political, and economic inequality. These elements came together to create a society bent on maintaining and deepening racial hierarchy as a fact of life. It's complicated—it was a complex system, as all systems are that seek to crush a minority through the oppressive force of a violent and intolerant majority. The Jim Crow South infused racial domination into every possible sphere of life, and the accumulation of these infusions built, brick by brick, the white-supremacist state.

Many aspects of this culture have never gone away, even if the tactics might have changed. There are people today, occupying positions of power in our society, who are trying to reconstruct this system of domination, starting, as in the nineteenth century, by stripping Black Americans of the right to vote. I'll come back to this later in the book, but it is important to make the point clearly here: these regressive steps must be vigorously resisted. We need to join now in protest and refusal of this vision of life. Anyone who thinks white supremacy will stop at denying Black men and women the vote is badly mistaken. Disenfranchisement is, as it was then, an evil step toward exploitation, humiliation, and sadistic violence. This is why our movement to fight for the vote remains a critical, if by itself insufficient, response to white supremacy. It is part of the bigger struggle for real freedom.

My grandparents were born in the South during the Great Depression. The Great Depression was a crisis for Black America, especially for poor, rural folk, of a magnitude that dwarfed the general crisis the nation was facing. In the 1930s, as now, crisis hits the most vulnerable the hardest—just look at the impact of the 2008 financial crisis or the Covid-19 pandemic. Black folk, especially in the South, were already languishing under Jim Crow when the bottom fell out of the U.S. economy in 1929. During the peak years of the Depression, unemployment among Black workers reached over 50 percent, double that of white workers. Those who managed to hold on to a job were at the bottom of the pay scale.

I like to look at photographs of those years across the South; it helps me better imagine the life my grandparents and great-grandparents must have been living at the time. One of my favorites is of three Black children gathered around a porch somewhere in the Mississippi Delta. In the foreground, there's a girl standing on the edge of the porch. She's shoeless, thin, probably ten or eleven years old. She's wearing a tattered dress, frayed and patched, made of some light cotton fabric with a check-ered pattern. The collar of the dress forms a V shape below her neck, ex-posing the austere lines of her collarbone and upper rib cage, a subtle, though jarring, sign of hunger. There's a play of light and shadow on her legs, moving up her right shoulder onto her hand, which sits, fingers curled, propped up by the elbow on her waist. The girl's face is somehow both impassive and highly charged; her eyes, piercing and aware, seek out their object to the left of the camera frame.

Behind and above her in the background, a boy, maybe eight years old, leans against the porch's post. He's also without shoes, and he gazes in the same direction as the girl. The look on his face is not one of stoic calm or clear-eyed assessment, as hers is. It is a look of anxiety and fear.

To the girl's right, occupying the photo's foreground with her, there's a third child, a boy wearing a pair of dusty overalls and a gray flat cap that's tilted down toward his left eye. The boy, around twelve, has his one visible sleeve rolled up to the elbow, exposing his wrist and fore-arm. His fingers, like those of the girl, are curled halfway into a ball. This boy is not looking off to the left, like the other two. He is looking directly at the camera. There is a confidence, a power, in the boy's gaze. It seeks out our eyes, demanding recognition, demanding voice, even if his lips are pressed firmly together.

A photograph of three children in the Mississippi Delta in 1936—three stories untold but intersected at a single moment by a photographer passing through the South on her way to California. What became of these kids? What happened to the girl with the sun-dappled face? To the young boy leaning against the post with his mouth agape? To the boy in the foreground with his angled cheekbones and his powerful gaze— the gaze of a knowing man, the gaze of a man with dignity? I look at that boy who's looking right back at me and feel like I know him. I know him because I am him. I know him because he could be my grandfather.

I know him because, like me and my grandfather, this boy had to live a lifetime before he turned fifteen, if he made it that far.

My grandmother, Mary Lewis, was born in Church Point, Louisiana, in 1935. When she was twelve, her parents took her, her five sisters, and her three brothers and moved to Beaumont's Pear Orchard. It must have been a crazy trip for the family to make in the 1940s. My great-grandparents had decided, like millions of others, to get on out of the rural South, to leave the cotton fields behind and to go in search of another, better life. It is easy enough to take a journey like this from Church Point to Beaumont for granted—it's a couple hours by car now—but that would be a major mistake. These migrations were acts of tremendous courage and were made in the face of danger.

Unfortunately, much of my family history has been lost to the past. Or maybe that's not the right way to put it. More accurately, this story and countless others like it were excluded from history, and certainly from most history books that are taught in our schools. History has found little space for the lives of ordinary Black folk like my grandparents and great-grandparents, especially those from the rural South. They appear as groups—slaves, tenant farmers, sharecroppers—but not as individuals, families, and communities. This is one of the reasons I was motivated to write this book in this particular way—to place my story, that of an NBA champion, in connection with these deeper forces that shape our lives. When I think about my grandmother's journey as the oldest of nine children in 1947, I encounter so many unanswered questions. Why did they leave Church Point? Was the decision made for a specific, immediate reason like job loss, debt, violence, or fear? Was it the result of long deliberation? Did they leave primarily to get out? Or was it, rather, a quest after opportunities, real or imagined, offered by a growing city within geographical reach? Was it hope that drove them—hope that Beaumont would provide the setting for a better life? Or was it exhaustion after generations of fruitless toil in the wake of the Civil War?

When they arrived in Beaumont, my great-grandfather somehow got himself a piece of land in the Pear Orchard. There, he built a house for his family. It was a low, ramshackle structure where nine kids and two adults packed into the small rooms. Eventually, my great-grandfather would build a second house on the land, nothing more than a shack, really, where my grandmother and grandfather raised their kids. This shack was the house I'd grow up in half a century later, a shack built by the hands of a former sharecropper, hands that only a few years before had been picking cotton in a Louisiana field. For me, like for so many people, the past was present.

The Second World War was good to Beaumont—to white Beaumont. The oil refineries, shipyards, and other industries grew to meet the demands of the war, attracting thousands of workers to the Gulf Coast. As people crowded into Beaumont, white residents of the city became increasingly concerned with maintaining the Jim Crow structures of white supremacy. Nowhere in the city was this clearer than on Beaumont's city buses, where white drivers and riders were focused on policing the color line. On the buses, this meant the division of the space into white and "colored" sections.

On July 27, 1942, Charles J. Reco sat on a Beaumont city bus with his knees over the border. Reco, who was a Black military policeman back in town on leave, refused to retract his knees when instructed by the driver. The driver then called for the police to come and remove Reco from the bus. When four Beaumont police officers arrived, Reco resisted. During the confrontation, Officer Billy Brown pulled his gun and shot Reco three times. Another officer, Ben White, added a fourth shot, while yet another white officer, Clyde Brown, beat Reco with his nightstick. Reco, miraculously, survived the assault. All of

the white officers involved in Reco's shooting and beating were exon-
erated a month later.

A year after the white officers attacked Reco, white anger seemed
to be spiking. On June 15, 1943, a white woman called the Beaumont
police to report that she had been raped by a Black man. The supposed
violation of white womanhood by Black men was the central white-
supremacist justification for terrorism. It played into many of the myths
of Southern racial hierarchy. It emphasized the vulnerability and deli-
cacy of white femininity, which, according to the racist ideology, was under threat from the Black man. It brought up notions of racial purity. It
created the space for the performance of white "honor," which was tied
closely to white masculinity and white power.

In other words, the issue of sexual relations between white women
and Black men contained a potent mix of white delusion and ignorance
and was used to justify extreme violence. Throughout slavery and Jim
Crow, white accusations of Black men's crossing of this sexual color
line led to tens of thousands of lynchings, beatings, riots, and countless other major and minor injustices, the most famous of which was
the case of the Scottsboro Boys.

Word of the alleged rape spread from the police station quickly throughout the city on June 15. By nighttime, thousands of white workers at the
Pennsylvania shipyards walked off the job and moved toward downtown
Beaumont, intent on exacting mob "justice." By the time the workers
reached the city center, the crowd had doubled in size. After learning
that the police hadn't yet apprehended a suspect, the thousands of white
people began to riot.

Groups of white rioters broke away from the center and entered the
city's Black neighborhoods. Black people who were caught on the streets
were beaten by the mob. Buildings in the Black business districts were
burned and looted. Black-owned restaurants, cafes, shops, funeral homes,
and offices were destroyed, a merciless assault on the already meager

Black middle class. At some point during the mayhem, the mob discovered that around fifty Black draftees were waiting in the city's bus depot for an early morning bus to Port Arthur, having just come from their physical examinations in Houston. As the young men waited, the white mob stormed the depot and attacked the new soldiers with pipes and other makeshift weapons, killing or severely injuring many of the men before they could begin their journey to serve the country in the Second World War.

When my grandmother arrived in Beaumont with her parents and eight siblings, the city was strictly divided along the color line. There was a white Beaumont and a Black Beaumont. Schools, churches, stores, restaurants, hotels, and businesses were segregated. Black businesses were concentrated in specific sections of the city, like along the Black-owned section of Forsythe Street. My grandmother went to work soon after the family arrived from Church Point. With eleven people to feed, her parents counted on her, as the oldest child, to help the family make ends meet. Wages for Black workers were low in the 1950s, and on average a Black worker made only half of what a white worker earned. Black workers were barred from better-paying blue-collar jobs and managerial work. Higher education in Beaumont, as throughout most of the South, was closed to Black students. Students who sought a professional career had to go elsewhere for education and training.

One of these students was Elmo Willard, who attended Howard University Law School in Washington, D.C., and helped prepare Thurgood Marshall for oral arguments in front of the U.S. Supreme Court in the case of *Brown v. Board of Education* in 1954. Willard would return to Beaumont and became one of the city's first Black lawyers—and one of the preeminent civil rights lawyers in the state. He would be part of the legal team that finally overcame white Beaumont's opposition to school desegregation in 1982 (close to thirty years after *Brown v. Board*)!

My grandmother worked hard, never earning more than forty dollars a week for cleaning homes. Together with my grandfather, she raised twelve kids in that second small house her father had built on Glenwood Avenue in the Pear Orchard. It was a complex family, and though my mama was my grandmother's child from another relationship, my grandfather raised her like she was his own, as he would later raise me.

My grandfather must have seen and experienced a lot during his life in Beaumont, though he didn't talk much about it. He was born during the Great Depression. He was eight years old when the race riot broke out in 1943. He played baseball and basketball for segregated Hebert High. Folks say he had skills, which earned him the nickname "Lefty."

He joined the military after high school and returned after his service to a Beaumont still segregated. He watched as the Civil Rights Movement expanded through the Gulf Coast and he lived through the violent, repressive white backlash, some of which spread throughout the state from Klan headquarters in nearby Vidor.

My grandfather didn't become a star athlete. He wasn't a leader in the Civil Rights Movement. He worked as a janitor and handyman for our church, earning around five hundred dollars a week at his peak. Despite the challenges he faced, he never broke. He worked damn hard his entire life. He had a moral core as hard as steel. It would be his values, more than anything else, that shaped my life.

THE PEAR ORCHARD, 1989

The Pear Orchard lies to the south of downtown Beaumont. It has been a Black neighborhood for over a century, since the brothers and former slaves Usan Hebert and Ozan Blanchette inherited the entire area from their slave-owning, white father at the end of the Civil War. Hebert and Blanchette sold plots to migrant families and donated land to build the first neighborhood school, which became South Park Colored School before it changed its name to Hebert High School, where my grandfather and mama went, and before it became Ozen High School, where I played ball. When my great-grandparents settled in the Pear Orchard, it was home to families arriving in the city from rural Texas, Louisiana, and Mississippi and from as far away as Georgia and the Carolinas.

Whether my ancestors bought their small plot of land from the Heberts and Blanchettes directly or from someone else, I do not know. How they had the money for the land is unclear, but the fact that they came from Church Point, acquired land, and built a house in the Pear Orchard is incredible, a testament to their will to survive against the greatest of odds.

The Pear Orchard, as the closest Black neighborhood to the Lucas Gusher, grew in relation to the oil boom on Spindletop Hill. Its residents were barred from the drilling rig, but many found work clearing roads, digging belowground tanks, hauling wood chips for the boiler, and cleaning tools. Many of the neighborhood's first residents, like Hebert and Blanchette, were former slaves and their children.

The Federal Writers' Project recorded stories from some of the former slaves living in the Pear Orchard in the 1930s. In the editor's notes, the Pear Orchard is called a "settlement," indicating its peripheral status in relation to the brick and stonework of downtown, white Beaumont— and it must have seemed a world away, with its groves of pear trees and its roads paved with oyster shells, which became muddy lanes with every heavy rain.

It is fascinating and important to read the stories of men and women in their eighties and nineties, former slaves, living in the Pear Orchard or elsewhere in Beaumont during the Great Depression. In one story, a man named La San Mire, a Pear Orchard resident, remembers picking up and burying dead soldiers from a Civil War battlefield forty miles away from the Louisiana plantation where he was enslaved. He recalls his master, Prosper Broussard, forcing his mother to the ground to whip her. When asked about school, he replies, "I hoed cotton and drove the oxen in the field."

Henry Lewis, whose mother came from Mississippi, was born on nearby Pine Island and was owned by Bob Cade. Lewis describes in detail one slave-era method of punishment. An overseer had cut a hole in a fence just large enough to encompass a slave's neck. The slave would be forced to lie on a board with his head through the fence to prevent him from moving. The overseer would take a whip with holes bored into it and beat the slave's body. The holes in the whip would cause blisters to rise on the skin, which the overseer would then cut open with a handsaw. Then the overseer would take a specially prepared mixture of water, salt, and pepper and, using a mop, apply it to the victim's wounds. The reason for the sadistic torture—an overseer's "bad humor," or a determination that the slave had an insufficient harvest for the day. In some cases, Lewis reports, an overseer would murder a slave. The only penalty for such an act was the necessity to compensate the slave's owner for the "property" destroyed.

The Pear Orchard was a settlement of former slaves and the children of former slaves before it grew into a Beaumont neighborhood of grandchildren and great-grandchildren of former slaves. Like my great-grandfather, migrants to the Pear Orchard built low, small houses out of the materials they could gather and afford. The neighborhood grew as more Black folk arrived in pursuit of stable work and an escape from the punishing conditions of field labor.

Houses like my great-grandfather's place have been passed down through generations in the Pear Orchard, often with multiple generations living together under one roof. It was in such a space that my grandparents raised twelve kids—kids sleeping six to a room and two to a bed. When I'd ask my grandmother how they managed it, how fourteen people could have lived in that house, she would say, "We had to figure it out."

Martin Luther King Jr. once said that the arc of the moral universe is long and bends toward justice. For decades, people in the United States have told themselves that the country overcame its racist legacy during the Civil Rights Movement. Nothing could be further from the truth. Today, Beaumont remains nearly as segregated as it was fifty years ago. During and after the 1950s and 1960s, white leaders in the city dug in and fought every attempt at integration and economic justice for Black residents. Though school desegregation can be traced back to 1954, Beaumont refused to take meaningful steps toward integration until the early 1980s—apart, that is, from raiding Hebert High School of its best teachers and sending them to the mostly white Forest Park. State and local housing authorities followed a similar playbook: obstruct at every turn.

When integration and desegregation started to come to Beaumont, they were met with new mechanisms of white supremacy. Unequal banking practices blocked Black business development and Black neighborhood revitalization. So-called white flight to surrounding towns and suburbs like Lumberton, Port Neches, Nederland, and Vidor increased. Racist real estate practices prevented the rise of similar Black middle-class spaces. When confronted with the issue of the white abandonment of Beaumont in the early 1980s in reaction to school desegregation, Dr. Richard L. Price, a prominent member of Beaumont's Black community, responded that there's no "Black flight" because "Blacks can't fly."

This brilliant quip says it all. For generations, white people held the best jobs, owned the most valuable property, received loans that Black folk couldn't, had access to better schools and higher education, controlled government and the police, and suppressed minority wages. And when changes still couldn't be held back, they used these tools to rebuild segregated societies in the suburbs, leaving cities and neighborhoods stripped of revenue and resources, causing a spiral of dereliction and economic decline.

The end of the civil rights era witnessed the beginning of another phase in the long history of white supremacy in Beaumont and throughout Texas and the country. White society, together with white elites, launched what amounted to a broad and deep assault on Black communities from Los Angeles to Boston, from Chicago and Detroit to New Orleans. In the 1980s, under the Reagan administration, the federal government added its support to the campaign to stoke racial fears, divisions, and violence by ramping up the "war on drugs," which was focused on Black communities.

At the same time, the economic agenda of the right wing intensified economic distress, undermined workers' rights, and withdrew government assistance, using racist rhetoric to paint Black people as lazy and freeloading. "The Welfare Queen" became the new public enemy number one, even though this character was more of a fiction than Snow White or Cinderella.

The connection between increased "law and order" and the demonization of Black welfare recipients was not accidental. It was a deliberate strategy, and its goal was the tearing apart of Black families and the destruction of Black communities—in other words, the breaking of resistance to white power. This strategy was embraced and expanded in the 1990s, as Bill Clinton and his Democratic allies doubled down on Reagan's "war on drugs" and continued to cut welfare programs, joining with Republicans to pass the "Crime Bill" in 1994 and the Personal Responsibility and Work Opportunity Reconciliation Act in 1996, two pieces of truly Orwellian legislation, both with disastrous consequences for Black communities in the United States. Structural racism was now one of few bipartisan issues in an increasingly polarized country.

Even in the face of this onslaught, the Pear Orchard, and many neighborhoods like it, have endured, though not without scars. Not only did the Pear Orchard survive but it also had the internal strength to raise me. I was two years old when my father, Kenneth Perkins, left Beaumont to go overseas to play basketball and disappeared from my life. I grew up without a biological father.

Three years later, on December 1, 1989, my mama, Ercell Minix, was shot and killed. There are no words to describe the devastation of losing my mama. It's not something to get over—it's a loss I carry with me to this day. Before she was killed, it was just the two of us. She wouldn't go anywhere without me. She'd tell people I was her son and her man, the only man in her life who mattered, the only man she wanted. Every cent she earned from her work as a beautician, she spent on me—spoiling me, loving me like only she could. Losing her was like seeing the sun go down and knowing it would never come up again. It was like all the beauty had suddenly drained out of the world. And she was beautiful, my mama, tall and elegant. Her beauty flowed outward from her generous heart.

"What if?" This is the question I used to ask myself over and over. Still do. "What if my mama was alive?" Would this happen? Would that happen? Would my aunties and uncles treat me like they did, always looking to discipline and punish me. If some of my uncles would see me outside the house a minute after the streetlamps came on, which was when I was supposed to come home, they'd force me to kneel on bags of rice with my arms stretched out, airplane style, for thirty minutes in the corner of the room, even though they knew my grandparents didn't care that I was a little late. They'd whip me any chance they got. "What if . . . ?" My high school basketball coach, Andre Boutte, had dated my mama when they were in high school. She was his first love. When I first went into Coach's office, I saw he had a picture of the two of them from those years stuck in the side of his mirror. "What if?"

It might be hard for people to imagine now, but as a kid I kept to myself. I was shy, a loner. Each day, my grandmother would put a jug of frozen water on the picnic table with a Styrofoam cup and I would be outside until those streetlamps came on. There was nothing for me to do inside anyway, and I didn't want to be there. I'd spend the days hunting for tadpoles in the swampy ditches, digging holes to try to catch a crawfish with a small piece of meat on a string, taking a stick around the side of the house to catch a possum, or, my favorite activity, hunting squirrels with my BB-gun rifle to protect our pecan tree.

I'd be on the small sandlot under our basketball goal for hours at a time, just dribbling a ball by myself. When it got too dark in the summertime, I'd take my game to the middle of the street, where a power line was hanging down and could be used as a hoop. I'd be dribbling hard in the street and would shoot over the powerline—buckets.

If I wasn't fooling around outside, I was working. I'd lug my lawn mower and jug of frozen water around the neighborhood doing lawns, or I'd be off with my grandfather fixing something in the church, or I'd be cleaning our already spotless house every evening and every morning, my grandmother making sure not a single particle of dust settled there too long.

When I was young, other kids would make fun of me. They'd see that my "play shoes," the previous year's "school shoes," had holes in the toes to make room for my growing feet. They'd notice that my pants were too short for my long legs, my sleeves too short for my long arms. If you've ever wondered where I get my quick-response skills, this is it: a motherless boy, shy and lonely, with holes in his shoes having to stick up for himself. I had to have wit and a thick skin.

When none of my aunties and uncles would take me in, my grandparents adopted me, saving me from an unknown fate. It was hard, but the community rallied around me. Our Mother of Mercy Church sheltered me. I would go to the church summer camp for free, to the church school without paying tuition. For eight years I was an altar boy, for four years an usher. The church was there for my grandparents, too. When my grandfather went over to work on the church grounds, there was always something to do, and he'd take me with him to help him out.

Pastor John would be there, too, the first Black pastor of a nearly entirely Black congregation. He brought the faith and its strong social and moral messages alive for me—his flavor, his delivery, was like nothing I had ever seen or heard. There was hip-hop sprinkled into his words, his tone. It was like he was breathing new life into an old and tired body.

Beyond church, I was playing sports. By the age of seven, I was playing basketball at the YMCA and football for the proud Washington Manor Panthers, a team sponsored by the apartment projects of the same name.

By the time I got to the seventh and eighth grades, I was meeting kids, mostly through basketball, who would become my lifelong friends. Some of my best friends, like Jason "Dab" Dabney and Brandon Chappell, were like brothers to me and accepted me for who I was. Dab was the closest to me in size, and he'd often pass off clothes or an old pair of his shoes to me. I'd wear them even when they were a size too small.

They'd have me over to their houses to spend the night, and sometimes I wouldn't go back to my grandparents' shack for a week. Their parents didn't mind and always welcomed me into the family—mothers, fathers, and grandmothers treating me like I was one of their own. Others might have made fun of me—my lack of designer clothes with fancy logos, pants that showed my ankles, rolls of pennies instead of bills to buy my lunch—but not these people.

And what did it matter anyway if I wore highwater pants and had a pair of Olajuwon shoes from Payless instead of a new pair of Jordans from Foot Locker? It didn't change the fact that in seventh grade during a game, I did a drop-step in the paint and put down a monster two-handed dunk, the first game dunk of my life. What a beautiful feeling it was!

In seventh and eighth grade I was playing AAU ball for the Houston Hoops with Hal and Josh Pastner, traveling to Houston every week and even once to Las Vegas on my own. Coach Boutte was starting to get deeply involved in my life, taking me to AAU games, letting me spend nights at his place, telling me about what could lie ahead with basketball if I worked at it and what this could mean to me and my grandparents, talking about how proud he knew my mama would be of me. He became like a father to a fatherless boy.

In all these ways, I was raised up instead of lowered down. There were headwinds, forces blowing back at me the whole time, but there was enough pressure in the opposite direction to keep me moving forward on the right path. I might have worked hard—and I did work damn hard—but I was also buoyed up by this community: Coach Boutte, my friends and teammates and their families, the folks at the church, my grandparents, and many more besides. I spent fourteen years in the NBA, and can tell you that every Black man who made it to the league was similarly raised up by a Black community—not a community defined by a map or a name, but a community defined by the generous hearts of its people, a community defined by history, culture, values, dignity, and love.

Perk's Guide to NBA Survival

YOU THINK IT'S HARD TO MAKE IT TO THE NBA, AND YOU'RE RIGHT. IT'S A GROWN MAN'S league. There are 450 roster spots in the National Basketball Association. Let me put that number in context. Out of the 450, at any given time, there are foreign nationals, the elite players from around the world. In a typical year, there might be about one hundred foreign players, counting players from Canada. This leaves 350 spots for players developing out of the U.S. basketball system. Each year, the NCAA's Division I teams are allowed to give basketball scholarships to thirteen players. This is already an elite class of athletes—less than 1 percent of high school players in any given year. College teams can also carry some "walk-ons," or nonscholarship players. Just taking the thirteen number, this makes 4,550 Division I scholarship players at any given time.

Then we'd need to add players who aren't coming from the NCAA system but are playing in a development league or are seeking to enter the league through some other nontraditional route. To make it into the NBA, a player typically must be drafted. The modern NBA draft has only two rounds, comprising sixty selections. If, as with the league overall, roughly a quarter of draftees come from abroad, this leaves around forty-five spots for American players. And this means, optimistically, Division I college players have less than a 1 percent chance of being drafted.

If getting drafted into the NBA is hard, making a roster and staying there is even harder. Survival in the NBA is a fierce struggle against the very best in the world; it is a struggle that takes place day after day, practice after practice, training session after training session, game after game. But that's only a part of it. The main struggle, the true challenge, is the struggle with oneself—and this chapter is my story of that inner struggle for survival.

THE MAKING OF AN NBA BODY

When I arrived in Boston in the summer of 2003, I discovered that what had previously been my biggest strength had instead become a severe and possibly career-threatening weakness: my body. My sweltering workouts in that Texas heat, which I'd been doing since before the NBA draft with Coach Boutte, had been cut short by a foot injury in summer league.

The problem was that my eating habits (already not great) and my training schedule went together like a pick-and-roll. When I stopped working out and went on eating just about every type of fast food and soul food a person can find in Southeast Texas, my weight rose quickly.

The issue of weight management for NBA players is a huge one, especially for a big fella like me. If an NBA player, especially a guy playing down low, doesn't weigh enough and isn't strong enough, he can't compete. He can't hold his own in the paint, can't play defense, can't rebound, and can't even set a quality screen. How else but with size and strength could a center or a power forward go up against the other big men in the game? Night after night, the likes of Shaq, Tim Duncan, Yao Ming, Dwight Howard, Zach Randolph, Ben Wallace, and many others were waiting to pound on you—and even smaller guys are tough as nails and damn strong. On the other hand, if you weigh too much, you also couldn't compete against these guys. They were big, yes, but most of them were also incredibly fast, quick, and skilled. If you're overweight and out of shape, then you're way too slow, not quick enough, not agile enough, and don't have the stamina to run the floor.

The very worst condition to be in was to be both overweight and not strong enough, and that was my situation when I arrived in Boston. As my grandmother would say, I was "dead bird, tall grass."

When the training staff first took my numbers, the stats were truly atrocious. My weight had risen to 330 pounds, and this was not muscle. My body fat had crested up to a flabby 29 percent. I was lucky the team didn't put me on the first bus back to Beaumont. I'm sure the thought crossed some of their minds, including my first NBA coach, Jim O'Brien, who told me straight up, in his typical blunt way, "Get in shape, Perk, or you're going to be out of here." I could tell from the jump that O'Brien was gunning for me. He was just waiting on me to fail, like so many others in the media and elsewhere, who took extra pleasure in the struggles, on and off the court, of any guy who was trying to make the leap from high school to the pros.

I had to get myself together and take care of business. I thought about what my grandfather said to me before I left Beaumont for Boston: "Time to get to work." That was it, and though it sounds straightforward, and on some level *is* straightforward, after years of dominating Texas basketball I had to make a radical readjustment in my thinking to confront a new and unforgiving reality. The reality was this: I wasn't good enough to get serious minutes in the league. If I didn't get it together, I would be out of the league and the latest cautionary tale about why high school players should never skip college in the first place. My body needed a total rebuilding. Respect in the NBA isn't a product of AAU, high school, or college success. Respect from coaches and teammates— and game minutes—is earned.

There are two ways to think about pride—and it can make or break you. There's the type of pride that provokes us to defend ourselves what-ever the case might be, to dig in and fight back whether we are right or wrong. This is the pride of Proverbs 16:18, and I knew my Catholic school lessons well: "Pride goes before ruin, arrogance before failure." Then there's the other kind of pride. This is the kind that pushes us to be better and calls on us to be the best version of ourselves that we can possibly be. I can't count how many times during summer league or those early months in Boston that first type of pride rose inside of me, calling on my memories of recent triumphs, the knowledge that at var-ious times during the previous years I'd been ranked the number two high school player in the country.

If this side had won out, I wouldn't have made it. I'd have stumbled before I even got started. Believe me, I've seen it countless times: guys who get stuck in this destructive mire of pride, digging a trench to defend themselves out of which they'll never escape—and soon they're gone, out of the game and out of the league. Instead of buying into the team game and finding a role, some guys couldn't get out of their own way.

Another rookie on that 2003 Celtics team had a voice-mail message that said, "You have reached 'I am Him.'" Could there be any better ex-ample of pride before the fall? Predictably, this guy's career never de-veloped as it should have. He got stuck inside the image of himself he'd constructed and needed, unable to see it was just a mirage. In later years, I'd try to guide the rookies and other young players to embrace the right mindset to make it in the NBA. This is because for the second type of pride to work, the kind that builds us up instead of tearing us down, it's necessary to get feedback from others. Everyone comes into the NBA as The Man, as a star, but in the NBA most of these guys are never going to be The Man, and are going to need to find their spot, to learn their role.

Luckily, even though I was eighteen years old during my first pre-season, I have always been something of an old soul, with respect for my elders. I knew I had to do way more listening than talking—and the

"talking" I had to do was with my play on the court and in the training room. It's funny looking back on it now from the perspective of being in the media, where nobody is really listening and everyone wants
to talk as much, and as loudly, as possible—myself included. Getting
a word in when Stephen A. Smith revs up can be as difficult as boxing
out Dwight Howard in his prime! The value of really listening, absorb-
ing, soaking in knowledge—this is what it's all about. And soaking in
knowledge that's hard to hear, that's uncomfortable—I'm talking about
hard but constructive criticism—this is the pathway to greatness for all
of us. It builds the second kind of pride. And I certainly heard plenty of
hard, constructive criticism during my first months as a Boston Celtic.

Perk, you got to lose some weight, big fella, you're too fat.

Perk, you got to work on your foot speed.

Perk, you got to get up and down the floor faster, you're way too slow.

Perk, you got to work on your hops.

Perk, listen, you got to control your eating habits. You can't eat like
this. You need to watch what you put into your body, because that's your
temple. "Does this mean no more deep-fried catfish?" Yes!

Perk, you got to be a true professional at all times, show up to work
on time, treat the janitor the same way you treat the principal.

I'd listen to what people were telling me—coaches, trainers,
teammates—and I'd say, "I got it." And I did get it. I watched the
veteran players and how they acted. Guys like Walter McCarty took me
under their wings. Paul Pierce guided me like he was my big brother.
He'd have me over to his place, what he called "Club Shiznit," and we'd
spend time kicking it in his man cave.

It was special for me to leave my town house and head over to Paul's
$3 million mansion. He had about five televisions going in the Club,
each playing a different NBA game, and we'd spend hours watching
basketball and eating food, breaking down certain players and situations, getting to know each other. Paul would ask me about how it was

growing up in Texas, about my family and my past. He'd tell me about his life in California, his move from Oakland down to Inglewood, about the relationship he had with his mother, who meant everything to him.

It might be a long road from Inglewood to Beaumont, but it turned out Paul and I had a lot in common. We grew up the same way—and these were the kinds of bonds that meant everything to me as a young player. Teammates became friends, friends became family. When we weren't watching games, Paul would get out the dominoes. When he'd try to pull some of his California dominoes style on me, I'd tell him about how we do things in Texas, that I put the dots on dominoes.

I was grateful to Paul, too, for always extending invitations to my friends who'd come from Beaumont to visit or live with me. He'd have all the players and their friends over to the Club for "fight nights" or other big pay-per-view events, and we'd chill there. One night, we decided we'd hit up a bowling alley and do some bowling. It was my friend Dab, Tony Allen, and me up against Paul and two of his boys. After a while, Paul must have gotten bored, because he began to lay down bets on each frame. First it was twenty dollars for a strike. After a few rounds, the bet grew to one hundred dollars. After losing a couple of rounds, Paul unzipped his money pouch and pulled out twenty thousand dollars in cash. He was ready to put it all on one frame, he said, twenty thousand for the man who would step up and try for a strike. That was too rich for me or Tony—and it was game over for the night.

During my rookie season, on one of those cold, snowy Boston days, Paul came into the locker room before practice and threw down fifteen hundred dollars in front of my locker. He bet me I couldn't go outside into the twelve inches of newly fallen snow in just my workout tights and give him one hundred push-ups. I said, "You've picked the right motherfucker today," and went and knocked out the hundred, pocketing the cash. Paul pushed me to take pride in everything I did, on and off the court. At the same time, no number of snow push-ups were going to make my 330-pound body NBA-ready. This was a job for professionals.

Another rookie in the Celtics' organization in the fall of 2003 was a guy named Bryan Doo. It was Bryan, and others like Walter Norton Jr. on the Celtics' athletic staff, who worked me, guided me, drove me, and ultimately helped me transform my body. By the middle of my rookie year, I'd lost around 60 pounds, got my weight down to around 270, and had cut my body fat from close to 30 percent down to 9.

The hard work I was putting into my body was translating directly to the court. I still wasn't seeing time in games, but "game time" for me was every day in practice. I threw myself into the different aspects of the game like I'd never done before. I was learning how to play the center position at the NBA level: learning how to read NBA offenses, how to anticipate where lines of attack develop, how to communicate and move on defense, how to get in the optimal position for a rebound. Danny Ainge added more detail: court spacing, defensive positioning. The amount I was taking in and processing in these first months in the league was incredible.

It felt good to be learning and growing. I could see it coming together, could feel how with each passing week I was stronger, faster, and smarter. My play in practice began catching people's attention. One day toward the middle of my rookie year, I arrived at our practice facility and nearly walked right into a shouting match between Danny and Coach O'Brien. They were going at it like I'd never heard either of them do before.

After a few minutes, it became clear they were yelling at each other about me! Danny had seen what I was doing in practice and thought the time had come to get me some minutes on the floor in games. Coach O'Brien disagreed. He felt like he should keep Tony Battie in the rotation as the backup to Mark Blount, our starting center. O'Brien was old-school and didn't think a rookie should be given anything, even if

I'd earned a shot. It gave me confidence to hear Danny talking the way he did, though it didn't change how I related to the coaching staff. If they wanted to keep playing Battie over me, that was how it had to be. I knew I'd have my day.

The incident did give me an interesting insight into how NBA organizations functioned and the divisions that could grow between a coaching staff with one philosophy and set of priorities and a front office with another. It was fodder for a later media career.

For a fatherless kid, I have been lucky to have some great father figures, starting with my grandfather and then Coach Boutte. Danny Ainge was another one, a real mentor and eventually a close friend. Like I said, Danny saw what I was doing in my training and at practice and advocated for me, eventually trading away Battie and firing Jim O'Brien before the year was out, though I doubt it had much to do with a nineteen-year-old rookie's minutes.

Beyond the court, Danny was a major factor in keeping me focused on the right things. For young players, the first years in the league are fraught with dangers and distractions. With the money starting to flow, previously unimaginable options start to open for guys in the league, especially guys without families. Daily, there are choices to make, and a guy can make the right choices or the wrong ones. Of course, nobody makes the right choice every time, but if a player wants to stay in the league, he better be sure that when he makes a wrong choice, it isn't too wrong. And things can go wrong in a hurry.

I'm writing this in the shadow of the death of Terrence Clarke. A Boston native, Terrence was on the cusp of his NBA career, after a year at the University of Kentucky, when he died in a car crash. We can think back to Len Bias, whom the Celtics drafted second overall in the 1986 NBA draft. Bias was a transformational talent and was going to be the cornerstone of the franchise as Bird and company headed toward the second half of their careers. Bias died a couple days after the draft from a cocaine overdose. I also think of Jay Williams, one of the most dynamic college players I've ever seen. His career was cut short by a motorcycle accident, though blessedly he survived to be here with us today.

These are extreme cases, for sure, but they are extreme cases of bad decision-making that plagues players, especially young players, every year. Danny approached this part of his job with open eyes, and he tried his best to steer guys in ways that maximized their potential for success in the NBA. Some hear it, some don't. With me, Danny stressed the importance of family, convinced me to avoid the type of partying that would negatively impact my play—telling me, for example, that I shouldn't go out drinking all night the day before a game. Solid advice. When he saw me wearing big clip-on earrings, he told me I didn't need to adopt a style just to try to fit in, that I should be myself. In the crazy, fast, money-flush NBA, Danny was a grounding force. He was steady, true, and honest. Being honest in a job like that is tough, and Danny always told it straight.

My rookie year was hard, but it was also one of the most important years of my life, maybe the most important year. I won't say it was the happiest or most enjoyable year (it was baked chicken and steamed vegetables, for God's sake—no carbs); the lows were pretty low, and the highs weren't that high. One of them was my first NBA dunk, in a preseason game against the Detroit Pistons. That was probably as good as it got on the court that year. But it didn't matter. I was building toward the future, and was satisfied with how far I'd come when the season ended. That year, we slipped into the playoffs as the number eight seed and were swept by the Indiana Pacers in the first round.

After a long season in Boston, I looked forward to heading back out to Texas. Whenever I went back during those first years in the NBA, I'd stay in my grandparents' house. It took me years to convince them to move out of their Glenwood Avenue shack, but it never crossed my mind to stay somewhere else. I'd make the rounds to the clubs, pull up at the park—go everywhere. I was young, I was living, and I liked soaking up a little of my local fame and notoriety.

Like I did during my high school days, I'd show up at the school gym at 7 A.M. to run with the team and play pickup with Dab, Brandon, and the other guys. Dab would often sleep over at my grandparents' place, because we were usually hanging out late into the night and working out together early in the morning.

Here I was, an NBA player, in the front room of that tiny house, sleeping head to foot with Dab on a full-sized bed while a kid my grandmother was babysitting was in the twin bed in the corner of the same room. I'd eat my favorite foods, which were impossible to get in Boston, like oxtails with rice and gravy, pig's feet, and crawfish. When I wasn't playing, I'd get food for the guys and we'd hang like we did before I left. It felt good to be among the people I grew up with, people who treated me the same way after I turned pro as they did before.

DOC RIVERS AND THE MENTAL GAME

Shortly after my rookie season ended, Coach John Carroll, who'd stepped into the head coaching job when O'Brien was fired, was let go. A few days later, the news came out. The Boston Celtics had a new head coach, Glenn Anton Rivers, better known as "Doc."

Doc had played thirteen years in the NBA, most of them as the starting point guard for the Atlanta Hawks alongside "the human highlight film," Dominique Wilkins. This meant something to the guys in the locker room. It's nice to have a coach who can draw on a depth of experience. He understood the game from the player's *and* the coach's perspective, which meant he could see the game as a whole and understood the specific roles of everyone on the court.

This is how he set out to build a team. He saw what roles would be right for certain guys, and he tried to put them in positions to succeed. I can remember, like it was yesterday, the first time Doc called me into his office after he arrived in Boston. It was one of the most important, formative moments of my basketball career. Doc said to me, "Perk, Ben Wallace has made a lot of money in this league. Ben Wallace has done a lot in this league by being Ben Wallace. You can do the same by just being Kendrick Perkins. Block out the outside noise, be the best screen-setter, be a shot-blocker, be a rebounder, anchor a defense, and you'll last long in this league. And finish around the basket when you get the opportunity."

As I sat there with Doc, I was no longer Kendrick Perkins, NBA player. I was transported back to Beaumont, to that kid listening to the simple and clear life lessons given to him by his grandfather. Doc was my newest elder—and I was hearing his message.

That meeting with Doc was the true beginning of my transformation into an NBA player. If year one had been about physical development—getting in shape, dropping weight, eating right, building strength, speed, and endurance—year two with Doc was about the mental game. My challenge was to learn how the NBA game worked on a micro-level by breaking down film, studying formations, filtering out media noise, eliminating distractions, establishing a routine, and locking in. It might sound easy—and it's easy to say, "Learn how to anchor a defense"—but actually anchoring an NBA defense, when up against the most potent scorers this planet has ever seen, is something else again.

The other big change between my rookie year and my second year was the arrival of my man Al Jefferson, the Celtics' first-round draft pick in the 2004 NBA draft. Jefferson, like me, was big, though more of a power forward than a center. Like me, he'd come into the league directly out of high school, where he'd been a scoring machine, putting up an average of forty-four points a night as he tore through Mississippi basketball. When he got to Boston, we quickly became close friends. Our houses were right across the street from each other, and if Al wasn't hanging out at my place, I was across the street kicking it at his. We were like family.

I think these pieces—Doc, Al, the work I was putting in on my mental game, the great chemistry on the team, especially among the younger players and between us and the vets—set the stage for a year of good basketball. Along with Al, we'd added Tony Allen in the draft, and midway through the year Danny brought Antoine Walter back to Boston from Atlanta. That season, we won the Atlantic Division and went into the playoffs as the third seed in the East. Al and I continued to grow throughout the year, he mostly on the offensive side of the ball, I on defense. We went to battle against the best low-post players in the game, and people around the league started to see that Boston had a nice young pair of bigs.

In the playoffs that season, we again went up against the Indiana Pacers. Though we were third and Indiana sixth, our records were separated by only a couple of games. In general, it was one of the most even years in the Eastern Conference that I can remember.

We entered game six of that series down three games to two. In the final seconds, we were up by a point and were inbounding the ball. The inbound pass went to Pierce, and he was immediately fouled hard by Jamaal Tinsley, who caught Paul's face as he swiped at the ball. Pierce, reacting in frustration, pushed Tinsley to the floor. The whistle blew, and Pierce was given a technical foul. One of the game's greatest-ever free throw shooters, Reggie Miller, went to the line and sunk the shot to tie the game.

For Pierce, the technical was his second of the game, and this meant automatic ejection. Because he had been fouled and was awarded foul shots, Indiana coach Rick Carlisle was free to choose a player from our bench to replace Pierce at the line. And who do you think he chose? Me.

I hadn't played a minute that game, and here I was, going to the line with the chance to win game six and send the series back to Boston for a decisive game seven.

Since Indiana would get possession of the ball after the shots, the refs cleared the floor. With the season hanging in the balance, I stepped up to the line alone, took a couple of deep breaths, calmed myself, and put up the first shot. Miss. The Indiana crowd was going absolutely nuts. It's okay, I thought, just focus on the next one. I got the ball back from the ref, gave it a couple of dribbles, set it in my hands, and put it up. Miss. So much for my first moment in the NBA spotlight.

Luckily for me, the shame didn't cut too deep—we went on to win the game in overtime. Unfortunately, we didn't come out to play with the necessary intensity in game seven and Indiana blew us out on our own floor, a dispiriting end to an otherwise great year. Despite the loss, and despite those lonely misses at the line in game six in Indiana, I felt like I was at the beginning of what would become a career in the NBA.

Think about this: I was just turning twenty-one years old when my third year in the NBA began. In the summer before that year, I'd stayed in Boston and had worked hard on my game. After two years of flying in for most weekends, my girlfriend, Vanity, had moved to Boston to live with me.

I'd gotten to know Vanity when I was in tenth grade. She was from nearby Port Arthur, and I'd first seen her at an Ozen High basketball game. I had a friend in Port Arthur, Calvin Jones, and I asked Cal what was up with her. Cal knew that Vanity worked at a nursing home. He went out there and told her that his boy Kendrick Perkins had seen her at the game and had wanted to holler up to her to get her number. Cal got her home number (no cell phones in those days) and I called her up. The rest is history.

Well, not quite. Vanity and I broke up during my second year in Boston.

It was a classic case of "the grass is always greener." It ended up being the best thing for both of us, because after that I knew there was nothing out there better for me. Vanity was it—she grounded me, kept me honest and real, and would soon be the grounding force for our family.

Together with Vanity's move to Boston, it was during this third year that the necessary components started to come together for me on the court. I was in better shape with every passing day, thanks to great people like Bryan and Walter on the athletic staff. My mind was locked in. I was breaking down a ton of film, learning, studying every nuance. I'd won Doc's trust, which meant I could go out on the floor and play without looking over my shoulder every time I made a mistake. And I was still making plenty of them, believe me.

In late November 2005, I earned my first NBA start, against Charlotte. I played twenty-five minutes, ended the game with seven points on three-for-five shooting and six rebounds. We won the game by a point. It felt great. Over the next months, my play took off, punctuated by a nineteen-rebound game against the 76ers. Unfortunately, though Pierce was having a career year, injuries and inconsistencies were hobbling us, and we struggled to win close games. We turned the ball over too much, had too many defensive lapses. With Al on the sidelines for much of the season, our offense, other than Pierce, sputtered.

For me, it was a strange combination of highs and lows. On the individual level, I was making strides, especially when Danny traded Mark Blount and opened up more minutes for me in the middle. On the other hand, basketball is a team game, and losing, especially for the Boston Celtics, puts tremendous pressure on the organization. We could all feel it. The media started to do what it does. Rumors were flying that Pierce wanted out. Others started flowing that Doc would be fired, or Danny, or both. These rumors echoed across television and radio. The "experts" were weighing in. At one point, fans even booed Doc in the arena.

I can remember how Doc reacted to the media chatter, how he helped us deal with it. He told me one time, "Hey, Perk, this is what you signed up for. You have to take the good with the bad; you have to deal with everything that comes with playing in the NBA. But Perk, guess what? At the end of the day, I'm still going to go to my house in Florida in the summertime, and I'm still going to be golfing every day. So let those motherfuckers talk." Though Doc might have had harsh critics in the media, he never, not for a single day, lost the guys in the locker room.

It was clear to people both inside and beyond the organization that my game was developing. After my third year, the Celtics picked up my fourth-year option at a salary of $1.7 million—nothing like numbers we're used to now, but a lot of lettuce in 2006 for a not-yet-twenty-two-year-old kid from Beaumont, Texas.

Just days before the 2006–2007 season, the legendary Red Auerbach passed away. This was a great loss for the organization and for basketball in general, and it was an ill omen for our season. We were the youngest team in the league that year. Imagine: I was one of the older guys, and I wasn't even twenty-two when the season began. Things turned bad quickly as Pierce went down to injury in early December, taking our leading scorer off the court for an extended time. We didn't have another guy on the team who even approached scoring twenty a night. Despite the mounting losses—and at one stretch of that brutal season we lost a franchise-record eighteen straight games—we were playing hard, fighting, and competing. Still, our losing streak seemed like it might never end, and it was broken only when Pierce came back and dropped thirty-two points on the Milwaukee Bucks.

The Boston Celtics might not have won a lot of games in the 2006–2007 season—we ended the year with the second-worst record in the NBA—but, man, did we have some fun. We were kicking it in the clubs, making it rain. Every fruit that the labor of the NBA gets you, we got it. There was one epic night in Memphis when a bunch of us hit up a club and didn't leave until we'd collectively dropped around $75,000. You'll have to imagine the rest of that story.

Other than having some of the best times of my young life, the other big thing that happened during the season was that I got a contract extension: four years and sixteen million. That's what I'm talking about— that was some serious NBA money.

Money is a blessing and a curse, and from early on in my career I understood that I needed to figure out how to best manage an NBA paycheck. My priority after I made it to the league was to make sure my grandparents were straight, and I took care of them right away. After that, I put myself on a monthly allowance, which during those early years was about $3,500 a month. I didn't have a credit card and only used cash. I knew I didn't want to have access to those NBA checks hitting my account. Being eighteen and coming from nothing, I would have blown the whole thing on cars, jewelry, and other nonsense. Coach Boutte hooked me up with a financial advisor in Beaumont, and we drew up a solid plan for those first years—and I still hold to the same principles today.

Beyond the court, I was getting out into Boston. When I'd have some free time or a day off, I'd jump in the Denali and cruise over to one of the Black neighborhoods, like Roxbury or Dorchester. I'd hit up my favorite soul food restaurant in Roxbury. It was nothing like real Southern cooking, but it did the job. Often, I'd pull up on a group of young guys hooping on one of the public courts or some old-timers sitting around on lawn chairs chatting, and I'd get out of the car and chat it up with them.

Those were some of my best experiences in Boston, just being with the people, talking about basketball, chilling in the different neighborhoods, getting to know the real city, answering the people's questions about the team. When people ask me about Boston and what the fans are like there, I don't only think about the Garden crowds, I'm thinking about these folks, too. It's easy to make broad generalizations and define certain cities in certain ways. It's much harder and truer to see

THE EDUCATION OF KENDRICK PERKINS

the complexities of places and their people. It seemed like every time I was leaving on one of these visits, they'd say to me, "Hey, Perk, it was great that you came down here. Maybe next time you can bring Paul Pierce with you."

If you want to see the many dimensions of a city like Boston, compare the experiences I just described to another one I had one night when I was out with my Celtics teammates and other friends. The crowd of us, Paul Pierce included, went to a club to hear some music. It was one of those clubs with a dress code, and we made sure we were looking good so the guys at the door couldn't make up a reason to turn us away. Still, when we got to the door—no luck. Dab and I decided to go to a piano lounge next door to chill and have a drink. That's where we met the club's owner, who also owned the piano bar and just about everything else on the strip. I tried to joke around with him and ask him why we couldn't get into the club, given how well we were dressed. He got a serious expression on his face and said to me, "To be honest with you, I don't want you guys in my establishment."

One day, I got into the Denali, drove north, and ended up somewhere I never thought I'd be: Vermont. I remember arriving in a small, quaint village, wondering whether the place was still part of the same country. Was I suddenly in Canada? Had I traveled to another universe, one full of wooden farmhouses, cows, cheese, and Boston Celtics fans? One thing I knew for sure—I'd never been so far away from Beaumont.

After the 2006–2007 season ended, all eyes in the organization were on the draft, and especially the draft lottery. The Celtics had the best chance of getting one of the top two picks. That year, the draft was considered weak, with only two players considered franchise-caliber stars. These included the big man Greg Oden out of Ohio State and a lanky sharpshooter from the University of Texas named Kevin Durant, who had a type of game the league had never seen before—six-ten with the skill set of a guard.

In other words, if the Celtics fell out of the top two picks, the draft would be more or less a bust. And that's what happened. We fell to fifth overall. Though Oden turned out to be plagued with injuries and a bust at number one for the Portland Trail Blazers, we know what Durant has become: a true NBA megastar. When we slid out of the top two in the draft, the chatter started again, and it was even louder this time. Rumors mounted about the fate of Paul Pierce, about Doc's position, about Danny.

To be honest, I was focused on my personal development as a player and wasn't really paying much attention to the big picture. From where I stood, we had a solid core of guys. We were young and inexperienced, but we had talent, especially with Rajon Rondo at the point and me and Al on the low block. That's what I saw heading into the 2007 draft—but that's not what Danny saw, and that's not what Doc was seeing. While I was seeing what was right in front of me, they were imagining an entirely different reality.

It would be nice to think that Danny had a master plan in mind the whole time, and maybe he did. He certainly put himself in position to execute deals when the opportunity arose, stocking high draft picks and developing young talent—in other words, acquiring tradable assets. Now was the time for him to play his hand.

One day that summer, as I was coming out of the gym after a grueling workout, I saw that Doc was calling. I picked up and said hello.

"I got to tell you something, Perk," he said in a serious voice.

"What's going on, Doc? What is it?"

"We've traded your man Al Jefferson."

The words stopped me in my tracks. Al Jefferson was my brother; he was family. "Don't do it, Doc. We'll get this thing together."

"We had to do it," Doc told me. "It will be okay, Perk. Kevin Garnett is coming to Boston."

I fought back tears. At that moment, I wasn't thinking about KG or basketball. I was thinking about losing my friend, my neighbor, and my brother. Believe it or not, it took a while for this new situation to settle in for me. I saw only the narrow path ahead—my guy Al was heading out of town. The team I'd imagined playing for had suddenly dissolved. Everything seemed unstable, tenuous, and unknown.

Soon enough, though, the new reality, Danny and Doc's reality, became clear. Ray Allen was coming from Seattle to Boston—one of the best shooters the game has ever seen. Kevin Garnett, KG, the Big Ticket, was on his way from Minnesota. With all his wheeling and dealing, Danny had still managed to keep his coveted point guard, Rajon Rondo, despite demands for him from all parties involved in the deals. And going into my fifth season in the NBA, I was about to be the starting center, the "Big Man," for a championship contender, for a Boston Celtics team chasing the franchise's seventeenth NBA title and its first since 1986, twenty-one long years ago.

3

Big Man

I WANT TO TELL YOU ABOUT A FAVORITE BOOK OF MINE. IT'S ONE OF THOSE BOOKS THAT'S so vivid it stays with you for your entire life. I read it in high school. I can remember when the books were passed around in English class and I held it in my hands for the first time, not yet understanding what incredible power lay inside. It was a creased, ragged copy, probably twenty years old or more—a public school book, a poor public school book. Its pages were yellow and brittle around the edges. There was a large piece of clear tape across the binding of my copy, holding it together. It, too, was yellowed from age.

But all that disappeared when I opened it up and started reading. Its action and characters made a deep impression on my consciousness and helped shape who I was becoming, at the age of seventeen, and who I am now. There is no character in a book more important to me, and maybe it's the same for many of you, than Bigger Thomas.

Bigger Thomas is twenty years old and lives in Chicago's South Side neighborhood with his mother, his brother, Buddy, and his sister, Vera. The family moved north from Mississippi five years before the story begins. Bigger's father didn't make it out of the Jim Crow South—he was killed by a white mob. The family occupies a one-room apartment in a rat-infested building, and still they are barely able to pay the rent. Bigger, who dropped out of school after eighth grade, is a frustrated, aimless young man. He's been committing petty crimes around the neighborhood with the members of his gang: Gus, Jack, and G. H. Their targets have always been Black businesses, but now Bigger has it in mind that they should pull off their first hit on a white target, Blum's Delicatessen. The four young men meet in a local poolroom, and Bigger announces that today is the day. The others are nervous, especially Gus, and Bigger is nervous, too, but he doesn't want to let on that he is. They agree to do the job in the afternoon, and part ways.

When the time comes to do the job, Gus is late. Bigger is anxious— anxious to do the job and not to do it, to call it off, to back out of it without having to back out of it, to save face. He's got an interview for a good job set up for later in the afternoon. Why should he take the risk? Because the target is white. Because it will show something—something to himself—to cross that line. Because of why it is a risk.

Gus finally arrives, and by this time Bigger is in a state of frenzy. He lashes out at Gus, attacks and overpowers him, pulls out his knife and threatens to cut him. It's a performance—a performance of his power, strength, and manliness, and at the same time a performance of his fear of the job they've agreed to do, and of his deeper fear of the white man, not of Blum but of those behind Blum: the police, the courts, and the prisons. Bigger knows the system. He's been caught in it before, as a juvenile, when he was sent away to the reformatory. He knows how thin the line is between freedom and unfreedom, even if he also knows that this so-called freedom isn't really being free at all. It is a life confined to the squalid realities of Chicago's Black Belt. He pulls back the knife. Gus flees the poolroom, pelting Bigger with a pool ball on his way out for good measure.

The Relief Society has set Bigger up with the job interview that afternoon—to be the chauffeur for the Daltons, a rich, white, liberal, and philanthropic family far removed from Bigger's life on the South

Side. Removed but certainly not unconnected, Mr. Dalton owns a real estate empire in the Black Belt, including the building where the Thomas family lives. Mr. and Mrs. Dalton are looking to "lift up" some of the city's Black people, and Bigger is one charity case out of many.

Bigger arrives at the Daltons' house late in the afternoon. Should he use the front entrance? He doesn't know what to do or how to behave. He's afraid of doing the wrong thing. He's afraid of being seen loitering in front of the house. He's afraid to enter the house, afraid of the unknown world that lies behind those walls—the white world. Fear, emptiness, discomfort, and self-loathing mix in him, forming a kind of psychological cement.

Bigger pushes on, makes his way into the house, and is taken to see Mr. Dalton. Mr. Dalton tells Bigger about the job. It doesn't require much, mostly driving the family around a few times a day, and the pay is good: twenty-five dollars a week. It'll take care of his mother, allow his brother and sister to finish school, and there will be enough left over for him to enjoy himself. Mrs. Dalton comes in during the interview, and Bigger sees that she's blind. The Daltons' daughter Mary appears, presses Bigger about joining a union, and then leaves Bigger and her father to their business.

When the meeting is over, Peggy, the white housekeeper, shows Bigger around the house. The chauffeur is also in charge of keeping the furnace stoked, so Peggy takes him down to the basement. She instructs him on how to add the coal, which is an easy pull of the lever. She tells Bigger how to get to the garage, then takes him up to his room. It's a large room, a room of his own with a bed he doesn't need to share with his brother Buddy. Alone now, Bigger is feeling pretty good, optimistic. Things finally seem to be settling down; his emotions are quieting, his anger and hate burning low.

That night, Bigger is to drive Mary to a lecture she's attending at the university. He pulls the car around at eight-thirty. Mary gets in and they start on their way. After some time, Mary tells him to pull off and to head in a different direction. He doesn't like it, doesn't want to do it, but agrees. What else can he do? They arrive at the address Mary has given him and she gets out and goes into a house. She returns a while later with a young man named Jan, a member of the Communist Party. Jan wants to drive the Buick. Mary gets in the front seat, and the three of them are crunched together. Jan and Mary want to eat at a Black restaurant, so Bigger guides them to Ernie's Kitchen Shack on the South Side. He's uncomfortable riding between two white people, and he can't stand the idea of entering Ernie's with them and sitting with them at a table while they eat their fried chicken. They're putting him at risk, with no sense of what it means for him. Why?

> They made him feel his black skin by just standing there looking at him, one holding his hand and the other smiling. He felt he had no physical existence at all right then; he was something he hated, the badge of shame which he knew was attached to a black skin . . . He felt naked, transparent; he felt that this white man, having helped to put him down, having helped to deform him, held him up now to look at him and be amused. At that moment, he felt toward Mary and Jan a dumb, cold, inarticulate hate.

Inside Ernie's they order fried chicken and beer. Bigger doesn't have an appetite. When his girlfriend Bessie comes by the table, he blows her off. Jan orders a bottle of rum and pours Bigger a glass. The alcohol starts to dull the sharp edges of his emotions, to wash away the fear and hate. When they're done eating, Jan takes the bottle with them to the car. They tell Bigger to drive around for a while. Mary and Jan stay in the backseat, drinking, making out, occasionally passing the bottle up to Bigger so he can take a pull of rum. Bigger coasts through the city. He's feeling fine now, relaxed, doesn't mind that the two in the back are getting pretty drunk, especially Mary. Bigger is drunk, too, but he can handle the booze.

Around two in the morning, Jan gets out to catch a streetcar back to his place. Bigger takes Mary home. Mary is far gone at this point. When they get out of the car, Bigger sees that she can't walk straight—she can barely stand. Bigger knows that if she makes a racket and wakes up her parents and they see she's drunk and he's been drinking, he'll probably be fired. Then again, if he helps her up to her room and they find him there with his Black hands on her white body, he'll definitely be fired, if not something much worse. Either way, there's danger for him—but then again, he thinks, he can't just let her pass out on the floor or risk she will fall down the stairs.

He helps her to her room, lays her down on her bed. As he's there above her, the blind Mrs. Dalton appears at the door. She calls out to Mary. Bigger imagines that if Mary talks, she'll give him away. Mary starts to respond, but Bigger covers her mouth with his hand. Mrs. Dalton approaches, again calling out to Mary. Mary tries to free herself, but Bigger takes her pillow and pushes it down over her head, muffling her voice. Mrs. Dalton keeps calling. Bigger is desperate now. He's pushing down hard on the pillow with all of his force. Mary's hands have grabbed onto his arm, digging their nails into his flesh, trying to claw herself free. She has no chance. Bigger Thomas is big and strong. He's fighting for his life—unaware that Mary is fighting for her own. Mrs. Dalton smells the booze in the air. Disgusted with her daughter, she turns and leaves.

Bigger is relieved. He lifts the pillow from Mary's face and gazes down at her. At first, he thinks she's asleep. But then he notices her chest isn't rising and falling. She's not making any noise, not drawing breath. She's not breathing. She's dead. He's killed her. It's an accident that is no accident, a murder that is no murder, or maybe it is, or maybe in part.

Bigger grabs Mary's body, stuffs it in her trunk, and brings it down to the basement. His plan is to bring her body out of the house to get rid of it, but then he sees the furnace. He opens the grate and pushes the body in toward the glowing coals. The shoulders catch in the hatch—the body is too long to fit. With his knife and a small hatchet he finds in the cellar, Bigger cuts off Mary's head. The headless body slides down into the flames. The head follows. Bigger pulls the lever and the furnace fills with coal as Mary's body burns.

Richard Wright's portrait of Bigger Thomas in the novel *Native Son* remains incredibly powerful. The force of the story is propulsive, sweeping the reader along in a torrent of action and emotion. Bigger's feelings of anger, shame, fear, and hate are just as current now as when the book was published in 1940. It's a sorry statement that Bigger's world is still our world, Bigger's fear is still our fear, and Bigger's fate is still the fate of way too many of America's Black men, who are battered and often destroyed on the cusp of manhood.

Bigger's path to manhood is blazed in violence. The killing, beheading, and burning of Mary Dalton is Bigger's "revolutionary act," a strike against white tyranny and control. It is an act Bigger thinks can win him his freedom, but Bigger's act is futile—there is no revolution coming from his violence. His violence is not self-creating but self-destructive. His desire to be human burns out in the flames of dehumanization. Giving himself over to the notion of the purifying force of violence, Bigger plunges into a spiral of destruction, raping and murdering his own girlfriend Bessie as he flees for his life. After this second murder, Bigger reflects:

> And yet, out of it all, over and above all that had happened, impalpable but real, there remained to him a queer sense of power. He had done this. He had brought all this about. In all of his life these two murders were

the most meaningful things that had ever happened to him. He was living, truly and deeply, no matter what others might think, looking at him
with their blind eyes. Never had he had the chance to live out the consequences of his actions; never had his will been so free as in this night and
day of fear and murder and flight.

Of course, Bigger is not free at all. He is hunted by thousands of
police moving systematically through the Black Belt in search of him.
Rather than being powerful, he is soon to become the ultimate symbol
of powerlessness: the convicted murderer awaiting death. If Bigger's self-
destructive nature is clear, if his failure to create meaningful change
is obvious, if his act of rebellion ultimately strengthens white society's
power over Black men rather than weakens it, if his portrait reinforces
rather than subverts stereotypes and prejudices about Black men and
Black masculinity, why does Bigger Thomas continue to loom so large
in the American imagination? Why is Bigger Thomas America's quintessential Black "Big Man"—a model resurrected time and again in both
the white and the Black imagination, from the Moynihan Report to the
lyrics of Ice Cube and Biggie Smalls?

Common to these visions is a fantasy of violence. There was violence
on Bigger's side as a means of acquiring agency. There was violence on
the other side as a means of domination, control, and the maintenance
of social, political, and economic hierarchy. Violence, then, becomes a
way of constructing identity, whether it is Bigger's violence as a young
Black man in Chicago in the late 1930s or the violence of a white Minneapolis police officer in the summer of 2020 pressing his knee on the
neck of George Floyd.

As a six-foot-ten, 275-pound Black man, the following question seems
vital to me, and not only to me but to my kids and the entire next generation. Can we imagine a model for a new Black "Big Man" beyond
Bigger Thomas? Or, as James Baldwin might have put it, can today's

Bigger Thomas (and there's a Bigger Thomas in each of us) overcome self-destructive anger and violence, despite the massive amount of violence coming at him from all sides, to move into love? "Big Man" is another way of saying "leader," and I don't mean a guy yelling and telling everyone what to do. I learned over a fourteen-year NBA career that leadership is based on deeper qualities, ones that have to do with character, self-knowledge, and the willingness and ability to adapt. A look at some of my favorite big men in the history of basketball can help us discover the type of leadership, of manhood, we need now more than ever.

BILL RUSSELL'S REVOLUTION

Nowhere in the world does size matter as much as it does in the National Basketball Association, but being big isn't nearly all there is to it—I know this better than almost anyone else on the planet. There is no player who captures the complexity of basketball's big man better than Celtics legend Bill Russell. For me, NBA history might as well begin on December 22, 1956, when Russell made his debut for the Boston Celtics against Bob (Robert E. Lee Jr.) Pettit (the son of a Louisiana sheriff) and the St. Louis Hawks. Russell was born just one year before my grandmother, in 1934, in Monroe, Louisiana. Like my ancestors, Russell's family worked the fields amid the horrors of the Jim Crow South, and like my great-grandparents, Russell's parents found their way out of Louisiana. The Russells settled in Oakland, California, in 1943.

Russell's mother and father got jobs in the shipyards, and things seemed to be going well for them. A year later, Russell's mother got sick, and soon she passed away, a devastating blow to the twelve-year-old Russell, just as it had been for me the day my mama was shot when I was five. Russell talks about how his mother provided a barrier between him and a brutal reality, remembers asking his mother's ghost not to leave him alone in this place, this world, a world full of mean, cruel people. I can relate—I had these exact same conversations with ghosts. Everywhere a boy turned in 1940s Oakland, there was cruelty and violence, like the time Russell saw an Oakland cop beating and dragging an eleven-year-old Black boy away to jail.

Russell wasn't a sports star in middle school or high school. It wasn't until after his senior year that he got offered a scholarship to play for the University of San Francisco across the bay from his home in Oakland. In those days, the big college programs either didn't recruit Black athletes or they had a strict but unwritten quota system in place to limit the number of Black players on the team. Opposing coaches would complain when the USF Dons took the floor with three Black starters: Hal Perry, K. C. Jones, and William Felton Russell. By Russell's junior year, a year after a medical emergency sidelined Jones for the entire season, the Dons were college basketball's dominant force. Perry, Jones, and Russell would blaze their way to two straight college basketball championships and a record-setting fifty-five-game winning streak.

In late 1956, Russell joined the Boston Celtics to play for Red Auerbach, alongside Bob Cousy and Tommy Heinsohn. During this thirteen-year career in the NBA, Russell would fundamentally change the game of basketball and demand a reevaluation of the status of the Black athlete in American society. Both Russell's on-the-court presence and his off-the-court actions offer a model for the life of a "big man" that takes us far away from the nihilistic, self-destructive violence of Bigger Thomas.

One of the things I love about Bill Russell is how he changed the game of basketball. It's possible Russell had the single greatest impact of any player on professional basketball, and he did it not on the offensive end, not primarily as a scorer, even though he could certainly score the ball. When we think about the NBA greats from generations past—Magic, Jordan, Bird—we tend to think of offense, those sublime dunks, amazing passes, fallaway jumpers, and, as of late, breathtaking three-pointers by the likes of Steph Curry, Damian Lillard, Kevin Durant, and James Harden.

Bill Russell wasn't an offensive star. He was no Wilt Chamberlain or Kareem. Unlike those other guys, Russell changed basketball with his defense and his rebounding. On the glass, Russell was a monster. He would pull down twenty, thirty rebounds a game, night after night. His 21,620 career rebounds are bested only by Chamberlain. To really appreciate the scale of Russell's rebounding numbers, just compare his dominance of the boards with some of the great rebounders who followed him. Tim Duncan, who played nineteen seasons to Russell's thirteen, finished his career with around 15,000 rebounds. Shaq, who also played nineteen seasons, barely cracked 13,000. Patrick Ewing, a fifteen-year pro, grabbed around 11,000 boards.

It wasn't just that Russell rebounded the ball with incredible efficiency, it was that his work on the defensive glass was the cornerstone of a Celtics style of offense that transformed the NBA. Russell's rebounding allowed the Celtic guards to release early into spaces up the court, where they could receive darting outlet passes from Russell. This was the first step in executing the fast-paced tempo that would define Celtic basketball, a tempo that since Russell's rookie year in Boston would create the modern NBA on-court dynamic. It is the tempo Russell and the Celtics added to the game that transformed it from a game of set-pieces and deliberate moves to the fast, flowing, dynamic, athletic, and beautiful sport we love today. It is no surprise that Russell had this impact—he and K. C. Jones had already pioneered this approach to the game with the San Francisco Dons.

While Russell's rebounding became the foundation for the Celtics' fast-paced transition offensive, reshaping NBA basketball into a true full-court game, Russell's defense was even more revolutionary. Not only did he neutralize opposing centers, many of whom were stars before he entered the league, but he also made the area around the hoop unwelcome terrain for those who wished to test him. Before Russell, if a slashing guard or forward beat his man off the dribble, it was generally smooth sailing into a layup. This was no longer the case with Russell on the court. The Celtics' big man blocked shots with deadly precision.

Defense became Russell's calling card. Far from being only a question of power, defense for Russell was a complex process of establishing control of the court by eliminating opponents' strengths. It was this brand of total team defense that anchored the greatest run of any professional sports team in American history—eleven championships in thirteen years.

Beyond the winning, Russell's defense sparked innovation in how others played the game of basketball. The next wave of players would have to move faster, jump higher, shoot better, and be, in general, more creative on the offensive end of the court if they had any hope of surmounting Russell's dominance. In other words, the ripple effects Russell caused in the game led to the likes of Elgin Baylor and Oscar Robertson, and eventually players like Magic Johnson and Michael Jordan—guards and forwards who could challenge in the paint, often high above the rim.

Whether we're talking about rebounding or defense, what we're really talking about with Russell is a team-centered approach to the game, a basketball philosophy that became the cornerstone of my NBA life. Russell, of course, played the lead role throughout the Celtics' dynasty, but he still had a role to fill and knew he needed to inspire his teammates to do their part. Russell's understanding of the team concept on both ends of the court is, for me, the key to his on-the-court legacy. He saw how the game could be played better, he knew what he needed to do to allow this to happen, and he strove to be the best component of the best system rather than aiming to be simply the best individual player on the court. The greatest players, the greatest winners in NBA history, would re-create this model—from Magic and Bird to Jordan, Kobe, and LeBron James.

Many of us forget that Bill Russell, beyond the court, was one of the most important Black athletes in this country's history. At USF, he and his teammates ushered in a new age for the Black college athlete, playing key roles in transforming what had been a nearly all-white sport at the collegiate and professional levels to a sport dominated by Black players, many of whom were sons of parents who'd left the rural South during the Great Migration and had settled in the densely populated Black sections of American cities in the North and West, helping to define basketball as an urban game.

Nonetheless, resistance in the 1950s to these racial changes on the court was fierce. When the USF Dons were on the road in the Midwest or in the South, Russell and his Black teammates experienced firsthand the virulence of American racism, now enflamed and radicalized in the wake of the Supreme Court's decision in *Brown v. Board*, which struck at the heart of legal segregation and white-supremacist identity. In other words, Russell, K. C. Jones, and the other Black players on the USF team played the game of basketball in a cauldron of racist hate, meaning that they needed a type of focus and mastery over themselves that is hard to fully fathom, but which Black athletes today certainly can at least partly understand.

In Boston, Russell was forced to live a kind of divided life. The force of his character and the quality of his play had quickly and successfully integrated his Celtics team. Beyond the walls of the Boston Garden, however, the situation was very different. Throughout Russell's career, Boston remained a divided and racially segregated city, like so much of the United States. As he confronted racial hate at home and as he traveled around the country, often being denied service in hotels and restaurants, Russell could not be silent. So central were issues of racial inequality for Russell that even after winning the NBA championship in three of his first four years as a pro, he could say with utter sincerity that he felt as if he'd accomplished nothing.

After all, what did a ring mean to a Black man who lived in a country that espoused freedom but practiced racial terror? What did it mean to bring the NBA crown to a city and a region that segregated its schools and neighborhoods and discriminated against its Black residents? What did it mean for Russell to be a champion when white residents in his suburban Massachusetts town organized a movement to drive his family out, broke into his home, vandalized his space, and defecated in his bed? We can start to see what Russell's "nothing" meant.

Part of Russell's evolving consciousness was the deliberate assertion of a media persona at odds with expectations—white expectations—of the time. If the media wanted Russell to defer, he refused. If the local and national press wanted Russell to be grateful for his opportunities and wealth, he was instead defiant. The white media lobbed the typical criticisms of Black athletes at Russell, but Russell would never bow to the pressure—not to the Boston crowds, not to the national media, and not to the Celtics' management. So firm was Russell's commitment to his principles that he even refused to sign an autograph on a teammate's team picture because Bill Russell didn't sign autographs.

Russell's relationship to the media created an important model for the Black athlete, though not one that has been uniformly followed. Russell knew as well as anyone that his personal and political stances would unsettle or even outrage the white status quo. He knew his reputation among white fans and the media establishment would take a hit. Yet he acted out his consciousness anyway, never apologizing for being a strong, confident, powerful Black man.

In 1963, Russell joined Martin Luther King Jr. and hundreds of thousands of others for the March on Washington. Always the quintessential team player, Russell steered clear of the limelight, politely rejecting the organizers' offer to stand on stage with the civil rights leaders and instead occupying a seat in the second row. At the same time, Russell was conflicted about King's nonviolent approach. The movement leaders,

Russell thought, were staking everything on this oppositional tactic. If it failed to deliver, the movement itself would fail, and its leaders would be discredited. Russell was sympathetic with the more directly confrontational approach of Malcolm X, though he rejected the idea that white people were devils.

Still, he didn't shy away from proclaiming his truth—he disliked most of the white people he'd met and liked most of the Black people. It was a truth based on a rock-solid foundation of experience from Monroe, Louisiana, to Oakland, California, to Boston, Massachusetts. "Show me the lowest, most downtrodden Negro," Russell said, "and I will say to you that man is my brother."

There is no one ideal role model—no perfect Big Man to stand toe-to-toe with Bigger Thomas—but if there was, it just might be Bill Russell. He knew his life was bound to history and the structures of society, but he was vigilant in his determination that his life would not be determined by those forces. Freedom, for Russell, was not gaining agency by destroying oneself or others; true freedom was attained by acting as a moral human being, not apart from society but within and often against its pressures and forces. "All my life," Russell wrote, "I've tried to develop a personal responsibility for what I do . . . I have an extreme view of it, I guess. I alone am responsible for being a good human being."

KAREEM ABDUL-JABBAR'S INSIGHT

On June 4, 1967, a group of Black athletes gathered in Cleveland, Ohio. They met in the offices of former NFL running back Jim Brown's Negro Industrial and Economic Union. The purpose of the meeting was for influential Black athletes to try to convince the heavyweight boxer Muhammad Ali to take a deal offered him by the U.S. Army. According to the terms of the deal on the table, Ali would agree to perform in exhibition bouts to entertain U.S. troops deployed overseas fighting the Vietnam War in exchange for the government's dropping criminal charges of draft dodging against Ali. Ali, one of the most powerful and public opponents of the war, had refused the deal and had rejected the notion of collaborating in any way with the government and military. His stridency prompted anxiety among several celebrity Black athletes. They wanted to hear directly from Ali.

In attendance in Cleveland that June day was one of the most prominent big men in professional basketball, Bill Russell, there as an elder statesman and a leader of Black activism in sports. In addition to Russell, there was another big man, a nineteen-year-old center who played for John Wooden's UCLA Bruins. His name was Lew Alcindor, better known today by his Islamic name, Kareem Abdul-Jabbar.

The atmosphere at what came to be called the Cleveland Summit was tense. Military veterans among the attendees had little sympathy for the idea of draft evasion. Others wanted to see whether Ali was being sincere and standing on principle or if this wasn't a ploy to gain attention. Still others, including members of the Nation of Islam, had financial stakes in Ali's career and didn't want to see him jailed or banned from fighting.

If you look at the famous photo of the summit, Kareem sits on the far right in the picture, next to the group's leader, Jim Brown. His expression is serious, because even at this young age he knows this is a serious moment. After hours of debate, the group, which initially had come together to persuade Ali to take the deal, was instead persuaded by him, and now they were to announce to the country and to the world that the most famous Black athletes in America supported Ali in his stance against the Vietnam War. Ali had won them over to his side, and in winning them over, he had chosen his beliefs and principles over professional success and material reward. He had chosen to stay true to his moral center, even if it meant sacrificing his freedom and going to jail.

For the young Lew Alcindor, Ali's act of bravery and commitment became a turning point in his life. It was no longer good enough to play basketball while making halfhearted statements and performing ambiguous acts about the serious matters taking place in the country and the world. It was time to go all in, as Ali had, for social justice and world peace.

Kareem bridged two eras of basketball and American history. He came into the league in the fervent atmosphere of the late 1960s and the Vietnam War, participating in defining moments of social protest like the Cleveland Summit and the Olympic boycotts. In the NBA, he was the heir to Bill Russell and the new rival of Russell's greatest on-court nemesis, Wilt Chamberlain. During his time playing for the Milwaukee Bucks in the early and mid-1970s, Kareem witnessed the NBA expansion across the country and its merger with the upstart American Basketball Association, the ABA. He left Milwaukee for the Los Angeles Lakers in 1975, eventually teaming up with the 1979 number one draft pick, Magic Johnson, to win five NBA championships during his final ten seasons as a pro.

By the time he retired from basketball after twenty seasons in the league, Kareem had won six championships to go along with his three college titles, not Russell numbers but the next best thing. As of 2022, he continues to hold the record for most points scored in NBA history. For two decades, spanning the 1970s and 1980s, he was basketball's signature big man, and developed the single most recognizable offensive move in NBA history, the one-handed "sky hook," an indefensible shot that nobody before or since Kareem has been able to perfect.

Kareem, like me, was raised in a Black Catholic household, though he grew up in a place as far as possible from a neighborhood like the Pear Orchard. He was from New York City—Upper Manhattan, in proximity to the famous Black neighborhood of Harlem, where he hung out in jazz clubs and talked politics and literature. Harlem in the 1960s was one of

82   **BIG MAN**
the centers of Black activism in the country, and the force of the ideas of social justice and Black power grabbed him during his high school days.

In the summer of 1964, a seventeen-year-old Kareem would have a transformational experience, one so many Black Americans have had, when he was caught in a police crackdown at a protest against police violence in the Black community where he lived.

On July 18, Kareem was coming home from a day at the beach and decided to go to the site of the protest to get material for a story he was writing as a high school journalist. When he got off the subway at 125th Street, he found he was in the midst of the protest and that it was being confronted by the NYPD. The protest had formed in reaction to a white police officer's shooting and killing an unarmed fifteen-year-old Black boy named James Powell. Days of calls for action against the white officer yielded nothing, and now over a thousand people had gathered to demand justice.

As Kareem made his way toward the center of the protest, the police started to fire on the crowd. He had to run for it with the others and hid behind a lamppost in fear for his life. A police officer got on a megaphone and called on the protesters to "go home." Kareem vividly remembers the response from someone in the crowd, a response that steeled him at that moment and flooded his consciousness with the insight of an epiphany that would power his social activism for decades: "We are home, baby!" This might have been a particular voice, but it was also the response of the whole of Harlem. "We are home, baby!" This is the call of community activism and community pride.

The media treated Kareem in similar ways to how they had treated Russell and Wilt Chamberlain. The big Black man was always a target for criticism, an object of anxiety and fear for conservative and even liberal white America. Kareem's demeanor, his style of play, his statements critical of U.S. action in Vietnam, his stances on social justice, and his boycott of the Olympics made him a target of an enduringly racist society and press. Stereotypes were hurled across the country's newspapers, especially when an act of aggression or retaliation on the court could justify claims of deeper "character flaws"—like the assumption of a Black man's inner propensity for violence and aggression. Kareem's success, the general sentiment went, was the result of a physical gift. His shortcomings, of course, were said to be his own failings. Like Russell, Kareem was said to be ungrateful for the money and the fame—"gifts," it was clearly implied, bestowed by white owners and made possible by the loyalty of white fans.

It takes an awful lot to overcome scrutiny like this. We see athletes and others who break under this pressure, especially in today's social media environment. I've seen it up close in NBA locker rooms. Some players want to correct every misrepresentation or combat every insult, striking back at every offense. The problem is that in doing so, today's players too often become part of the narratives that others create and control. More than that, they start to lose track of their own selfhood and their own stories, so that the kind of deep introspective work that grounds Kareem and gives him a foundation for critical analysis and action is often lost in a maelstrom of tweets, posts, and the general confusion of social media. Too many of today's "Big Men" are reacting. Kareem teaches us, rather, to fix ourselves to our spot—to find our "home," as it were—so that we can let the hurricanes of social media, daily news, and racist hate speech blow past us. Then we can carry on in the direction we know is right. We carry on with purpose, poise, confidence, humility, and, like Kareem, a self-respect born from introspection and faith. Such is the meaning of the name he adopted: Kareem: noble or generous; Abdul: servant of God; Jabbar: powerful.

In the late 1960s, Kareem converted from Catholicism to Islam. While I continue to draw inspiration from the spiritual foundation built in the Pear Orchard's Our Mother of Mercy community, Kareem discovered his bedrock in the Qur'an and the community of Muslims throughout the world. One way is not better than another. The point I want to make is that at the heart of both of these religious systems, despite what many say and practice today in the name of faith, is that every single person, every human being alive, was made in God's image. In other words, equality is the central principle of faith. It is not "freedom" or "democracy," it is equality. This equality is not a matter of politics only—this equality is divine.

HAKEEM OLAJUWON'S ARTISTRY

I came into this world not long after the Houston Rockets took Hakeem "the Dream" Olajuwon with the first overall pick in the 1984 NBA draft. As much as I grew up in Beaumont, I also grew up in "Dream Land." Olajuwon, my childhood hero, was taken two picks ahead of the University of North Carolina's Michael Jordan. With the number two pick that year, the Portland Trail Blazers drafted the imposing seven-foot center Sam Bowie out of Kentucky to play alongside Olajuwon's former college teammate Clyde Drexler, drafted the year before. With Olajuwon and Bowie going one-two, the NBA, it seemed, would continue to be a big man's league.

Olajuwon grew up in Lagos, Nigeria, playing soccer and team handball. He didn't pick up a basketball until he was seventeen years old. His story is amazing. It is so different from the stories of top recruits in the United States, especially now, but even when I was coming through the youth basketball system. Today, kids are targeted from early on, even in middle school, and coaches and scouts start to cultivate relationships with them and their inner circles.

Olajuwon took to basketball quickly, no surprise given his incredible athleticism. After playing only a year, he was placed on Nigeria's national team and went to play in a Pan-African tournament in Angola.

There, the coach for the Central African Republic, Christopher Pond, counseled Olajuwon to move to the United States to play college ball and connected him with University of Houston's head coach, Guy Lewis.

Lewis agreed to take Olajuwon, a decision that would result in one of the best runs in college basketball history—three consecutive trips to the Final Four. Though he never won a national championship, Olajuwon proved dominant, living by the wisdom of his first coach on the Nigerian national team: "This is the paint. You know, it's painted red," Coach Ganiyu Otenigbade told the young Olajuwon, "because that's blood. It's very physical in there. And you, in your position, rule that lane. You rule the court. You rule the middle."

Olajuwon's freshman year at the University of Houston was solid, if not dominant by Coach Ganiyu's standards. Olajuwon ruled the lane on defense through physicality and shot-blocking, and ruled the paint on offense through intimidating dunks. In the summer between his freshman and sophomore years, he trained every day with NBA great Moses Malone. It was here, with one of basketball's legendary centers, that Olajuwon became a true "big man."

A solid argument can be made that Hakeem Olajuwon is the best big man in the history of the NBA. He had the defensive tenacity and instincts of Bill Russell. He had the physicality and power of Wilt Chamberlain. He had the shooting touch of Kareem Abdul-Jabbar. But what set Olajuwon apart from even these greats was his unbelievable arsenal of moves—his footwork, his ability to face the basket and beat his man off the dribble, his lightning-fast drop-step, his fadeaway jumper, his misdirection. The combined effect of these skills made Olajuwon dominant in an era of fierce competition, ranging from the likes of Moses Malone, Kareem, and the Celtics' frontcourt of Bird, McHale, and Robert Parish, to Patrick Ewing, to a young Shaquille O'Neal.

Hakeem's ability to combine a range of exceptional skills allowed him to weave together a new style of play. This is the definition of an artist, and Hakeem is the most artistic big man ever to play the game of basketball. Just go back and look for yourself. Watch Olajuwon in action—see the way he overcame the physical onslaught from Pat Riley's New York Knicks in the 1994 NBA Finals, how he outdueled Ewing, held his position against Anthony Mason, endured wave after wave of double-teams and punishment. And if this isn't enough, go to the next year's playoffs, when Hakeem led the sixth-seeded Rockets past Karl Malone and the Utah Jazz, then past Charles Barkley's Phoenix Suns, then past twin towers David Robinson and Tim Duncan on the way to the finals, where he met a young Shaquille O'Neal, the most dominant force the game had ever seen, and utterly destroyed him. A person would be hard-pressed to find a more impressive playoff run in the history of professional sports.

Olajuwon was a basketball artist—but what makes an artist great? I don't have a clear answer to this—nobody does—but here's my take based on a decade and a half of watching the NBA game up close. First, an artist has to put in the work, and Olajuwon certainly did. Whether in practice or in games, Olajuwon never cut corners, never took a day off. He demanded as much or more of himself as he did of those around him, leading his teammates through his example. But this isn't really it; a lot of people work hard and hold themselves accountable to their teammates. No, what made Olajuwon an artist was his ability to innovate, change, and grow. It was his refusal to remain stagnant. Year after year, he added to his game, so that by the time we see him in the 1994 and 1995 finals, his repertoire of offensive attacks is so extensive that he simply could not be guarded. Even those Knicks, a defense led by Riley and Ewing, one of the best, couldn't stop him.

Where does this desire to innovate come from? On the one hand, it comes from a kind of mental flexibility—the ability to reimagine how present circumstances might be different in the future, and how we might get to that future. On the other hand, innovation, imagination, flexibility—these things seem to me rooted in something deeper. And for Olajuwon art was rooted in faith. To be an artist, one needs to believe fully in oneself—and I don't mean belief in oneself as an egoist or a narcissist. It's the confidence and belief of a painter when he makes a brushstroke. It's the belief of the hip-hop artist in the line, the rhyme, the rhythm, the beat. It is the faith of the worshipper in the righteousness of the prayer. Artistic innovation rooted in faith in oneself: this is what Olajuwon means to me. Every move he made on the court, he made because he knew it was right.

BECOMING BIGGER

My mama was six-foot-one, my father six-six. I was never small, but it was in middle school that I really began to grow and tower over even the other tall kids on the court. By eighth grade, I was six-seven. Growing like that was good for life on the court, but off the court such a growth spurt caused me problems. My shoes were always too small, and my grandparents couldn't always afford new ones. My pants, even when newly bought, would quickly become too short, rising over the ankles to become the dreaded "highwaters," at the time an embarrassing sign of poverty and an utter lack of style.

In high school, my combination of size, strength, and skill was overwhelming to most of my basketball opponents. On the court, I led with my play. I had the respect of my coaches and teammates. I started to see myself, for the first time in my life, as a leader. I began to get glimmers of the idea, nowhere near fully formed, that the term "big man" was not only a description of size. "Big Man" was also a way of talking about importance. In other words, it was a way of talking about power.

What did it mean to think about power as a poor Black kid without parents growing up in a racist society? Despite the support and love I got from those around me, I still carried Bigger Thomas inside of me—his frustration, his rage. These were strong feelings, able at times to drown out the other side. In pivotal moments on and off the court, I could sense Bigger rising inside me, and I was able to draw strength from his rage.

There's nothing more dangerous to be in America than a Black man, an heir to Bigger Thomas. During slavery, control over Black men was an obsession for plantation owners, who devised methods of labor organization, oversight, and punishment to try to prevent revolt. Revolts that did happen, like the Stono slave rebellion or Nat Turner's heroic campaign, were met with incredible force and an enduring legacy of violence and administrative and penal control. In the aftermath of Stono, slaves were forbidden to assemble, and the practice of manumission (slave owners granting slaves freedom) was dramatically reduced. In the case of Nat Turner's rebellion in 1831, the reprisals were swift and bloody. Local white militias formed, and not only in Turner's Virginia. Throughout the South, combinations of army regulars and militia members attacked innocent Black communities, killing hundreds. Paranoia about the power of the Black man in the South knew no limits.

After the Civil War and Reconstruction, white society, first in the South and then nationwide, sought to control and punish the Black male body. Why? Black men were not disproportionally criminals, and yet the prison system throughout the South and increasingly in the rest of the country incarcerated mostly Black men. Why? When the lynch mobs formed and attacked like demonic hordes, they found, strung up, and killed mostly Black men. Why? When local, state, and federal police began their "war on drugs," the majority of those arrested and put in jail were Black men, even though the majority of drug crimes are committed by white people. Why?

One reason is the way white society has seen Black men from the days of Nat Turner until today. We are seen as threatening, dangerous, aggressive, and potentially violent. None of these descriptions are accurate, but they have deep roots in bigoted ideology and continue to be expressed in popular media. In an interview on public television shortly after he won his second consecutive NBA championship, Hakeem Olajuwon was asked—or not asked, but told—by Charlie Rose, a mainstay of liberal media, that previously he had been an "angry young man." This was in 1995, not 1955 or 1905. Not passionate, not committed, not hungry or gritty or scrappy, but "angry," which means out of control, unpredictable, violent, and threatening. This is how racist ideas infiltrate and construct our thoughts. We need to do much better.

Beyond the racist bigotry, the war on Black men in America is about power and wealth. While the racist stereotypes of the Black man as a violent threat create the public acceptance of police abuse against Black men and their unjust incarceration, the carceral mechanisms themselves strip Black men of their voting rights and press them down to the bottom of the economic ladder. In this way, the country maintains its supply of cheap wage labor, the modern version of debt peonage and sharecropping.

This is the big picture. It is a combination of racist ideology, power, and greed. When these elements remain concealed or implicit, Americans can try to convince themselves they live in a "color-blind" society. At certain moments, however, events of racial terror occur that shock the national consciousness and the consciousness of the world. The murder of George Floyd in Minneapolis in 2020 was such an event. Another happened near Beaumont in Jasper, Texas, during the summer after my eighth-grade year. It was a defining moment in my life and shaped the way I understood the society that surrounded me.

It was in the early hours of Sunday morning on June 7, 1998, when James Byrd Jr., a forty-nine-year-old Black man, left a party to make his way home. Though he'd had a lot to drink, Byrd was sure he could make it home by foot. As he walked through Jasper's streets, a pickup pulled up next to him. There were three young white guys inside. They offered him a ride. Byrd, most likely recognizing one of the men from around town, agreed and hopped onto the back of the pickup.

Instead of driving Byrd home, the three men, two of whom were avowed white supremacists, took him out into the thicket. Once far away from town, the two white supremacists dragged Byrd from the truck and started beating him. Byrd, though drunk and a sufferer from chronic arthritis, fought back bravely and desperately. This strength inflamed the men even more. They got him to the ground, kicking and hitting him. One of the men then took a can of black spray paint and sprayed it directly into Byrd's face, blinding him—an act they admitted was meant to humiliate their victim.

But the humiliation didn't stop there. Once a kick to the head had knocked Byrd unconscious, the men took off Byrd's pants to expose him, chained him to the back of the pickup trunk, and sped off, dragging him behind, skinning Byrd alive. When Byrd's body slipped off the chain, they backed up over him, crushing him under the tires, then re-chained him to the truck and continued. Through all of this, James Byrd Jr. had managed to keep himself alive. But not for long. The three men in the truck had no mercy. They made it out of the dirt back roads and onto the asphalt and concrete. James Byrd Jr.'s body was ripped apart. In a final act of white-supremacist furor, the men deposited the mangled remains of Byrd's body in front of a Black church, to be discovered as men, women, and children arrived for Sunday service.

I'll bet that every Black man in America, when he heard about what happened in Jasper, Texas, that day, felt the presence of Bigger Thomas inside himself. I know I did. How else can a fourteen-year-old process an event like that? "Bigger Thomas" is a shorthand for our inchoate response—rage. Bigger Thomas is the raw energy and power of every Black man in the United States and around the world who has felt debasement and humiliation—and much of white supremacy is based precisely on the desire to debase and humiliate.

On the other hand, Black men are not Bigger Thomas. We are not and never will be mirrors of the white supremacist's actions and imagination. We act daily to maintain our agency and the type of personal responsibility for ourselves and others that Bill Russell expressed through his words and actions. As Black men, we probe ourselves with the type of introspection shown by Kareem Abdul-Jabbar. We understand that to know ourselves is the first step to knowing about the world. And we strive, as big men, as leaders, to be artists like Hakeem Olajuwon. We're not afraid to innovate, to take risks—and this book is itself a risk—to think differently, to change our minds, to accept outside wisdom, to learn from others, while at the same time believing in our words, actions, and prayers.

This combination of agency, introspection, and artistry shapes the raw energy and power of our inner Bigger Thomas and transforms it from a negative force to a positive one. I don't want to be misunderstood. I am not talking about "taming" this energy and power, and I'm not talking about repressing our rejection of a racist history and the status quo. I'm talking about letting the energy flow, giving this incredible power its due, its outlet, in ways that support, build, and grow our communities, families, and selves—that draw together "teams" made up of all genders and races. In this sense, being a Black man in America will always be a Big Man's game.

4

The Run

THE OTHER TWO

THE BIG THREE ARE GREAT, BUT DO THE CELTICS HAVE A POINT GUARD? GARNETT IS A BEAST in the paint, but do the Celtics have a center? These were the questions the media and the whole basketball world were asking as we headed into training camp in the fall of 2007. Talk of the Big Three—Paul Pierce, Ray Allen, and Kevin Garnett—dominated the NBA conversation. The city of Boston was alive and crazy with anticipation for the season. It was an atmosphere unseen since the days of the original Big Three of Larry Bird, Kevin McHale, and Robert Parish.

The intense focus on Pierce, Allen, and Garnett helped forge a powerful bond between me and the other supposed question mark in our starting five, second-year point guard Rajon Rondo. Defiant, Rondo and I started to call ourselves the "Other Two."

I remember Vanity telling me during Rondo's rookie year, the year before KG and Ray Allen arrived, that Rondo was the best point guard on our team, better than Sebastian Telfair, who was starting over him at the time. "I don't know about that," I'd tell her, "I haven't seen enough yet." But damn, Vanity had it right—and she saw it early. She saw what Danny saw. There was something about Rajon Rondo that was special. Danny had been saying it for the whole year after he'd sat across from the young Kentucky point guard and seen the look in Rondo's eyes. It was a desire to take it all in, a thirst for knowledge, and a vision for the game.

Rajon Rondo grew up in Louisville, Kentucky, raised along with his brother and sister by a single mother, Amber, who gave those kids everything she could. Let me say this up front: Rondo can be a little asshole. He's one of those guys who thinks he knows everything, which is doubly irritating because he is almost always right. It is a quality that occasionally makes you want to strangle him. On the other hand, when you were in a tight spot on the court, you were glad he was on your side, and when he'd huddle us up to let us know what he was seeing or thinking, everyone listened to what he had to say, including Paul, Ray, and KG.

Still, I used to joke with his mama and ask her how on earth she put up with him for his whole life. She'd laugh and say, "Well, I'm wondering how y'all can put up with him now!"

There was some truth to his mama's words. During Rondo's rookie year and heading into his second season, now the undisputed starting point guard of a championship contender, there was friction between him and Doc. Rondo and Doc were two strong-willed point guards. Both saw the game deeply, though not always in the same way. Many times, Doc would call out a play and Rondo would change it on the way up the court, which frustrated Doc. If Doc would say "Go right," Rondo, defiant, would go left.

The scouting from Rondo's Kentucky days filled in the picture—Rajon Rondo didn't respect authority. But that's not really it. Rondo didn't respect authority for authority's sake, and he wasn't about to submit to it if the person above him, in this case Doc, had it wrong, especially when he, Rondo, knew what was better.

For Rondo, this desire to go his own way wasn't about arrogance or resistance for the sake of defying authority, though I'm sure for Doc it felt that way at times. The fact was that Rondo had probably broken down more film than anyone on the team, including most of the coaching staff. In my fourteen years in the league, I never knew another player who studied the game harder than Rondo. The result of this dedication—combined, I have to say, with God-given vision—was that Rondo would see things developing on the court more quickly than just about anyone else. He'd make the necessary adjustments, putting us in the best position for success on each trip down the court.

In the league, we call this "basketball IQ," or basketball intelligence. Some of it, as I said, has to be natural. People like Rondo, Chris Paul, Magic—those guys have the mental flexibility to see the complexity of what's going on in front of them. It takes an incredible amount of mental flexibility, what we could also call "imagination," to assess a situation and make the right decision to meet it in a matter of seconds. Remember, each possession in the NBA is, at most, only twenty-four seconds long, meaning that if it takes a guy ten or fifteen seconds to figure out what's happening and what the right decision is to meet the challenge, it's already too late. Three, four, five seconds and then the play needs to happen, the ball needs to move.

The difference between a rapid assessment and distribution of the basketball and one that takes too long is the difference between a good and a bad shot—and ultimately a winning and a losing team. This is one of the reasons Rondo has always been a winner, especially in the playoffs, when defenses lock in and decisions are much harder to get right.

Scenes flood to mind of Rondo on the Celtics' team airplane during the 2007–2008 season. We're being rowdy—shirts are off, playing cards are out. The "billionaires' table" is heating up—KG, Paul, and myself are talking trash, shouting, laying down big bets, whether we're holding a fistful of aces or just bluffing our way through it. Across the way, others are playing for lower stakes. The music is blasting.

I turn halfway around and see that Rondo is sitting by himself. He's got his laptop out. He's studying something from one of our last games,

or from our next opponent. Every now and then, he'll call us over. We
know that if he calls, it means he's found something important. All of
us—including KG, Ray, and Paul—pause what we're doing and huddle
around our little brother. He's heading into something deep, breaking
it down, telling us what he sees, what we should do about it. Whether
it's something big or small, it's usually brilliant. We tuck the gem away
and head back to our game, leaving Rondo to hunt for his next treasure.
The same dynamic happened on the court. Rondo would huddle us up
and break down what he was seeing, or he'd draw up a play for the next
possession—and damn if it didn't work most of the time.

Rondo and I became close over that year. It was to the point where if
you saw Rondo, you probably saw Big Perk walking next to him. Our families were tight, and like I said, I always looked forward to when his mama,
brother, and sister came to town. During the off-season, I'd head down
to Louisville with him and we'd kick it in his old neighborhood. Rondo,
for his part, came to my basketball camp in Beaumont and put on a show.

GLADIATORS

I had one concern as our new team boarded a flight for Rome, Italy, where
we were scheduled to spend ten days training in prelude to an exhibition
game against the Toronto Raptors. This concern was a big one, and it was
called KG. In a game in February of the previous season, Garnett and I
had gone at it, both verbally and physically, to the point that it seemed
like the hostility might boil over. It probably would have boiled over if
we weren't on the court in an NBA arena. Neither of us forgot it, and
when KG first came to Boston, as I learned later, he asked Pierce, "What's
up with your boy Perk?" Even though Paul vouched for me, there was
a cold hesitation between us when we first met. This coolness lingered
through our flight to Rome.

It might seem strange that my strongest memory from my fourteen years in the NBA is of a practice. But it was not just any practice—it was the first practice of our 2007–2008 season in Rome, the first practice playing with KG and Allen, the first practice with Eddie House and James Posey, with Glen "Big Baby" Davis and the other rookies on the squad. It could be that we were fired up to get going, just to get after it following so much talk, media chatter, and anticipation.

Maybe the guys were nervous. I know I was. I was anxious about how I would measure up in a lineup with three all-stars and future Hall of Famers. I was anxious about how I would gel with KG, especially given our history as opponents. I was anxious how life on the low block would be without my man Al Jefferson, who'd been my partner for the previous three seasons.

For practice that day, Doc split us into first and second units. And we went at it. I'd never seen basketball played like this—not on the fiercest blacktop in Texas, not in the NBA, including the playoffs. Nowhere. For hours, we pounded one another; we were relentless. I don't think anyone held anything back in this gladiatorial combat. The small local gym became our Colosseum. It was old-fashioned basketball at its finest, which means one or two steps away from being an all-out brawl. At some point, Doc blew the whistle. He knew it was something different. He told us we had to quit before someone got seriously hurt. We wanted to keep it rolling, but Doc wasn't having it. He canceled the afternoon session, too, and told us to chill and get some rest.

That one practice set the tone for our preseason and for our entire run at the NBA championship. On the court, we played hard, we fought for every inch. Off the court, we bonded like no team I'd been on. When the dust settled, the Other Two had held our own. I could tell right away after practice that I had earned KG's respect. He didn't need to say anything—it was in his look. In retrospect, this moment went far beyond basketball. It was the beginning of a lifelong friendship, a unique brotherhood. Who would have imagined, only hours earlier, that KG and I one day would huddle together in a Denver hotel room, crying our eyes out like babies, when the news broke in 2011 that I had been traded to the Oklahoma City Thunder?

During those first days of training camp, I'd become mesmerized by Garnett's workout regime, which he commenced with his trainer when practice was over. After a few days, Paul came up to me as I sat there watching and asked me what I was looking at. I told him I was seeing how KG did his thing. Pierce wasn't having it. "This man is a future Hall of Famer," he said, pointing at the Big Ticket. "He's not going to come and invite you to join him. If you want to work out with KG, go up and ask him."

I got up and approached as KG was pushing through a grueling set of exercises. I asked if I could join the workout, and I was greeted with the biggest smile I'd ever seen in my life. Only KG can smile like that. I jumped to it, and you can probably imagine what came next. I'd just signed up for what was one of the world's toughest workouts. Man, did I come to know some pain—but I'd push through it with KG throughout training camp and into the regular season. If I thought I was in shape before, this was next level. It taught me a critical lesson: that whatever point I'd reached, there was always another, a higher, a deeper, a better version of myself possible. On this and in countless other ways, KG was showing me the way.

The impact of Kevin Garnett on the team was so massive it is hard to put into words. If there was a culture change when Doc Rivers arrived in Boston, then it is safe to say the arrival of Garnett was like a revolution, an event that leaves nothing unchanged. The first thing KG did when he arrived was to make sure the whole team knew he was going to be the third option on offense. With Rondo running the point, the offense would work through Pierce and Ray Allen as the primary scorers, cycling through those options to Garnett. He wasn't looking to dominate the ball and didn't care how many shots he got up. He told us he'd take what came to him in the rhythm of the game.

I knew right away he was no ordinary superstar. To me personally, KG made it clear that we were a partnership on the inside, and that if we could rule the paint, rebound, block shots, prevent guards from turning the corner on the pick-and-roll, we'd be doing our job. Sacrifice, unselfishness, team-first—the Big Ticket saw the whole picture, understood basketball as a complete game, didn't care one bit about his stat sheet. He wanted his legacy to be measured in team success, in wins, in what we'd do in the playoffs.

Off the court, Kevin Garnett is one of the best human beings I have ever met. His generosity is legendary—new suits for the rookies in Rome, designer watches for the entire Celtics staff. The combination of his dignity, work ethic, intensity, kindness, and fun-loving spirit centered our team, sharpened our collective focus, and drove our will to be the best. I'll just say this about KG. If I saw someone pointing a gun and about to fire at him, I'd jump in front of him and take that bullet without thinking twice. I can't say that about too many people. And I know KG would do the same for me. More than that, I know that if anything were to happen to me, KG would be the first person to make sure my wife and kids were straight. That's the kind of man he is, and that's why I can call him a member of my family to this day.

We had a special group of guys in 2007–2008. Take Leon Powe, for example. Leon, like Paul, was born in Oakland. While Paul's mother moved him and his brothers down to Inglewood, Leon's mother found herself and her kids out on the streets, living out of her car, homeless. This is poverty in America, folks—it is unforgiving and cruel, and its primary victims are children like Leon Powe and his brothers.

Leon and I are the same age. We'd met on the AAU circuit, at the elite camps, and in the McDonald's All-American Game in 2003 when we were seniors in high school. The commonalities went deeper. Our fathers had left us when we were each around two years old. Our mothers were gone, Leon's mama passing away when he was in high school. Whereas I came from high school into the NBA, Leon suffered an injury, which derailed his chances of being drafted. Instead, he got a scholarship to UC Berkeley and established himself as one of the premier players in the Pac-10. Leon knew how to play tough, defensive-minded, physical basketball. This was the basketball that counted in Oakland, and Leon's toughness steeled him through incredible childhood hardship and multiple serious injuries on his way to the league. He was drafted in the second round, usually an inauspicious start to a very short NBA career, but Leon, being Leon, overcame it.

I could tell stories like this about so many of the guys—Tony Allen, James Posey, Eddie House, Glen Davis. These were guys who'd battled through hardships, who'd overcome incredible adversity. I hope that each of these guys gets the chance to tell his full story. I hope that we're awake enough to really listen to every one of them. It was a physically tough, mentally strong group—a team of gladiators. This was a team with championship DNA.

DEFENSE, DEFENSE, DEFENSE

Our season opener was against the Washington Wizards in the Garden. It was a packed house and the fans were fired up. It was a playoff atmosphere. I'd started plenty of games before over the previous couple of seasons, but never a game like this one. It felt different, and it was different. Being announced in the Garden in the starting lineup together with Rondo, Pierce, Allen, and KG was wild. The press had talked, the coaches had done their thing, we'd trained hard, but after all of it—the trip to Rome, the intense practices, the media focus—we still hadn't played a single meaningful game of basketball. Now we were about to test ourselves against one of the top teams in the East.

A day or two before the opener, Wizards guard Gilbert Arenas started talking, saying that the Celtics might look good on paper but we hadn't done anything real. He doubted we'd live up to the hype, and he guaranteed a Wizards victory. That was all we needed to get our blood flowing—though, truthfully, we didn't even need that. We were already pumped up and ready to get at it. But thanks to Arenas, we got a little extra push.

Besides Arenas, the Wizards had big Brendan Haywood, a physical center. I knew I'd have to play hard to establish myself on the floor with this team. It helped that the second time down the court, I took a gorgeous dish from Rondo and scored my first bucket of the season. Washington hung with us for about a quarter, but when Ray Allen and others started to get hot from the outside, we busted the game open. By the third, we were up by twenty and closed out the game with stout defense, never allowing the Wizards to make a serious run. It was a sign of things to come.

We dug out a hard win against a tough Toronto Raptors team, then blew out Denver and Atlanta on our way to winning our first eight games. Through the first thirty games of the season, we were 27–3, a long way from the dismal record of the year before. I can tell you the main reason we were winning at what was at that time a record-breaking clip. It was defense. We were simply the nastiest defensive team in the history of NBA basketball. Over those first thirty games, for example, only four opponents had broken one hundred points on us. At times, our efficiency on the defensive end was out of sight, like when we held the New York Knicks to fifty-nine points. I'm talking about for the entire game.

From the jump, our goal was to hold opponents to under twenty-five points per quarter. If a team did better than that in one quarter, it meant we had to lock in harder, communicate better, play tougher and smarter. It was quarter to quarter for us, not game to game, throughout the season and into the playoffs—from the opener against Washington to the last game of the finals against the Los Angeles Lakers.

In addition to KG, Allen, and the other new players, over the summer Doc had brought in another key member of our team, an assistant coach named Tom Thibodeau—"Thibs." I can say without exaggeration that Tom Thibodeau is one of the greatest defensive minds the game of basketball has ever seen.

Defense in basketball, at any level, including the NBA, looks to the average fan, and even to many serious students of the game, as reactive. The offense does something and the defensive players respond in relation to it. This is partly true, of course, and this kind of purely reactive defense is how many teams in the league play, especially during the regular season. Truly special defenses, on the other hand—and I'm talking about the "Bad Boy" Pistons, Pat Riley's Knicks, Jordan's mid-1990s Bulls, or our Celtics team—anticipate offensive strategies and attempt to dictate the style of play to the offense. In these cases, the offense, far from controlling play, is actually reacting to the power of the defense. This is the type of active, aggressive, offensive defense that is often the key element of a championship team. Championships are built on the defensive side of the ball.

Tom Thibodeau is a fanatic for defense. When he showed up in Boston, I could hardly believe the guy was for real, but he was the perfect coaching reflection of Kevin Garnett, and the combination of Thibs and the Big Ticket would form a defensive nucleus the likes of which the NBA had never seen. For Thibs, it started with study—and, man, could he study! He knew the offensive tendencies of every single player in the NBA in minute detail.

I'm not just talking about the stars, the big-time scorers. No, I'm talking about everyone from Kobe and LeBron to the guys on the very end of the bench who never saw the court. I'm also not talking only about tendencies on the ball. Thibs saw the whole picture, on and off the ball

habits, offensive sets, structures, and movements. As you can probably imagine, this was a bewildering amount of information, but the key
to building the type of defense Thibs wanted to develop in Boston was
for us to internalize this huge amount of information so that we didn't
need to think about it on the court as plays developed. We needed it to
become second nature. It got to the point that Thibs could call out the
play the other team was going to run as they brought the ball up the
court, which gave us the maximum chance of defending it with success.

Success, however, lay in execution and attention to detail. Imagine,
we're up against the defending NBA champions, the San Antonio Spurs.
The Spurs ran a lethal pick-and-roll with Tony Parker and Tim Duncan.
This combination destroyed LeBron's Cavaliers team in the 2007 NBA
Finals, sweeping the series 4–0.

The dilemmas defenses faced with the Parker-Duncan pick-and-roll
were many. The first issue was preventing Tony Parker from coming off
the screen with the ball and either driving to the hoop for a layup or
pulling up for an easy mid-range jumper. This is easier said than done—
Tony Parker was lightning-quick. Any hesitation—and I'm talking a
fraction of a second—was out of the question. At the same time, too
much attention on Parker could allow Duncan to pop free in the confusion of the switch. Duncan was deadly from the elbow, or he'd roll to
the hoop into the lane for an easy bucket.

Making matters worse, if a defense collapsed on Parker and Duncan, one or the other would kick the ball out to the perimeter, where
the likes of Bruce Bowen or Manu Ginobili could kill you from outside.
Nor was Parker one-dimensional coming off the screen. He possessed
an arsenal of moves. He could change directions on a dime and could
read and adjust to a defense as well as anyone.

How can you stop this potent combination? The short answer is that
Thibs prepared us for every single nuance of the play, presenting us with
scenario after scenario during practices, walk-throughs, and in film

sessions. If it was KG on Duncan in a high pick-and-roll, he'd show and stay high to prevent Parker from popping off from the perimeter. This meant I'd have to be ready to slide over and pick up Duncan's roll out of the screen—prepared, if need be, to guard him one-on-one on the low block. If I was on Duncan, I'd execute what's called a "drop," meaning I'd come up level with the screen to let the guard get over the top. When Duncan would start his roll, KG would give Duncan a bump to slow him down, then get out quickly to one of the shooters. This bump would give me enough time to get back on Duncan, while my work on the screen would give the guard time to square up Parker and deny him a lane into the paint.

In a matter of seconds, you know the result of hesitation or a mental lapse—it's called a highlight film. Playing high-level, consistent NBA defense is about five guys executing every single time down the court with knowledge, focus, and intensity.

Luckily, we had two of the most intense motherfuckers the game has ever seen: Thibs on the bench and KG on the floor. These two made sure we'd be ready for whatever was coming our way, and if a guy wasn't ready or didn't execute—and it didn't matter if this was a starter or a guy coming off the bench—he'd be damn sure to hear about it.

"Perk, you got to do a whole lot better than that," KG would bark out at me. "We aren't going to win anything with you playing like that." I'd hear him. I'd hear it from KG, Thibs, and the other lockdown defenders on our team, like James Posey. I'd see it in the eyes of Paul and Ray, who suddenly were playing the best defense of their careers.

But my work paid off. I remember Danny coming to me at some point during the season to show me the numbers indicating that I was one of the top big men in the league at guarding the pick-and-roll. That's a perfect example of learning how to be a star in your role. No fan or member of the media ever sees stats like that—and this was before the analytics age in basketball anyway. Defending against the pick-and-roll didn't earn an assist or a rebound or a point, and not even a steal or a block most of the time. It was one component out of many that earned a stop, an extra possession—and a championship run is built brick by brick, making one stop after another, winning one possession at a time.

An NBA season is long, grueling, and unpredictable. Rondo would miss a few games on one of our road trips, including a Sunday tilt just before New Year's Eve against the Lakers. KG, too, was out now and then, addressing some nagging injuries. We had occasional lapses, like losing three out of four following a big win against the Detroit Pistons, our fiercest conference rival. We had our only three-game losing streak during a February West Coast trip.

Aside from these few down moments, our intensity and focus rarely wavered. The regular season was our laboratory. We tested out every aspect of our game, especially on defense. The amazing thing was that our first practice in Rome set the tone for our practices for the entire season. Our practices were like playoff games. We used to go at it so hard that when Doc would blow the whistle and shout, "I said practice is over," we'd shout back at him, "No, man, you're going to give us one more motherfucking quarter."

It was vicious. We went at the second unit, and the second unit went at us. It got to the point that even after we'd come off the court from a regular-season game, we were already thinking about scrimmaging in practice the next day, ready to bust the other unit's ass. Our games in practice were so intense that they could have been nationally televised.

Then there were what we called the G-Unit runs—one-on-one battles on the low block, first to five wins. G-Units were for the bigs: myself, Glen "Big Baby" Davis, and Leon Powe. The thing about the G-Units was that anything went—no fouls were called. We were throwing elbows and generally getting physical; fights would break out, training us for battle, for keeping our mental focus in the midst of the greatest amount of pressure possible.

This intensity, purpose, and mindset prepared us for the grind—and though we didn't win every game that season, had off nights shooting and what have you, nobody can say we took a single night off in 2007–2008. We brought it night in and night out, brought it from the practice court to the Garden, from the Garden onto the road, where we relished the role of being the villain, the Goliath to all wannabe Davids. None of those other teams had a slingshot.

We ended the regular season with the number one–ranked defense in the league and, in my opinion, the best defense of all time—yes, better than the Detroit Bad Boys, better than San Antonio, better than Chicago or those rough and rowdy Knicks teams in the 1990s. We were, in the words of KG, "a pack of wild hyenas," ready to attack anyone, absolutely fearless.

How long did it take to build that defense? All damn year, including the playoffs. Defense isn't something a team builds and that then sustains itself or gathers its own momentum. No. It needs to be constructed possession after possession, through focus, determination, self-discipline, communication, and trust. It's amazing to me how many people in the media still can't see how a championship team is built. They see scoring, shooting—the occasional spectacular block or steal. But it's defense that wins out in sports, whether it's on the gridiron or the hardcourt.

We closed out the season with sixty-six wins. This was the best record in the Eastern Conference and the top record in the NBA overall, which meant home-court advantage for as long as we survived in the playoffs—and we were planning on going the distance. For guys like myself, Tony Allen, and Rondo, the difference between the previous season and this one represented the largest year-over-year improvement in NBA history.

I have to say one last thing about the regular season. Despite the warfare in practice between the units, despite the gladiatorial G-Unit runs, we had so much fun together as a team off the court that year. If we'd get together for some event, or if we'd be on the road and go out to dinner, everyone was expected to show up, and if someone didn't, that mother-fucker would hear about it the next day. The intensity and seriousness of purpose on the court was matched by our play off it, and this balance is how we were able to maintain our level of production and stay sane.

MENACING GESTURES: ROUND ONE, THE ATLANTA HAWKS

Our first-round opponent in the 2008 playoffs was the Atlanta Hawks. The Hawks were a young team. They were athletic and energetic as hell, but inconsistency and inexperience had dogged them throughout the season, resulting in a weak 37–45 record and an eighth-place finish in the East. Talent they had in bunches, with guys like Josh Smith, "Iso" Joe Johnson, Mike Bibby, Josh Childress, and a rookie big man named Al Horford.

We'd handled our business against Atlanta in the regular season, going 4–0. We'd won all four games by double figures, two of the four in outright routs. But that was the regular season, and what a team's done in the regular season doesn't matter one bit when it comes to the NBA playoffs. The playoffs are, as we were soon to find out the hard way, a different animal entirely, especially on the road.

The Boston crowd was going crazy when the series opened. It was clear that the city had been starving for over twenty years from a lack of relevant basketball. We showed up for them in game one, playing lock-down defense, preventing the Hawks' young stars from finding any kind of rhythm. Game two was no different, and in general we were tougher, stronger, and executed better than Atlanta in both games. The Hawks didn't seem to have enough to hang with us when we were locked into playoff mode.

The beginning of game three in Atlanta pointed to more of the same. In the first half of the first quarter, we pulled out to a double-digit lead.

My guess is that we were two or three solid possessions away from a knockout blow and on our way to a sweep.

Then something happened. Just when we had this young team on the ropes, closing in on putting them away, they dug in. They started making shots, taking it to the hoop and picking up fouls on our starters, myself included. Their defense came to life. They made stops, blocked shots, and created turnovers that led to easy fast-break points. At the end of the first quarter of game three, we'd given up thirty-two points, an atrocious quarter for us. The Hawks had fought back and taken a six-point lead.

We clamped down in the second quarter and went into halftime with the game tied. In the third, our offense stagnated. We couldn't hit shots, stopped playing solid team basketball, and settled for bad looks. Not surprisingly, we fell behind by ten heading into the fourth. Though our defense was great in the final quarter, holding Atlanta to eighteen points, we couldn't get anything going offensively. We scored only nine-teen ourselves and lost game three by nine. Josh Smith, whom we'd held to six and thirteen respectively in games one and two in Boston, torched us for twenty-seven. Johnson added twenty-three.

At the tail end of game three in Atlanta, with the outcome of the game no longer in doubt, an incident occurred that most people have probably long forgotten or never registered in the first place. Even as a player, I hardly took note of it, in the midst of the intensity of the se-ries. In retrospect, though, it is worth thinking about.

With twenty-two seconds remaining in the game, Al Horford hit a jumper and started to jaw at Paul Pierce. Doc had called a time-out, but instead of going immediately to the bench, Paul, who didn't take kindly to the rookie's trash-talking, moved toward half-court to stare Horford down. Then Paul made a kind of hand gesture in Horford's direction, his thumb and forefinger formed into a circle with his other three fingers extended. Nobody on the court, including the refs, took note of it. The refs didn't give Paul a technical foul.

Afterward, however, chatter started in the media that Paul had flashed a gang symbol at Horford to intimidate or even threaten him. Over the next couple of days, "experts" weighed in that the hand sign was a signal taken from the L.A. gang the Piru Bloods, a gang prominent in Pierce's childhood neighborhood of Inglewood, California. The NBA commissioner's office, led at the time by David Stern, reacted on the morning of game four of our series by issuing Paul a $25,000 fine. Stern's office justified the penalty by claiming Pierce had made a "menacing gesture."

I need to take a step back and have us consider this situation. We were in the midst of a heated playoff series and at the end of a physical, hard-fought game, Paul and Al were going at it. It was getting hot, but it was also nothing beyond the ordinary. It was so ordinary that nobody on the team or in the stadium noticed the encounter when it happened. Paul made the gesture, no doubt about it—it's on film. Al, when asked later about it, claimed he had no idea what it meant. Pierce, on his side, adamantly denied that it had anything to do with a gang sign.

On its face, the idea that Horford, who didn't know what the sign meant, was "menaced" by Pierce's gesture is ludicrous. But it goes deeper. Paul Pierce was an NBA superstar. Yes, he grew up in a tough L.A. neighborhood, and yes, of course there were gangs in that neighborhood. But Paul Pierce was never in a gang. He was hooping. He was in the gym, working hard to pull himself and his family out of the steel trap of inner-city poverty. Paul could have stayed in L.A. for college. He could have gone to UCLA or USC, but he didn't. He shipped himself to Kansas to play for Roy Williams. He did this because it was the best move for him and the best move for the development of his game. We know how it ended up. Paul was recently, and deservedly, elected to the NBA Hall of Fame. How many gang members do you know who are in the Hall? The answer is none.

For some, none of it matters—not the knowledge of who Paul Pierce is, not the understanding of the many ways Paul gives back to his community, not the general understanding of what it takes, what sacrifices are necessary, to make it to the league and to stay there for nineteen years. Decades of performance and behavior don't outweigh the power of prejudice. For David Stern and the commissioner's office, the instant the chatter started that a player had flashed a "gang sign" on the court was the instant the player, in this case Paul Pierce, stopped being a human being, stopped being my brother, and became, in the eyes of those folks, a "Black man"—meaning, for them, a threat, a "menace," even a potentially dangerous or violent criminal.

Folks, these issues run deep, and if we are not careful, thoughtful, and aware, we will never escape the vicious cycle of prejudice and inequality. Stern told the Associated Press that his fining of Pierce was an act meant to protect the game: "We're not going to let it degenerate into something else. Period." What did Stern mean by "something else"? Was the commissioner of professional basketball suggesting that the game was going to turn into gang warfare? Did David Stern really believe that Black athletes in the league, without his steady, guiding hand, would "degenerate" and become the street thugs some imagined we were beneath the uniforms? This was white management seeking to control and police Black bodies, plain and simple—to define our actions, punish our behavior, and assert a set of social norms over us that are nothing more than the bedrock of a racially hierarchical society.

As the team prepared for game four, none of us, Pierce included, cared or thought about the fine or the commissioner's comments. In fact, fines by the league were a sort of badge of pride in our locker room, as they were usually assessed for tough, aggressive play that might have crossed (or at least approached) the line—a line we didn't mind crossing now and then, when need be.

In game four, we got off to a hot start and ran up a lead, only to have Atlanta battle back. Again, in the second half we came out strong, pushing our lead to ten in the fourth quarter. Then the Hawks' Joe Johnson caught fire. He was shooting the lights out, slashing to the rim, drawing fouls, and in general playing out of body. Our defense was far from awful, but the extra intensity and precision we'd honed game after game during the season wasn't there. Johnson ended the game with thirty-five points, lifting the Hawks to the win. The series was headed back to Boston tied at two apiece.

Back in Boston for game five, we took care of business, blowing out the Hawks for our third decisive home-court win of the series.

Game six in Atlanta was fiery. Both teams went at it, and again we opened up a big lead, and again, as in games three and four, the Hawks fought back. We took a lead into the fourth, but couldn't hold it. The Hawks pushed ahead in the final minutes. With about a minute and a half remaining, I grabbed an offensive rebound and got fouled. I went to the line and hit both shots, pulling us within two points. On the next possession, Johnson got Posey in the air on an up-fake and hit a nasty three. Paul responded with about a minute left with a three of his own. Johnson missed a jumper, and we got the rebound with a chance to tie the game or take the lead. Doc drew up a play to get Ray a good look at a three. The play worked perfectly, but Ray was unable to connect. The Hawks managed to hold on to game six, and we were heading back to Boston for a decisive game seven in the first round of the playoffs.

The anticipation for game seven was brutal. On the way home from Atlanta, Doc didn't say a thing. KG was silent—and when KG is silent, everyone is silent. There was no music, no card-playing, nothing. Shirts remained on throughout the flight. We knew we were the better team. In each game in Atlanta, we had built a big lead, only to falter when the Hawks made their run. In an NBA playoff game, the team that's down almost always makes at least one big run at you. Championship teams have to know how to absorb it, weather it, and then how to respond with greater force, putting the opponent away. But were we a championship team?

There were two days off between games, two long, torturous, and restless days. I didn't turn on the TV. I didn't watch any of the other playoff games. I didn't read the newspaper. I could barely sleep on the night before the game. It was hell. Round one would come down to one game, winner going on and loser going home. The entire basketball world was in a state of shock. Could the Boston Celtics, the best team in the league, really lose to this sub-.500, young, inexperienced Atlanta Hawks team? Were the Big Three really all that? Was KG a clutch performer? Were these guys winners? Was Doc a playoff coach?

I'll say this: the Hawks were balling out. People like to say that in the NBA playoffs the better team always wins, but this doesn't mean the winning comes easy. This series was a case study in a less talented, less experienced team pushing a series to the limits by playing inspired, tough basketball. Those Hawks players weren't going to lie down and just let us stroll out of the first round. They were men with pride and determination. They meant to play to the bitter end.

Heading into game seven, I could tell it was no normal atmosphere, even for Celtics basketball, even for Celtics playoff basketball. From Danny to Doc, from KG, Ray, and Paul to Big Baby, we were completely locked in. Nobody was talking. Doc didn't give a big speech. KG didn't say anything. It was silent intensity staring out of each guy's eyes. When the lights started flashing and the smoke was filling up the Garden as the starting lineup was announced, as the green and white towels were waving by the tens of thousands, we knew what we had to do. It was time to get it done. We were going out there to spank that ass.

It took a couple of minutes into the first quarter for us to get it going, but when we did, we turned it up to a level of intensity the Hawks hadn't seen before. I busted out my best quarter of the series, scoring eight points on my way to a double-double with five blocks. Our defense overwhelmed Atlanta. With three minutes left in the third quarter, they had thirty-four points total. Our lead grew to nearly forty. This was a lead no team was going to overcome, and we had no intention of letting them back in the game, giving them any hope at all. We kept the intensity and put the Hawks away in dominant fashion.

THE DUEL: ROUND TWO, THE CLEVELAND CAVALIERS

The dust doesn't settle for long in the NBA playoffs. There are no easy series, no pushover opponents. Fans most often remember the finals, and they forget about the bruising series that led there, series going six or seven games in the second round or the conference championship. After surviving Atlanta, we knew what was in store for us. LeBron James and the reigning Eastern Conference champion Cavaliers were headed to Boston. This was going to be a showdown, our league-best team facing off against the NBA's premier player. When the best player on the floor is on the opposite side of the ball, it's an inherently dangerous situation, and LeBron James is dangerous.

Game one was ugly. Both teams dug in defensively and made it hard for the other team to get clean looks. Absolutely nothing in the paint went uncontested. On the perimeter, we hounded LeBron with a combination of Paul, James Posey, and even KG. The result was one of the worst playoff performances of LeBron's career. But despite his shooting a woeful two of eighteen from the floor and zero of six from behind the arc, the Cavs didn't quit. They fought through the poor shooting and stayed in the game.

On this night, it was our reserves who bailed us out. Sam Cassell and James Posey made a series of clutch shots to push us into the lead in the final minute. On Cleveland's last meaningful possession, down by two, LeBron got the ball up top with Posey on him. Posey's defense had been tenacious all game, and this possession was no exception. No matter how well you play The King, nobody in the league, then or now, can stop him one-on-one. When LeBron started to make his move at the end of game one, Posey, following our game plan, funneled him into the lane, where I picked him up for the double-team. I just tried to crowd LeBron to make his shot difficult, careful not to foul. Posey and I had done just enough: LeBron's driving layup came off the rim. We rebounded the ball and the game was sealed. 1–0 Boston.

We opened game two with a slow start, and the Cavs built a ten-point lead at the end of the first quarter. With our starters on the bench, the second unit—Posey, Cassell, P. J. Brown, Leon Powe—brought us all the way back to even by midway through the second. Again, as in game one, the play was physical. We continued to hound and harass LeBron every time he touched the ball, to contest each shot he took with multiple bodies. It continued to pay off, as he went six for twenty-four from the field. This offensive inefficiency allowed us to build a lead, and by early in the fourth we were up by twenty. Posey kept the pressure on LeBron, and in general our defense held Cleveland to under 40 percent shooting. The Cavs scored a mere 72 points in game one, 73 in game two. This was defensive mastery at its finest. 2–0 Boston.

In Cleveland, our struggles on the road continued. The Cavs blasted us in game three, despite our solid defense on LeBron. In game four, we again contained LeBron, holding him to seven for twenty from the field, but didn't have the offense going and fell by eleven, 88–77. Series tied 2–2.

Game five in Boston delivered what every Celtics fan had feared from day one against the Cavs: LeBron went off. The league's leading scorer finally came to life, scoring thirty-five points. But it wasn't enough, not in Boston with our intensity spiking and the Garden hopping, our fans going nuts. Paul answered with a big game of his own. 3–2 Boston.

We returned to Cleveland with one thought on our mind. We needed to put this series to bed to avoid the damn stress we'd had in the first round. "For real," we kept saying to each other, "for real" we need to come in with the same intensity we had at the Garden and end this thing in six.

But LeBron and the rest of the Cavs had something to say about that. LeBron poured in thirty-two, and they ground out a win in a low-scoring affair. Series tied 3–3.

Game seven was back in Boston. We knew it wouldn't be like the Atlanta series—the Cavs and LeBron would be ready to play. LeBron had heated up in games five and six. We knew he'd be coming at us. We knew that on any given night, in any single game, LeBron could just about will his team to victory. Added to that fear was the fact that our offense hadn't clicked. Though we'd won three of six, we hadn't yet cracked even ninety points in a single game in that series. Ray, Paul, and KG had each had moments, but we hadn't yet played a complete game on the offensive side of the ball.

We came to play in the first half of game seven, pushing the lead to thirteen. But LeBron is just too damn good to go out like that. By the middle of the third, he had thirty points and the Cavs had closed the gap to three. At the end of the quarter, we were clinging to a five-point lead.

The fourth quarter of game seven was a dizzying quarter of basketball. The atmosphere in the Garden was tense. LeBron hit back-to-back threes. Pierce, on his way to a monster game, responded to the one-on-one duel with his signature pull-up jumpers. At the three-minute mark, our lead was three.

It didn't last long. LeBron stripped Pierce and went coast-to-coast for a thunderous dunk to cut the lead to one with two-twenty left on the clock. At the minute-thirty mark, Paul took the ball at midcourt, guarded one-on-one by The King. Paul drove the lane, kicked it to Eddie House in the corner, who swung the ball to the veteran P. J. Brown. Brown nailed the jumper—lead back to three, 91–88.

This is quintessential NBA playoff basketball. Everyone on the court has to be ready to perform, and championships are achieved as much by guys like P. J. Brown going 4–4 in the fourth quarter of a game seven as by the Big Three or anyone else.

The Cavs moved the ball well on their next possession and found De-lonte West open for a three. Shot went up. Miss. There was a scrum for the rebound, resulting in a jump ball. The big Zydrunas Ilgauskas won the tip and sent it back to his teammates, but at the very last second Paul dove between the Cav guards, grabbed the ball, and got the time-out. Fifty-eight seconds to play.

On the next possession, Paul took the ball at the point, with Le-Bron on him. Paul ran down the clock, drove to the right, then passed it back to KG at the top of the key. KG couldn't knock down the jumper. The Cavs had the ball again, still down by three. LeBron drove to the basket and put up a wild shot. KG grabbed the board, sent the outlet to Paul, who found Ray Allen streaking down the side of the court. Cleveland fouled Allen with eighteen seconds left. Ray, one of the NBA's all-time best free throw shooters, connected on both, pushing the lead to five. A late Cavs three made the final seconds more interesting, but foul shots by House and Pierce closed the deal. LeBron had been dominant, pouring in 45. Paul Pierce went toe-to-toe with him, ending with 41—and, more important, securing us the win. In my eight years in Boston, I saw Paul Pierce have many great games, but this was the game that defined "The Truth." It was one of the greatest basketball duels I'd ever witnessed, and at the end of the day Paul Pierce had the last bullet in the chamber. 4–3 Boston. We were moving on.

MY PERSONAL REVENGE TOUR—DETROIT EDITION: ROUND THREE, THE DETROIT PISTONS

"Rest is not an option, so don't even think about it," KG said as we headed into the Eastern Conference championship series against the Detroit Pistons. I think we often overlook how good this Pistons team was. They'd made it to the conference finals for five consecutive seasons.

Twice, they'd advanced to the NBA Finals. In 2004, they'd won it all. The Pistons' lineup was battle-tested: Rasheed Wallace, Tayshaun Prince, Chauncey Billups, and, of course, the assassin Richard "Rip" Hamilton. Unlike the Cavs, Detroit brought a balanced attack. Unlike the Hawks, they had the most experienced core in the league.

In game one, we kept up our defensive intensity from the Cleveland series. After an even half of basketball, we pulled ahead behind twenty-six from the Big Ticket and twenty-two from Paul. My minutes were up from the previous series, and I grabbed ten boards in the opener. We won it by nine. It looked to be more of the same—unbeatable at home in the Garden. Then came game two, and here fate dealt us a blow. Rip Hamilton went off, and Detroit accomplished the rare feat of scoring over one hundred on our defense. It would be our first home loss of the 2008 playoffs, despite Ray Allen having his best playoff game to date. If we were going to win the NBA championship, we'd have to start winning on the road.

The next day in practice, as we were gearing up to head to Detroit for game three, Thibs and Doc were running through scenarios related to how to guard Chauncey Billups when he tried to back our guards down into the post. Rondo made it known that he was completely uninterested in what was going on. He had his head back and wasn't listening to the coaches or watching the play. Doc shouted over at him, "Rondo, what the fuck is the problem?" Rondo just kept saying "Man" and shaking his head, blowing Doc off. The rest of us jumped in.

"Rondo, man, what's up, what you on?"

"What the fuck are we going over his play for? Billups hasn't done shit. We should be going over floppies and pin-downs for Rip Hamilton, because he was the one busting Ray's ass."

"Rondo," Doc said, heating up, "I'm trying to coach you!"

"Whatever," said Rondo.

Doc ran up to Rondo and got in his face. It looked like they were about to fight. They were nose to nose, going at it, jawing. We had to jump in and break the two of them up. This was conference championship basketball, and a team facing adversity with its back again against the wall.

I hate to go against Doc on the record, but in this case my little brother Rondo had it right. Rondo played forty minutes in game three, and we stole back home court with a convincing 94–80 win. I had my best night of the playoffs thus far, with twelve points on six-of-seven shooting, ten rebounds, a block, and a steal.

Detroit bounced back in game four, turning it up in the fourth quarter and evening the series. The Pistons were more aggressive, physical, played harder. Nothing comes easy in the playoffs. Nothing.

Game five of the Detroit series had a game-seven feeling. A loss in Boston would have sent us back to Detroit with a veteran Pistons team poised to close us out at home. I'd been feeling good and playing well throughout the series, but there was just something different about game five. My teammates found me a couple of times in the paint early in the first quarter, which got me going. I was playing tenacious defense on the other end, rebounding the hell out of the ball. By the end of the first quarter, I'd already notched a double-double: ten points and ten boards.

In the third, I picked up where I'd left off. I was scoring, blocking shots, even made a steal from behind the arc and took the ball coast-to-coast, drawing the foul—and you better believe I knocked down both of those foul shots! Ray Allen's shot had come to life and helped power us to a big lead going into the fourth. The Pistons made a push in the final period, but it wasn't enough.

In the preseason, Rasheed Wallace (who's my boy now!) had said that the Celtics didn't have a real center, and in general the Pistons didn't show me any respect. I think that's what gave me the extra motivation to elevate my game. By the end of game five, I had made 'Sheed and the other Detroit bigs eat those words.

Back in Detroit for game six, we were determined to end it. We'd had enough of game sevens. We kept saying to each other, *We are not going back to Boston—we need to end it here.* Detroit was up heading into the fourth, and they kept coming at us. Again, as it had been all year, it was our defense that won it. We made stop after stop after stop after stop, holding them to thirteen points in the fourth. We finally pulled ahead and never relinquished the lead, winning the game and the series. I played forty-one minutes in game six, by far my highest total of the playoffs. This time, we were not heading back to Boston for a game seven. We were heading home as the Eastern Conference champions with home-court advantage in the finals against the Los Angeles Lakers.

Two thousand members of the media were there to greet us on arrival in Boston. The circus was in town—it was time to get ready for this wild ride.

THE END OF THE RUN: THE FINALS, THE LOS ANGELES LAKERS

The finals were a rematch of the NBA Finals of twenty-one years before, when Magic Johnson and the Los Angeles Lakers ended the original Big Three's dynasty by beating Larry Bird and company in six games, including the famous ending of game four with Magic's last-second hook shot to win it in the Garden, devastating the hometown crowd.

Celtics-Lakers is hands down the most historic and important rivalry in American professional sports, and 2008 was no exception. The Lakers that year had the league's MVP, the incomparable Kobe Bryant. Kobe had led the Lakers on a dominant playoff run through the Western Conference, including dispatching the reigning NBA champion San Antonio Spurs in a mere five games. We'd handled our business in our two regular-season meetings with the Lakers, but both games came before they acquired Pau Gasol, and in any case that was the regular season, and this was the NBA Finals.

If we'd faced championship pedigree in Detroit, the Lakers were on a whole other level, led by a backcourt of Bryant and Derek Fisher, both of whom had already won three titles. Like LeBron, Kobe had the potential to take over a game and will his team to a win every time he stepped foot on the court. If he was at the top of his game, Kobe could dominate a series.

Our defense was up to the task for the opening game of the finals in Boston. This was the toughness we'd been cultivating all year. It wasn't just toughness in our starting five—we were deep, and every player on the team was a dog, could be physical on defense, could battle. Behind me, we had Leon Powe and P. J. Brown, both of whom stepped up big-time throughout the playoffs and in those first two finals games. Behind Pierce was James Posey, one of the scrappiest, most clutch players who's ever laced them up. Behind Ray Allen and Rondo were Eddie House, Sam Cassell, and Tony Allen, giving us a combination of shooting and lockdown defense.

Kobe got his points in game one, though he had to put up twenty-six shots to come away with twenty-four points. Those were numbers we could live with. In game two, we built a huge lead, but the Lakers came storming back. Kobe had a better night, scoring thirty on more efficient shooting, but we managed to escape with a six-point win. We headed to L.A. with a 2–0 lead.

Kobe took over in the first game back in L.A., scoring thirty-six and leading the Lakers to a win. The next game in L.A., game four, was awful for me personally. In the third quarter, I fouled Lamar Odom as he was driving to the hoop and injured my shoulder. In the meantime, the Lakers had built a seemingly insurmountable lead, pushing it to twenty with about seven minutes left in the third.

Then Doc made a key adjustment. He subbed in Eddie House and James Posey to play with the Big Three, with the idea that the additional shooting might create more space on the court and allow our offense to find some rhythm. The move paid off. The court spacing gave Pierce room to drive to the hoop on the next possession. At the five-minute mark of the third, House nailed a three and connected again a few minutes later as we began to chip away at the Laker lead. The quarter ended with an absolutely huge dunk by P. J. Brown. We'd cut the lead to two points heading into the fourth quarter.

The fourth was a battle. Kobe and Paul were going at it one-on-one. KG was heating up. The first six minutes of the quarter we would pull even, but we couldn't manage to take the lead. With a Kobe dunk at mid-quarter, the Lakers went up by four and looked to be taking control. The next time down the court, however, Posey hit a three, which put us right back in it. With five minutes remaining, House rolled off a Ray Allen screen, took the pass, and hit a mid-range jumper. We had our first lead of the game, 84–83.

Allen stole the ball on the Lakers' next possession, then converted on an up-and-under layup, pushing the lead to three. A Lakers miss gave us the ball back and the Big Ticket took care of it, scoring in the lane over Gasol. Kobe was battling, getting to the line and keeping L.A. in it. They had cut our lead down to two when James Posey stuck another huge three from the corner with a little over a minute to play. Derek Fisher responded with a long two, but on the next possession Pierce was fouled by Kobe and knocked down both free throws. Our lead was still at five, with forty-six seconds to go.

Kobe wasted no time on the next possession, slashing into the lane and feeding Gasol for the dunk on a nice drive-and-dish. Our lead was back to three. Ray took the inbound pass from KG and dribbled down the shot clock under heavy pressure from Sasha Vujačić. Vujačić couldn't keep Ray in front of him as Ray cut into the empty paint and finished beautifully with his left hand with fifteen seconds to go. Fittingly, one of the engines of our comeback, Eddie House, iced the game from the foul line to put the finishing touches on one of the greatest comebacks in NBA Finals history, pushing the series to the brink with a 3–1 lead.

Game five was also in L.A. Unfortunately, I was on the bench in street clothes, nursing a left shoulder sprain. This game, like the previous one, went down to the wire, and we had a chance to tie it in the final minute, but Kobe made an incredible defensive play to swipe the ball away from Paul with catlike speed. Lamar Odom scooped up the ball and fed it up the floor to Kobe, who finished with a high-flying dunk, crushing any chance we had for a final rally. The series was headed back to Boston for game six, and I was determined to make the start.

We came out to play in game six. Our defense was humming, and finally, after all these long, grueling weeks of playoff basketball, our offense matched or even exceeded it. Ray Allen was on fire, hitting seven three-pointers, which was at the time a finals record. Pierce was slashing and distributing, outplaying Kobe on the offensive end and doing his best to limit "the Black Mamba" on the defensive side of the ball. The Lakers hung with us for about a quarter, but then we busted it open, expanding our lead to over thirty in the third.

Even at that point, nobody let up. We were contesting every pass, every shot like it was still a close game. We were determined to close out the series with unrelenting force. And that is exactly what we did. Steals, blocks, assists, rebounds—we dominated that game completely. My own minutes were down because of the shoulder, but I still made a contribution. When Doc subbed out Ray, Paul, and KG with a few minutes to go, the Garden crowd went wild. The guys on the bench were celebrating. Before I knew it, Vanity was there handing me our baby, and those final seconds ran down with Little Ken sitting snugly in my arms, celebrating right on with us.

5

Fatherhood

FATHERLESS SONS

THE NBA IS A FRATERNITY OF FATHERLESS SONS AND FATHERLESS FATHERS. IF THIS IS A generalization or an exaggeration, it isn't one by much. Of the starting five on our 2007–2008 Celtics team, only one guy, Ray Allen, had a relationship with his biological father. The rest of us—me, Paul Pierce, Kevin Garnett, and Rajon Rondo—had little or no memory of a biological father. The same basic ratio was true of the others on the team. These realities and their consequences were clearly on Doc Rivers' mind when he said in a recent interview, "We have a lot of black players without fathers. And to me that's a story that needs to be talked about . . ."

I agree with Doc. We need to open up this topic and take a deep look at it, but once it's open, we'll find that the subject of fatherhood in the Black community runs as deep and heavy as the Mississippi River. The issue touches on just about every aspect of players' lives. When the dominoes fall, they lead into nearly all facets of society. That's why, I suspect, the topic of fatherhood is often avoided or treated superficially in media conversations in the world of sports and the NBA, where I have a front-row seat. That's why so many destructive stereotypes worm their way into popular culture.

Fatherhood is not an easy topic. It's painful; it cuts; it opens old wounds. It raises fresh anxieties about who we are. It makes us question everything as we search for our personal truth. The discussion of fatherhood in relation to the Black community has been polarized and polarizing, like so much of American life. I want to get beneath this discussion to find the human level, because the discovery of humanity is what fatherhood should be—must be—about. I can testify that it's been this way for me, a father to four beautiful kids.

THE "BLACK FAMILY" IN THE AMERICAN IMAGINATION

What does it mean to be a father as a Black American? What does it mean to be a father in general? There is no single answer to such a question. The answers are as diverse as the souls that reside inside of us. This beautiful and at times terrible diversity of fatherhood has been a playground for social scientists and politicians for well over a century. The importance of pioneers like W. E. B. Du Bois, E. Franklin Frazier, Joyce Ladner, and many more cannot be ignored.

At the same time, social scientists and politicians have played significant roles in turning fathers in the Black community into the "Black Father," mothers into the "Black Mother," families into the "Black Family," and predominantly Black urban spaces or communities into "Black Slums" or "the Ghetto." Once stereotypes are created, it takes a whole lot of hard work to break them apart.

This chapter must engage in a little demolition work to clear ground for building something new. I want to shatter this stereotypical "Black Father" to discover the human, me, Big Perk, in his shadow. Just think of how large the figure of the "Black Father" must be to cast its shadow over me.

In terms of the "Black Family" in the United States, the starting point often has been the following question: what is wrong with it? The question implies that the Black family somehow deviates from "normal" white family models. The "normal" American family for many is not only white, it is the suburban, white, middle-class, nuclear family. This idealized "normal family" is built around a patriarchal breadwinning father and a domestic, child-rearing mother: the father goes to work while the mother stays home to raise the kids.

This model might seem familiar to us, but it was a recent invention, and no sooner had it established itself as a dominant ideal in American life than it started to fall apart. It fell apart because it was never the truth for most people, of any race or ethnicity, in our country. But despite its highly questionable status, this notion of "normal" family life deeply impacted how people thought about Black families.

The first studies of the "Black Family" told the following story. The nature of the Atlantic slave trade and the history of American slavery made life for African Americans fundamentally different from life for other groups. While these other immigrants came as families and forged ethnic communities in the country, often continuing to speak the languages of their homelands for generations, the slave system created a violent break between African life, languages, and cultures and American life under slavery. African family traditions were lost or destroyed. According to the pioneering Black scholar E. Franklin Frazier, the brutal transition from African freedom to American slavery meant, above all, the disintegration of a slave's notion of family.

For Frazier, this disintegration stopped only when slaves began to build nuclear families as they assimilated into the world of their oppressors— meaning as they took on the trappings of white, Christian culture. This process of assimilation into the masters' culture, to Frazier, came with major problems. The masters might have encouraged the adoption of their culture among slaves in some respects, but they also prevented slaves from achieving the vision of life this culture purported to support.

The white plantation household was built around the powerful male head of the family, the patriarch. It was precisely this white patriarch who made it impossible, Frazier writes, for Black men to establish themselves as heads of households during slavery. For one, these Black men were at the physical and legal mercy of the slave owners. They could be sold at a moment's notice, beaten for anything or nothing, and killed without threat of penalty. Second, the white slave owner exercised his power over Black women in the form of sexual abuse and rape. Frazier concluded that instead of forming nuclear families based on the white, patriarchal model, Black families during slavery developed around the one type of bond that endured during these bleak times—the bond between the mother and the child. In other words, Frazier argues, white families were patriarchal, Black families were matriarchal. In Black families, the mother reigned supreme.

The idea of the matriarchal Black family, born in times of slavery and compounded by Jim Crow and the effects of the Great Migration, has played an enormous role in shaping our thinking about American society and our Black communities. We hear echoes of it constantly in and beyond discussions of NBA players and their single mothers. The arguments made by Black scholars like Frazier and Du Bois pushed for Black male empowerment.

By the 1960s, a more problematic understanding of Black life started spreading. It was partly based on this earlier work, but it introduced new and dangerous concepts into the discussion. It wasn't just that the Black family was thought to be matriarchal—now the Black family began to be described as deviant and *pathological*. What does it mean in plain terms to be pathological? It means to be sick.

The Civil Rights Movement and urban politics in the 1960s brought a more intense focus on Black communities. The earlier Black voices on the subject—Du Bois, Frazier, Richard Wright—were joined by many others during the tumultuous years of the Black freedom struggle and white backlash. It was this background that set the stage for Black psychologist Kenneth Clark's powerful indictment of structural racism in New York's Harlem neighborhood in his book *Dark Ghetto*.

Clark had been working on the ground in Harlem for many years, studying the psychological effects of segregation in New York's urban environment. Clark, together with his wife, Mamie, rose to prominence during legal debates about school desegregation. The Clarks' work, foremost their famous "Doll Tests," had been used in cases challenging segregation's "separate but equal" foundation, including the most famous school desegregation case, *Brown v. Board*.

The Doll Tests argued that the mere fact of living in segregated society resulted in damage to the psychic development of Black children. In these tests, the Clarks showed Black children dolls that were identical in every other way besides their color—one doll was white, the other brown. They found that though the children identified themselves with the brown doll, they preferred to play with the white one, assigning positive characteristics to the white doll and negative characteristics to the brown doll. Clearly, the Clarks argued, the kids' preferences reflected the value system they had internalized while growing up in a divided and racially hierarchical society.

The effects of "separate but equal" in the Jim Crow North and South, the Clarks' experiments indicated, were very deep, penetrating children's unconsciousness in ways that had not previously been appreciated. Racism, according to the Clarks, was not limited to the legal, political, and economic realms—it had devastating consequences for identity, self-esteem, and psychological well-being. As a Black father of Black children, I have a hard time thinking about the Clarks' work without feeling deeply disturbed.

Dark Ghetto was Kenneth Clark's study of his neighborhood of Harlem, New York, a predominantly Black area gripped, Clark thought, by crisis. The Clarks had worked for years in Harlem by the time *Dark Ghetto* came out in 1965, helping to found Harlem Youth Opportunities Unlimited (HARYOU). (It was this organization that employed the young Lew Alcindor as a student journalist during the summer of the

Harlem riots.) Harlem's crisis, Clark thought, was not caused by its inhabitants. The creation of the "dark ghetto" and the crises that gripped it were the results of the pervasive racism that structured American life. Black people, Clark asserted, were trapped in these "ghetto" spaces by what he called "invisible walls."

Nowhere was the psychological impact of American ghettoization larger, Clark believed, than in the Black family. For Clark, life in the "ghetto" was especially tough for Black men. The result of this impact was what Clark described as "the pathology of the Negro family." About Black men, he wrote, "The pressure to find relief from his intolerable psychological position seems directly related to the continued high incidence of desertions and broken homes in the urban ghetto." The Negro family, Clark wrote, agreeing with Frazier, was held together by the mother. For male children, according to Clark, this lack of a "strong father figure" posed an acute problem and caused the perpetuation of family crisis from one generation to the next. For Clark, the pathology of ghetto life was not the result of inferiority or any inherent pathology of Black people living it—it was the product of a brutal racial system. The issue was not Black people's choices but white society's intolerance and economic exploitation.

Despite Clark's best intentions, there are some important problems with the way he discussed Black life in Harlem in *Dark Ghetto*. First, by labeling Black life as "pathological" or sick, Clark opened the door to much more troubling uses of the pathological model of interpreting Black families, one that would gain widespread notoriety in the aftermath of what came to be called the Moynihan Report. Second, Clark, like Frazier, took the presence of strong Black women in families and communities as a weakness rather than seeing it, as it should be seen, as a strength; anyone married to a strong Black woman like Vanity knows this beyond any doubt. Finally, Clark's analysis of the "dark ghetto" presented Black life as a world apart. The "ghetto" came to be viewed as dangerous, immoral, disintegrating, bleak, scary, and bad.

Though Clark's book is nuanced, emphasizing community resilience and local, grassroots empowerment, the image of America's "urban ghetto" was starting to crystalize in the national white imagination as a space of immorality, violence, and crime. Soon, the urban space—coded as Black—would become the nightmarish "other" of white suburban America, and the "dysfunctional" matriarchal Black family the opposite of the stable white patriarchal family. By the 1980s, most people would forget about Clark's argument that these "ghettos" are best understood as walled-off "colonies." They would forget Clark's description and indictment of the structural racism in American life (those invisible walls). They would remember only the pathology. Instead of understanding the problem socially, they understood it as a sickness of the people themselves. If Black communities were in crisis, people argued, the people in the Black communities themselves were to blame.

From a sophisticated understanding of how a racist society functions and its impact on communities and families, the discussion moved increasingly toward a simplistic type of "blame the victim" attitude. This took place largely because of the migration of these ideas from people like Clark to white politicians, who were all too ready to mobilize white fears of the Black freedom struggle to push a new type of racist agenda under the guise of "law and order" and color-blindness. An important step in this direction was taken by the so-called Moynihan Report.

In 1965, Daniel Patrick Moynihan issued a report called *The Negro Family: The Case for National Action*. Moynihan, a strong supporter of civil rights, was pressing President Lyndon Johnson for economic initiatives to help Black Americans create the conditions not just for opportunity, but for equality and prosperity. For Moynihan, following Clark, Frazier, and several prominent white sociologists, the main obstacle for Black Americans in the quest to achieve real equality was "the deterioration of the Negro family." Like Clark, Moynihan saw the problem in spatial terms. The dysfunction was located "on the urban frontier." Relegated to a position outside of mainstream (code: white) society and into this "frontier" space, the Black family, thought Moynihan, was caught in a "tangle of pathology." At the heart of this "pathology"—no surprise—Moynihan saw the Black mother.

If the matriarchal structure of Black families was the central problem, according to Moynihan, then the cause of this problem had to do with absence of Black men as fathers. "Negro children without fathers," Moynihan wrote, "founder—and fail." For Moynihan in 1965, prospects for the rehabilitation of Black men to the status of patriarch in Black families appeared grim. In what he saw as the crisis of Black families in American cities, he warned that "the tangle of pathology is tightening."

Criticism of Moynihan's report came from many directions. Black Power leaders argued that problems for Black folk were not internal to Black families or even to the Black community. They were not a result of a "tangle of pathology" but rather a tangle of racist policies, racist culture, and the structural racism that infiltrated every layer of the American economy. Focusing on Black family dilemmas exclusively or even mainly was, for them, missing the point entirely. If there was pathology, it was what was directed at the Black family, not what was happening in it. Black families and communities, rather, were struggling mightily against a multifront assault of racial oppression to survive.

The report also generated a strong reaction from Black women, who rejected its male chauvinist, patriarchal logic. Black men, they argued, should not be empowered at the expense of Black women, as Moynihan and others maintained; instead, Black women should be supported as pillars of families and communities. They found the language of "pathology" and "matriarchy" sexist, insulting, and profoundly misguided, and felt that in fact, the reverse was true: it was not that Black families were too matriarchal, it was that the very model of American family life—the white, suburban family—was *too patriarchal*. And now men like Moynihan were trying to push this patriarchal model onto Black women, even if this meant increased hardship and poverty.

Feminist critic Michele Wallace captured this frustration with the male-dominated analysis of Black life, lamenting, "Rather than carve a piece of pie for the black man out of the white man's lion's share, they preferred to take away from the really very little that the black woman had and give that meager slice to him." When I read these words, I can't help but think about my mama, who raised me until I was five. She put herself through beauty school and then went to work as a beautician, often taking me with her to the salon, where I'd play quietly and watch her do her thing. My memories of my mama are not of a failed "matriarch" who needed a man to keep us off the welfare rolls. They are of a beautiful, strong, generous, and independent Black woman who was more than capable of creating a loving, supportive home for her boy.

Instead of fixating on Black women as scapegoats for America's problems, Wallace and others argued, people should face the real problem—and this was the systematic exploitation of America's poor, who were disproportionately Black and female. Women, Black women above all, didn't need to be pushed out of the labor market so that they could stay at home and fulfill the role of housewife. And they didn't need blame or patriarchy. What they needed was affordable childcare, better wages and an end to employment-based discrimination, opportunities for career advancement, better access to education, including higher and professional education, and food and housing assistance.

At the heart of much of the reaction to Moynihan's "solution" to what he saw as a deepening crisis of pathology on the "urban frontier" was a distrust or rejection of the core ideal Moynihan and others like him embraced so vehemently: the white middle-class family model, with a male breadwinner and a female homemaker and mother. In fact, this "ideal" was just that, a fantasy driven largely by media and advertising. The reality was that white middle-class families had plenty of problems of their own—alcohol and drug addiction, domestic violence, mental health crises, debt, and so on.

Equally damaging as Moynihan's labeling of the Black family as pathological was the development of the notion through the press and popular culture that the predominantly Black "urban frontier" was fundamentally different from other places in America. These spaces would become coded as deviant, dangerous, dysfunctional, and criminal, and this type of thinking would lead white society and its political leaders to move in the opposite direction from the one Moynihan originally desired. Instead of embracing programs for creating opportunity and a foundation for real social equality, white society rejected any notion of its responsibility or culpability for the realities of Black American life.

Those "invisible walls" Kenneth Clark identified as bounding Black urban space were about to get a whole lot higher, with the coming of a conservative reaction to the Black freedom struggle and the expansion of social welfare programs: the Reagan Revolution. The invisible walls, beginning in the 1980s and lasting until this day, would be increasingly patrolled by America's internal border control force, also known as the police.

FATHER'S DAY, 2008

On June 15, 2008, Father's Day, we lost game five of the NBA Finals to the Lakers. On that same day, presidential candidate Barack Obama went to the Apostolic Church of God in Chicago to give a sermon on fatherhood to the church's congregation and, now on the biggest media stage, to the world. In our Celtics locker room, we'd been following Obama's campaign very closely, and I, as a new father, was particularly interested in what he had to say on this occasion.

Obama's Father's Day speech was powerful. He opens with a reference to Jesus' Sermon on the Mount from the Gospel of Matthew, a work I knew inside and out from Catholic school. Toward the end of the sermon, Jesus tells his listeners that those who hear and obey his word will be like the wise man who built his house on a foundation of rock. Whatever comes, be it rain, winds, or flood, it will not destroy this home, because it rests on a solid foundation. A man who hears Jesus and does not obey his word, on the other hand, is like the foolish man who builds his home on sand. When the strong winds blow and the floodwaters come, this home will be swept away.

It is this metaphor that Obama uses to discuss the Black family in his Chicago speech. A foundation of stone, for Obama, means a two-parent family with a mother and father living together to raise their kids. The house built on sand, he implies, though doesn't outright say, is the single-parent household—and these households have trouble withstanding the "storms" of everyday life. For Obama, these "houses of sand" are particularly vulnerable, because the fathers who should provide their families with strength and support are absent. These houses, he suggests, are led by mothers. The ghosts of Moynihan and company are clearly still haunting us.

Obama emphasizes the word "responsibility" when addressing Apostolic's congregation. He urges Black men to take responsibility as fathers for their children "no matter what the hardships," because their involvement can break the cycle of broken families and poverty. Obama is picking up a well-worn discussion, one most famously articulated in the Black community by the now fallen star Bill Cosby. In the preface to Cosby's comedic self-help/advice book *Fatherhood*, the well-known critic Alvin F. Poussaint writes, "Being a good provider . . . did not mean that a father had to raise you to the level of even the lower working class. What it meant in my neighborhood was that the father had a job and kept the family off the welfare rolls."

Obama agrees with Poussaint in the main, tempered by the important recognition that government also has a role to play. What has happened to these fathers, these Black men, in Obama's imagination? Obama argues that these Black men are not acting like men at all, but like boys. They lack the maturity and the courage to embrace their roles as fathers. For Obama, too many Black men are "MIA"—missing in action. Instead of stepping up, he says, they shirk their responsibilities, and when pressed, they blame social injustice or racism. These are "excuses," in Obama's speech, not legitimate reasons. At one point in the speech, he asks rhetorically, "How many [Black men] are languishing in prison instead of working or at least looking for a job?" It is as if the incarcerated people Obama is talking about have chosen to go to jail rather than to work. This is very strange logic, one deeply embedded not only in a problematic racial history but also in the type of 1980s economic thinking that purported to be "color-blind" while demonizing the Black and minority poor.

The most troubling part of Obama's speech comes toward the end, when he mentions an act by the comedian Chris Rock. In one segment of his "Bring the Pain" stand-up routine, Rock has a running joke that certain Black people brag about things that others would consider normal. Obama uses the example of incarceration, citing Rock's quip that when he hears Black men boast about staying out of jail, he responds, "You're not supposed to be in jail!"

Rock's punch line, unlike Obama's speech, is a joke—and this particular joke works, because on a deeper level it is a parody of a tragic situation, the underlying and contradictory truth that, as currently constructed, American society seeks the incarceration of Black men, especially in poor communities. Under the prevailing social logic, these men actually are supposed to be in jail. This is why so many of them are there, why so many prisons were built nationwide in the 1980s and 1990s. Excellent research has demonstrated clearly that Black men are not choosing incarceration by committing more crime. It is our society that has made it a central priority for at least the last forty years to lock up Black men.

Not only does Obama ignore this reality in his speech, he doesn't make the connection between the massive number of incarcerated Black men and the "war on drugs." Rock, on the other hand, addresses the issue with his typical bluntness: "The war on drugs is bullshit. It's a way of getting more of us motherfuckers in jail. That's all it is." Rock has it exactly right.

As has been abundantly demonstrated, American poverty—especially poverty and unemployment in urban Black communities—is not a matter of choice or lack of a will to work. It is not an issue of "personal responsibility," and certainly not one of "courage." Rather, these are complex economic and social issues that connect to deeper structures, including educational opportunities, deindustrialization, public transportation, and criminal justice. Rock searches for humor amid the hardships and tragedies of Black life in the United States.

I love and have immense respect for Barack Obama, and I can understand he was speaking not only to the Apostolic community but to the whole country on that Father's Day. In 2008, he had a job to do—to get elected as *the first Black President of the United States*. I still savor those words. On the other hand, nobody denies that men need to be responsible as fathers—and the vast majority of Black men strive to do just that. The discussion of "responsibility," however, was manufactured to serve as a screen for a deep and violent attack on Black communities and as a way of denying the complex structures of racism in our country. We need to find a different way of talking about fatherhood.

JAMES BALDWIN AND THE SUMMER OF 1943

There is great power attached to fatherhood in most, if not all, cultures, whether it be in a father's presence or in his partial or total absence, and it could be said that in some cases the power of absence is greater even than that of the fullest presence. Absence—and I'm not just talking about fathers now—can create a vortex, as the removal of the center of any structure creates a void or a wound. Presence, meanwhile, pushes outward toward the very edge. At its best, paternal presence helps to create a zone of safety and love. This zone forms part of the foundation of our families and communities and offers us the model for an ethical, moral life. At its worse, this full, expansive presence is another way of saying tyranny.

As a father, I'm constantly thinking about these issues. How should I be there to guide and nurture my kids? What steps should I take to protect them, to shield them from evils and dangers out there in the world? Believe me, there are plenty of them in Texas, especially now that people can carry handguns without a license. Who knows how many guns will end up in our schools? On the other hand, how can I give my four kids the freedom to search and grow on their own? When we have such important, fundamental questions, it's wise to seek out others—a different kind of elder—who can help shape our view of the world. And there might not be two wiser guides in our country's Black history than James Baldwin and Ralph Ellison.

In *Notes of a Native Son*, James Baldwin puts his finger on the moment in his life when the presence of his father turns to absence: his father's death in July of 1943, just days before Baldwin's nineteenth birthday. As Baldwin describes him, his father was cruel and bitter. He'd grown up in New Orleans (another Louisiana family), was the son of former slaves, and moved north like so many others during the Great Migration. He settled in Harlem, where he ministered to an ever-shrinking congregation in small church spaces throughout the neighborhood. His mix of religious and everyday rage cast a shadow of terror over his wife and children, James being the oldest of nine.

This was the presence that Baldwin grew to hate and that drove him from the family house at the age of seventeen to live on his own. Only later, and upon reflection, could Baldwin attempt to find his way through his hate to imagine the roots of his father's psychic turmoil: "I began to wonder what it could have felt like for such a man to have had nine children whom he could barely feed." This is an important question, one all of us need to be asking. I grew up watching Black fathers and Black mothers—and my own grandparents—struggling with just this issue: how to live a *dignified life* as a poor Black person in the United States. How can we escape or blunt poverty's violence? And make no mistake, poverty is a structure of violence.

Baldwin's father seemed to be losing his mind during the year after James moved out. He'd have long periods of silence, which were broken by short and seemingly random religious exclamations. Eventually, convinced that his family was trying to poison him, he refused to eat. After he was committed to a psychiatric hospital, the doctors discovered he was suffering from advanced tuberculosis and that it was too late for any meaningful medical intervention. When Baldwin went to the hospital to visit him for the first and only time, it was clear to him that his father was going to die.

Baldwin's escape from his father's house set the stage for his first full encounter with the world beyond family life. This meant, above all, his first true adult experience with a kind of unfiltered racism. The impact of this encounter on Baldwin was profound. He describes this exposure to the force of American racism as if he had "contracted some dread, chronic disease." And what did it mean for Baldwin to have such a "disease"? He lets us know: "There is not a Negro alive who does not have this rage in his blood—one has the choice, merely, of living with it consciously or surrendering to it. As for me, this fever has recurred in me, and does, and will until the day I die."

As Baldwin's father wasted away in the hospital during the summer of 1943, racial tensions in Harlem were rising. Police were flooding the neighborhood streets. The war had thrown Black and white workers together, while the training of Black soldiers in the military stoked white fears. The tension would explode on the evening of his father's funeral, the same day Baldwin turned nineteen. As Baldwin was downtown celebrating his birthday, a white police officer shot and killed a Black soldier in Harlem's Braddock Hotel. Harlem exploded in anger.

From the death of his father, to a birthday, to a riot, there is one more major piece to add to Baldwin's incredible story about those days. His mother gave birth to his baby sister, Paula, on the day of his father's death. It was the birth of a fatherless child.

His father was gone. The man who had somehow shielded Baldwin from the "sickness" of racism had passed away. The man he hated more than anyone else on earth had departed life. The hated presence of his father had given way to a strange, yawning absence. And with it, the meaning of Baldwin's hatred for his father had started to disintegrate. The place where that hate had lived inside of him was transformed into emptiness. Judgment of his father and his father's life suddenly seemed pointless—for who can know what it is really like to walk in someone else's shoes? *Thou knowest this man's fall*, Baldwin's father had been fond of quoting, *but thou knowest not his wrassling*.

Hate. It is such a powerful emotion. Our world seems consumed by it. Many among us become gripped by its power. Hate provides an easier solution than many others in dealing with our feelings. The channel it has cut allows our immediate emotional responses to freely flow. Baldwin's task in his essay about his father's death, the Harlem riots, and the birth of his little sister into a fatherless world is a confrontation with this hate. In his father's absence, Baldwin's hatred for him starts to turn into a hatred for the world, but this diffuse and all-consuming hatred or rage, for the great writer, cannot be the end point. If we are brave enough to confront it, it can point the way in a better direction. This is what Baldwin writes in one of the most profound and important paragraphs in American letters:

Ellison's thoughts turned to two deaths—the death of his father when he was around three years old, and the assassination of Abraham Lincoln. Ellison's nightmare had woven these tragedies together.

When the dream begins, Ellison is walking on Classen Boulevard in Oklahoma City, where he was born and lived his early years. The scene in the dream is surreal. Birds are swooping down to the sidewalks to feast on catalpa worms that are covering the ground, oozing and sliming all over the place. There are sounds from a clarinet; a huckster calls out in the distance. Ellison realizes that he's on his way to see his father, even though he knows his father is dead. Almost at once, he sees a familiar man moving toward him, but as the man approaches, this familiarity fades and the man becomes a stranger. Ellison makes his way into a city square and sees the same man standing on a balcony and looking down at him. A cryptic message resounds from a loudspeaker. When it falls silent, Ellison notices he's standing in front of a hostile crowd. He runs.

He's in Washington, D.C. It is no longer the 1950s. Signs of the nineteenth century surround him—horse-drawn carriages, gas lamps, and women in long, rustling skirts. Ellison is no longer a grown man but a slave boy dressed in one of those single-piece tattered cotton outfits that young slave children wore. To his shame, he has no shoes, pants, or underwear—it is the shame of feeling inferior, the shame and humiliation of poverty. I know this shame well. It has stayed with me from my early years walking around the Pear Orchard in a pair of ruined shoes.

Another crowd has formed in Ellison's dream-Washington. It is gathered in front of a building as a body, covered with a sheet, is being carried out on a board. The sheet starts slipping away, gathering around the tall man's feet. The crowd grows vicious. It lunges at the corpse and starts to cut and tear away its clothing piece by piece. These fragments of cloth become the souvenirs of a demented carnival of death. The people in the crowd are ecstatic as they celebrate the murder of their hated President, Abraham Lincoln, the man who, in their eyes, launched the war to destroy the South, the man who set the slaves free.

Four "ragged Negro men" are carrying the board with Lincoln's corpse, which is dressed now only in undergarments; the rest of his clothes, including his famous hat, have been torn away. The men place the body on a railway baggage wagon and continue to pull it through the mob, heading toward the Washington Monument. The mob is unrelenting. People take turns kicking and beating the dead body, shouting "coon" at the assassinated President. Ellison watches, horrified and fascinated, unable to fully comprehend or believe that Lincoln is truly dead.

As the dream skips forward, the four Negro men, now holding shovels, beckon to Ellison to peer over the edge of a huge hole in the earth. He looks down and sees the crowd sitting at a table. They are making a "ghoulish meal" of something concealed beneath a white sheet. The thing under the sheet starts to stir and expand. Could it be that the mob is set to feast on the decomposing corpse of Abraham Lincoln? The ground gives way beneath his feet, and Ellison wakes up with a terrible fright.

Ellison's dream of the angry, hate-filled crowd abusing, and potentially cannibalizing, Abraham Lincoln's body is interrupted at one point by a memory. In it, Ellison is a small child. He's with his mother at a hospital, and they are taking leave of his father before surgery, which he will not survive. Ellison watches as the nurses wheel his father away in a metal hospital bed. It would be the final time he'd see his father alive. Years later, Ellison recalls his mother telling him that because the family had no money for a proper burial, his father's body had remained unburied for days, rotting and stinking in a back room of the funeral parlor.

Two deaths. Two corpses. Two men, his father and Lincoln, both denied dignity in death. Ninety years after Lincoln's murder, Ellison reflects once he wakes up and shakes off the residual terror of his nightmare: "his neglected labors withering . . . in the fields; the state fallen into corruption, and the citizens into moral anarchy, with no hero come to set things right." The result of an American parricide is an orphaned nation. White America, the mob, has become, in Ellison's dreamscape, a fatherless people, and white society, a grotesque carnival of sadistic evil.

But the fatherless son, the dreamer, Ralph Ellison, has not succumbed to the same fate. If Lincoln's absence has resulted in the rise of hate and a lust for revenge among the mob, Ellison's father's absence has created a space for a presence of another kind: "For in effect he only perished, he did not pass away. His strength became my mother's strength and my brother and I the confused, sometimes bitter, but most often proud, recipients of their values and their love . . ."

Ellison is onto something quite special here—*fatherhood as a zone of love, fatherhood as a zone of values*. In this sense, the fatherless Black boy in Ellison's dream is far less of an orphan than those in the white mob, which has not only killed its symbolic father but has defiled his memory, replacing his values of unity and equality with racial divisions and notions of hierarchy, replacing his love with hate.

We can't end on hate here, not with this essay. Instead, I want to give some space to Ellison's beautiful writing:

> . . . I had been bemused by a recurring fantasy in which, on my way to school of a late winter day I would emerge from a cold side street into the warm spring sun and there see my father, dead since I was three, rushing toward me with a smile of recognition and outstretched arms. And I would run proudly to greet him, his son grown tall. And then I could awake at last from the tortuous and extended dream that was my childhood with my father gone. So urgent had been my need for a sense of familial completeness, to have our family whole and happy as it had been until shortly before I saw him placed at last into the earth, that this thin fantasy had been made to serve for the man of flesh and blood, the man of the tales, the ghost stories, the gifts and strength and love.

FATHERHOOD AS PRESENCE

My mama fell in love with a man named Kenneth Perkins when she was around twenty years old. Perkins was a basketball player, at six-seven the starting forward for the local Lamar University team. By all accounts, he was a solid player, and he and my mama must have made a striking couple. Kenneth Perkins didn't give me much. He abandoned me when I was two years old. He did give me my last name, from which I derived the signature nickname "Perk," or "Big Perk." I like to think that there's a world between an ordinary Perkins and a Perk—and that was the distance I traveled in Kenneth Perkins' absence.

That's not to say I traveled the road from Perkins to Perk alone. After my first son, Kendrick Perkins Jr. ("Little Ken"), was born, before the team left for Rome to begin the 2007–2008 season, Vanity started talking to me about reaching out to and getting in touch with my biological father. He was my father, but he was also a man I didn't know. He'd disappeared from Beaumont and my life before I remember him ever being there.

If it had been just me, I never would have done it. He left me. He did nothing for me. For him, I might as well never have existed. He was a man named Kenneth Perkins. He graduated from Lamar University in Beaumont, and when he wasn't drafted into the NBA he moved to New Zealand to play ball over there, leaving me behind with my mama. He made a career playing for teams like the Canterbury Rams and the Nelson Giants of New Zealand's National Basketball League. That was it. He wasn't a father to me. What kind of father wouldn't come back for his child after he'd learned his boy's mama has been shot and killed? What kind of father would sneak in and out of Beaumont without going to see his son?

When I was a junior in high school, he showed up for the first time at one of my high school games. He came up to me, introduced himself, and I shook his hand. Thinking he was a rich, professional basketball player, I asked him if he'd brought me something—maybe a car or some cash. It would have been the first thing he'd ever given me. That he didn't have anything for me—not even a joke or a warm response—became completely clear when he turned around without another word and walked out of the gym.

I was twenty-two years old when we got back in touch. Our first phone conversation was awkward. What was there to say? He could offer apologies. We could make small talk, but there wasn't any history there. He'd missed too much time. There were no shared moments to go back to, no lessons he'd taught me. The simple fact is that there was no depth to our relationship, no deep emotions to fall back on to help overcome the gap between us, a gap that seemed just about as wide as the distance between Beaumont and Christchurch, New Zealand, home of the Canterbury Rams.

It was hard growing up and hearing the talk around town about my father, knowing what he was doing with regards to me—meaning doing nothing. My grandfather did a hell of a job stepping in and being a father to me, but even as a child I knew it wasn't the same thing. I could see around me the value of having a dad there. I could feel the way things were with my friends and their fathers, and in this way I could feel strongly, painfully, what I was missing out on. This sense of what was missing would only grow when I had kids of my own.

The loss of a father brings the pressures and the hardships of the world closer in. When Doc Rivers talks about NBA players with problematic relationships to male role models, I think that this is part of what he's after. Many, though certainly not all, of the Black fathers of NBA players were lost to the streets or otherwise not part of their kids' lives. Many were out there trying to provide for their families, trying to make it in any way they could, and often the only way for them to get ahead was to get involved with things that led them astray.

As players, we'd share these stories. We knew where the other guys had come from, what circumstances they'd grown up in. I knew that the guys in the locker rooms with me in Boston, Oklahoma City, Cleveland, and New Orleans didn't have a Plan B if Plan A—earning a living by playing basketball—didn't work out. I knew they didn't have a Plan B because I didn't have a Plan B.

Throughout my life, I have seen for myself how hard it is for Black men to make it in our system. Friends of mine have done all the right things. They've done well in school, graduated from college with a bachelor's or a master's. They've flown on the right path, then discovered that jobs for young Black men are hard to come by, especially the professional jobs they've worked for and are qualified for.

Often, these guys take a job below their level of training. When they have kids, they try to make it on their low-wage jobs, but at the end of every month find themselves with only twenty dollars left in their wallets. There's no cushion. Any setback means either a second job or debt, and you pick your poison, being ground down by endless hours of low-paid labor or mired in crippling debt without hope of pulling yourself above water again. Or both. There's a modern version of sharecropping going on throughout America, folks. These are the real conditions for young Black fathers—the choice of squeezing water from a stone at places like Walmart or a Shell gas station or turning to life on the streets and risking jail or even death. Let's tell these stories, real stories, around the Father's Day table.

When the world closes in and pressures grow and options narrow, you need two things to make it—besides a whole lot of luck. The first thing you need is good people around you. The second is a kind of toughness that is born of adversity, a toughness that shows one the way through self-discipline and steadfast belief in the correctness of one's path. As I've said before, I had some great people around me, both as a kid and as a young adult trying to make it in the NBA.

My grandfather was a rock—he gave me more than I'll ever be able to fully capture here. When I asked him to be the best man at my wedding, it was because I knew that without him—without his guidance, love, strictness, and discipline; without his daily example and core values—I wouldn't have been standing there about to marry Vanity. God only knows where I would have been.

Behind my grandfather, there was Coach Andre Boutte. Coach Boutte was one of my most trusted guides, in life and basketball. He encouraged me to come to him with any problem and tried his best to solve it. If I needed anything, material or otherwise, I could go to him and he'd provide for me, like getting me a new pair of shoes or some workout clothes; he even bought me my first car. During those early years in the league, I could call him up and he'd hear me out, listening to my fears and frustrations, helping to stabilize me, working with me to find the right way of seeing things, guiding me to find the next step.

In the absence of my father, there was space for the presence of some amazing elders, including men like Danny Ainge and Doc Rivers, or the veterans on those early Celtics teams, or the Big Ticket himself. In the absence of a father, my teammates turned into my brothers. It's not a cliché—or maybe it is. But who cares if it is? Sometimes clichés are right on the money. Some might call this "social" or communal fathering, but for me it's about presence. Presence means being there to give to others, to provide care, perspective, love, warmth, and support. It means facing challenges together so that the one in need doesn't have to face the world alone.

When I looked around the locker room at my championship teammates, I could see a bunch of guys who'd found enough of this presence to keep persevering and to overcome the many challenges that lay in their paths. But let's be real—these challenges were often painful and very hard to overcome. I'm talking about poverty. I'm talking about unsafe neighborhoods, crime, and violence. I'm talking about peer pressure. I'm talking about a vicious cycle of failure and a lack of opportunity, causing frustration and anger on all sides. I'm talking about mental health crises, exploited mothers, siblings making bad and often disastrous choices. I'm talking about trauma.

NBA stories, NBA books, might read like tales with happy endings—the kids who made it out of the 'hood and struck it rich and became famous. We need to remember that this is only one thread of a bigger story, and the bigger story does not have a happy ending. The one thread of success gains its meaning only from the tens of thousands of broken lives, from the tens of thousands of people and families in crisis. It is only by reflecting as deeply as possible on the nature and reality of this crisis that we can understand that Celtics locker room—or any NBA locker room. It was a team of men who'd had to damn near become men on our own. We had to face down adversity from an early age. We had to be tough. We had to find the discipline and strength within ourselves to pursue excellence.

Maybe more than that, though, this was a group of guys, myself included, who had to do what James Baldwin was talking about. We had to face our own hate—that self-destructive emotion that blocks introspection and growth—and we had to turn it into something positive, something generative that would allow us to find peace of mind and to forge the type of community of trust and love a team needs to succeed at the highest level. This type of work isn't a process that happens once and then is over. It is a process you need to commit to every day of the season—or, to put it in wider terms—every day of your life.

The locker room prepared me for fatherhood, if it's possible to say one can be prepared for fatherhood before it happens. I found real presence there—learned how to listen, how to sacrifice, how to care about something bigger and more important than myself. I'm not talking about wins and losses—though winning isn't bad—I'm talking about the importance of the people, the unit, the work, the shared experience. Being a teammate in the NBA means getting to know guys on and off the court. It means supporting them, respecting them, treating them with dignity, holding them accountable, learning to talk to them so they can hear you. It means patience and trust.

I'm a father of four beautiful kids. My oldest, Little Ken, was born at the start of the 2007–2008 championship run. When my wife was pregnant with Little Ken, I would watch as her belly got bigger, but what was coming never fully hit me. She's pregnant, whatever, I'd think, and I'd just continue to do my thing. But when you're in the hospital and holding your child for the first time, that's something else. I can honestly say that from the first day Little Ken was born, I started to look at my life totally differently. There was suddenly something in the world so much more important than I was—this child. His needs, and the needs of all my kids, came first.

That first year of Little Ken's life was one of the best years of my life. Vanity, always a night owl, would be up late with the baby or would get up in the night to feed and take care of him. That meant that mornings were mine. I'd wash and prepare his bottles and we'd hang together until it was time for me to get to the gym. Vanity would take Little Ken to every home game, and there was hardly a game that went by without at least one shot of him on the JumboTron, doing his thing. The Garden's fans embraced him, one season ticket holder even getting a gold necklace for him with my number 43 hanging from it. It was a gesture Vanity and I will never forget.

Another thing happened to me after Little Ken was born. It wasn't only that I knew there was a person in the world whom I'd give anything for—it was that this perspective expanded to include people in general. Having kids calls on a deeper humanity within us, moving us to try to see and understand other people's unique situations, to empathize with them—to have true feelings about what they are really going through. This humanity has to be the foundation for our shared community.

Presence as a father draws on this renewed sense of humanity and the ability to step outside of myself and meet others where they are, kids and adults included. It draws on the love I have for Vanity and my kids. But presence isn't, or can't be, just a set of feelings or emotions. Emotions, when they are not matched by actions, don't really matter. A presence based on a deep sense of humanity, on the recognition of the inherent equality of all people, on a love that's generous and giving— this presence needs to be enacted throughout one's daily life.

We've seen already how Baldwin's father, no matter what his feelings or emotions, oppressed and terrorized his family through his presence— his humanity and love, warped, as Baldwin sees it, by desperate conditions, frustrations, and fears. We see in Ellison's essay how the mob's presence degenerates into hate and violence—and we see, alternatively, how the brief presence of Ellison's father in the life of his family created a zone of love so powerful that it could stay with his boy, Ralph Ellison, throughout his life, giving him hope and a model for a type of society beyond racial hierarchy, violence, and hate.

When I think about Ellison's memories of his father, my mind turns to my mama. The zone of love my mama created for me has been both present and painfully absent since I was five years old. For most of my life, I kept these feelings private, even from Vanity. They felt like my most personal and precious possession—something I buried so deep inside me I didn't know how exactly to access it.

Then one night in 2007, as we drove from the Garden after a game to celebrate my birthday, I couldn't keep my feelings inside a second longer. The yearning I had to share my life with my mama was so intense I thought it might split me open. Little Ken, Vanity, my NBA brotherhood, Doc—I wanted her to see all of it and to live this life with me, this absolutely blessed life, even if just for a moment. Before I knew it, I was crying like I'd never done before. Decades of living with the tragedy of her death came pouring out of me as Vanity sat beside me, holding me, keeping me steady.

My mother's presence in my soul, even in her absence, is a North Star.

I think of this often as I tell myself that a real, guiding fatherly presence also means having the courage to pull back and give kids space to grow and find themselves. My four kids are all different. One might be more introverted, bookish, quiet; another louder, more social. One might prioritize sports, another studying. Whatever the case may be, as a father I need to step away from what I did or how I am, to allow the kids space to be themselves—and then it is my job to be present in the spaces they start to carve out for themselves and to support them in their individual journeys.

All of us saw how Dwyane Wade supported his daughter Zaya. He opened up about how his past had shaped his ideas about the LGBTQ+ community. Like so many people react when confronting new and challenging situations, especially ones rife with emotion, D-Wade could have acted out of fear and ignorance. He chose a different path—embracing Zaya's truth, challenging himself to overcome his own fear and ignorance, and setting a standard for all of us inside and beyond the basketball community to emulate.

Now that I'm retired from the NBA, I'm around the house more. This adds challenges to my relationship with Vanity, and we get into it now and then. On the other hand, I am around to coach my son Kenxton's AAU basketball teams, to take our twins, Zoey and Karter, to gymnastics meets, and to do the little things day in and day out that make a family unit what it is—Christmas pictures, Easter egg hunts, trips to the park for family runs, making sure the kids do their nightly push-ups (that's right!), and on and on. It is the small things that make the difference.

As a member of the media now, I have been watching closely how today's players have become more public in their roles as fathers. It's great to see guys like Steph Curry, LeBron James, Julius Randle, and Russell Westbrook embrace their roles. The list could go on and on—how many Celtics fans out there aren't touched by seeing the relationship between Jayson Tatum and his son, Deuce?

It's time to move beyond categories, generalizations, outdated ideas, and concepts about Black fatherhood that are mired in past racist discussions and media presentations. There's no such thing as *the* "Black Father" or *the* "Black Family." There are only millions of individual Black men and Black women fathering and mothering under the specific conditions of their lives. For many fathers in Black communities, these conditions are extraordinarily tough, and we, as members of a shared human community, need to approach them with empathy and love, trying our best to build them up and to help them flourish, rather than being part of a system that judges them, punishes them, and contributes to dragging them down.

This is also part of being a father to our kids, knowing that our kids inhabit a much larger world than our house or our neighborhood. As fathers, we need to do our part to make that broader world better and more just. To go back to Doc Rivers' statement, we need to talk about these issues—as members of our communities, as players, and as men. But we need to talk about these issues in the right way, so that we can strengthen our communities, address problems at their core, and create the type of presence for our kids and *all kids* that enables them to live happy, healthy lives.

6

Empty Center

I'M FLOATING THROUGH SPACE, WEIGHTLESS. THE PAIN IN MY SHOULDER HAS MIRACU-
lously vanished, despite the injury I suffered a few days before. Around me, I sense the Garden crowd, but though the people are cheering our championship victory, I can't hear it. The world has gone silent. I sink into a pleasant, gentle feeling, falling deeper and deeper into a thickening mist—Celtic green. It's cool and pleasant against my warm skin, beckoning me into the heart of sleep. This is good, I think; this is how it feels to be an NBA champion.

"Wake up, motherfucker! Wake the fuck up!"

Through the thinnest slits I see the fuzzy outlines of a roundish form floating in front of me. It's nothing, I tell myself, just a small glitch in my dream, one of those unpredictable intrusions, and it's silent now, fading into the background. I close my eyes and again the mist rises around me.

The loud voice returns, barking out with what seems like a vaguely familiar intensity, "What, you can't handle it?! You soft?! Do you want me to get you a pillow?!"

I open my eyes now and the fuzzy ball comes into focus. It's a gleaming bald head, attached to a long, ropy body. KG is above me, smiling.

"Naw, I'm good," I say, and let out a soft laugh.

I sit back and take what KG is holding out to me between his thumb and forefinger. I put it to my lips and take a pull, filling my lungs with the sweet smoke for what must have been the hundredth or thousandth time that night, slowly exhaling into the hazy air of Paul's "Club Shiznit." While I have it, it occurs to me, I might as well indulge. I take a couple more short hits and fully open my eyes.

We've been at it for so long I've lost track of the hours. It seemed like another lifetime when we'd arrived here after leaving the locker room and the media circus to kick it at Paul's place—bottles popping, laughing, reminiscing, just trying to feel every second of it, embracing each moment, not letting it slip away. Somehow the hours have turned into days, days folding back into seconds, obliterating time, a shot clock always counting down and always resetting, endlessly, back to twenty-four seconds, time circling around instead of spreading out along its line.

Through the windows, I see light coming in. It's already morning, I think, the morning after closing out the Lakers to win the championship. Some of the guys are sprawled out on sofas or slumped deep into one of Paul's cushy chairs. Two or three of the fellas are helping themselves to the remains of the lavish spread, enough food to last for days.

I gaze up at KG as he takes a hit and lets the smoke out slowly. A thought comes to me, a conclusion, that there's probably nobody in the world who could be more intense than KG after nine or ten straight hours of smoking weed. At this moment, the idea seems like the funniest notion in the world, and from deep inside of me I can feel it coming—one of the biggest laughs I've ever had. It erupts from my mouth like a goddamn earthquake. Through my watery eyes I can see that KG has also busted up. Despite the laugh, of course, he's able to continue to berate me for passing out at the party.

"You still want that pillow, motherfucker?"

But he can hardly get it out before the laughter seizes him completely and he falls on the sofa next to me, ash sprinkling over me and the sofa like charred snow.

The laughter fades away. I think my eyes are closed again, but at this point I can't be sure of anything. The mist rises; the world is silent. I'm slipping away toward that beautiful, distant horizon. This must be, I think, where NBA champions reside.

THE QUEST FOR A DYNASTY

After we won the championship, KG pulled me and Rondo aside and told us to savor the moment, to not take anything for granted because this was a special time and there was no guarantee we'd be back here, and in any case there's no feeling like that of the first time winning it. I took what KG said to heart and really lived every second of that summer—the parade through the streets of Boston, the appearances at local events, going to Fenway Park to be honored by the Boston Red Sox.

When our championship bonuses came in, I decided it was time to blow some cash. Rondo and I went to a Boston area car dealership and spent our entire bonuses on new Bentleys. I got myself a blue four-door and Rondo, as you'd probably imagine, pulled off the lot behind me in a sleek two-door black model.

When we got to the practice facility, KG was there. "Oh, you boys just doing it big, huh," the Big Ticket said to us, "pulling in here in back-to-back Bentleys." Life as an NBA champion had begun.

The question on everyone's mind after our championship year and heading into the 2008–2009 NBA season was whether our team could evolve from a champion into a dynasty. If winning an NBA title is hard—and it is a process that requires an extraordinary combination of talent, work, and luck—then running it back and doing the whole thing again the following year after a shortened off-season is exponentially harder.

The first challenge of repeating is the obvious one: keeping the core members of the team together. The nature of the NBA's salary cap makes this difficult, because on every championship team there are guys whose value has been raised considerably during the run. These guys look to get paid. After our 2008 championship, Danny managed to get Eddie House and Tony Allen under contract heading into the summer, but he lost one of our essential pieces, James Posey.

Pose was key to our championship success in countless ways. His tenacious, scrappy, and tough defense allowed us to throw multiple top-notch defenders at LeBron James and Kobe Bryant, taking pressure off Paul. His energy on the defense side of the ball was unmatched. He fought through screens. He dove onto the floor after every loose ball. A championship team needs a certain level of physical and mental toughness, and that's exactly what Posey brought to us from his title-winning days with the Miami Heat. Beyond these attributes, Posey was a key factor in Doc's scheme to play what might have been the first true "small ball" lineup in the NBA. Because Pose could guard the four, the power forward position, Doc was able to slide KG over to the five and have Posey float out behind the arc on offense as a three-point threat. This opened up space for our guards to lob it into the Big Ticket, and it created great lanes for the pick-and-roll.

This "small" lineup added an important dimension to our offense, forcing opposing teams to adjust to multiple looks. In general, Posey was a perfect fit for us. He played great with KG, was a stout warrior in Thibodeau's defensive army, and was a natural leader in our locker room, bringing an infectious energy to our work every day. And this is it, folks, this is precisely the type of guy a team needs to have a high level of success in the playoffs. While most of us don't think much about it, the truth is that there aren't many guys floating around like James Posey, guys with two NBA championship rings on their fingers. The loss of Posey would be felt even more strongly when KG went down with an injury later in the year.

I know Posey would have wanted to return to Boston—and I know

Danny would have liked to keep him. In the end, though, Danny didn't match the offer Posey got from New Orleans. This seemed like a major mistake, and still does—one of the few important calls Danny didn't get right during my time with the Celtics.

Besides Posey, a couple of other veterans took off after the title run or shortly into the following season. Both P. J. Brown and Sam Cassell decided to hang up the sneakers and walk away from the game. Again, these weren't starters, but like I said, winning an NBA championship requires everything to go right and for the team to get contributions from everyone who gets meaningful minutes. If you look back at our 2008 playoff run, you'll find games we just don't win without P. J. Brown and Sam Cassell, without Eddie House's instant offense and James Posey's clutch three-and-D play, without Leon Powe or even yours truly, Big Perk, going off for twenty or a double-double.

Besides Posey, Sam, and P. J. Brown, we had everyone back for a run at a second consecutive title. Our starting five was fully intact, and with a year of playing together as a unit under our belt, we felt great. Coming off the bench, we had a crew: Eddie House, Big Baby, Leon Powe, Tony Allen, and, of course, Brian Scalabrine. Even without Posey, Sam, and P. J., this was a veteran crew with a ton of experience. Everyone had bought in for the next season and believed in the system Doc had built with us.

The main thing that changed from our championship year to the following season was that in 2008–2009 we didn't practice. The previous year, our practices had been probably the most intense part of the season. It was a process of building a tough, winning culture, learning how to play with and for each other—a process of forging our team in sweat and blood. Once this culture was in place, once we'd collectively earned Doc's trust, and he ours, we turned toward the longer-term vision. The question was not how to win today but how to sustain our success over the next two, three, or even four seasons.

Doc knew he had guys who'd hold each other accountable. He knew we'd get our work done and take care of our bodies. On the other hand, if we came out bullshitting and messing around, not doing what we were supposed to be doing, he wouldn't hesitate to call us out and get that whistle blowing.

I was locked in as we headed into the 2008–2009 season. There's something about a championship aura that sticks to you and gives you extra confidence. Now that we'd reached the NBA peak, my next goal was to make an All-Star Game. Every night when we were at home during the 2008–2009 season, I was at the gym with Rondo working on my game.

KG started to work intensively with me one-on-one on my post-up game. He showed me different techniques to get the ball on the low block. "Look, Perk," he'd say, "you don't need a hundred different moves down here. What you need is a solid go-to move, and you need a counter." At the time, my go-to from the right block was two dribbles to the middle into a jump hook. On the left block, it was two dribbles to the middle and a turnaround jump hook from the baseline with my right hand. As a counter, I developed a short turnaround jumper over my right shoulder. This simplification allowed me to master these few moves, and the results speak for themselves. That year I shot around 58 percent from the field.

The other factor in my development throughout the 2008–2009 season was my 8 A.M. sessions with Thibs. I was more or less required to be at his office door first thing in the morning. Thibs was so old-school that he was probably the only guy in the NBA still using a VCR and tapes to break down games. We'd go through my film, every damn move I made on the defensive end of the court. The result was that my growth on the defensive end far outpaced my offensive development.

Thibs was instrumental in this process. We talked about anything and everything you can imagine, down to the smallest detail of positioning and defensive timing. We talked extensively about the dynamics of the pick-and-roll, about how to meet an opponent and drive him off his position on the low block. We talked about denying the entry pass, rotations, when to go up for the block and when to stay planted.

These sound like basics, like the stuff you learn at a youth basketball camp, but let me give you a little kernel of Big Perk wisdom: the perfection of the basics is actually the hardest thing to do in sports, and these basics are not "basic" at all on the NBA level. My work at them allowed me to thrive as an NBA starting center who did the things that didn't show up in the stat sheet, though at points during the 2008–2009 season I was near to the league lead in blocks per game, finishing the year averaging two a night.

We opened the 2008–2009 season against LeBron and the Cavs. It was a low-scoring game, but we went on a run in the third and put them away. We beat Chicago in our second game before we flopped in our road opener against the Indiana Pacers for our first loss of the year. After six consecutive wins following the Indiana game, we fell to the Denver Nuggets. Both losses were the result of cold offense; our defense was still as good as ever. Following the Denver game, we went on an epic run. We pulled out an overtime win against the Bucks on the road and then played dominant basketball from mid-November until Christmas Eve, winning nineteen straight games and capping the stretch with a blowout of the Philadelphia 76ers at home in the Garden.

At this point in the season, we were a gaudy 27–2 and looked to be on the way to challenging the Bulls' record of seventy-two wins in a season. KG, Paul, and Ray had their eyes on it, and in the locker room we knew we had a strong shot at it. We were coming to play every night with no sense that we should pull our foot off the gas. This wasn't a squad that had "load management" in its DNA, especially if that meant missing or losing a game.

Looking back, it could be that this was the high point, the pinnacle of the Big Three era in Boston Celtics basketball history. We'd come together the previous year and had won the championship. We were locked

It was on the 28th of July, which I believe was a Wednesday, that I visited my father for the first time during his illness and for the last time in his life. The moment I saw him I knew why I had put off this visit so long. I had told my mother that I did not want to see him because I hated him. But this was not true. It was only that I *had* hated him and I wanted to hold on to this hatred. I did not want to look on him as a ruin: it was not a ruin I had hated. I imagine that one of the reasons people cling to their hates so stubbornly is because they sense, once hate is gone, that they will be forced to deal with pain.

This phenomenal insight cuts deep. There is, Baldwin tells us, no truth in hatred. Hatred is the opposite of truth, because it pushes us to turn away from ourselves and to strike out at another in an attempt to destroy the thing we cannot tolerate. It is only by relinquishing hate that our energies can once again turn back toward ourselves, allowing us to feel pain, to confront our true emotional and psychic selves. I fought this same battle between hate and truth for years when thinking of my own father, who abandoned me, leaving me, like Baldwin's baby sister, a fatherless child. It is damn hard, but this process of feeling pain and moving toward a deeper truth can spur our inner growth and healing. This is true, Baldwin tells us, when it comes to our closest relationships—our families—and it is true when it comes to our engagement with the world.

RALPH ELLISON'S DREAM

In 1956, the writer Ralph Ellison sat at his desk in the American Academy in Rome, Italy, and tried to comprehend the angry reaction throughout the United States to the Supreme Court's decision in *Brown v. Board* to desegregate schools. Awakened out of a deep sleep by a nightmare, in and ready to run it back a second time, despite the roster changes. Our system was working. Individuals like myself and Big Baby were improving by leaps and bounds, working hard to match the level of intensity and focus set by KG. Our defensive numbers were as good, or better, than the previous year—not least because of the incessant rewinding and fast-forwarding of Thibs' VCR.

Doc's trust in us by Christmas 2008 was total; even the tensions between him and Rondo had eased. A championship will do that. Doc continued to give Rondo more freedom, and Rondo couldn't help but demonstrate his high level of basketball intelligence day in and day out. I have no doubt that this was a team on its way to repeating as NBA champions, and if we could have stayed healthy, we would have won three straight titles and would have been ranked among the elite dynasties. On a personal level, my conditioning was better than ever. My minutes were up, and I was posting the best numbers of my career.

Even with Doc, Paul, Ray, and the other guys, the emotional heart and soul of our team was KG. The Big Ticket's focus and intensity, more than any other factor, had carried us to our championship the year before. So you can imagine how it felt to us when KG went down with an injury midway through the 2008–2009 season. It was a devastating blow. But the rest of us were determined to overcome it, especially if we could last long enough in the playoffs for KG to come back. Even without KG playing the back half of the season, we finished the year with sixty-two wins and secured second place in the Eastern Conference with home-court for at least the first two playoff series.

As in 2008, to open the 2009 playoffs we faced a young, athletic, up-and-coming but inexperienced team: the Chicago Bulls. Like the 2008 Hawks, this Bulls team had gotten off to a slow start, but they had come on late in the season. The Bulls had the versatile and sharp-shooting veteran guard Ben Gordon and an athletic center in Joakim

Noah. But what really made them dangerous was a wily player named Derrick Rose, the NBA's Rookie of the Year.

Unlike the Hawks team of the previous year, the Bulls could compete in the playoffs on the road—and they challenged us every damn game of that first-round series, whether it was in Chicago or at home at the Garden. If I'm not mistaken, Derrick Rose set the record for points in a playoff debut in game one, leading Chicago to a win on our home court. True, we were playing without KG, but we were still the number two seed in the East and were fully expecting to make a deep playoff run. After that first game, however, everyone in our locker room knew we were in for a battle just to make it out of the first round. Rose and those boys weren't going to let up or back down. They had no fear of us.

We came back to even the series in game two when Ray hit a game-winning three. In the next game, we went on the road and dominated, the only blowout of the series. The Bulls evened it up with a double-overtime marathon in game four, a prelude of things to come. We returned home to Boston and took care of business in game five, but needed overtime to do it, and the minutes were starting to pile up. Our starters were logging over forty minutes a night, closing in on fifty in the overtime games.

Game six was one of those unforgettable NBA epics. Ray Allen poured in fifty-one points in what was an utterly astounding performance. Despite it, we fell to Chicago in triple-overtime, 128–127, an unlikely hero, the Bulls' John Salmons, scoring thirty-five points.

We finally managed to put the series to bed in game seven. I posted a solid double-double with fourteen points and thirteen boards, including five on the offensive glass, to go with a couple of blocks.

Unlike the previous year, when the seven-game series with Atlanta seemed to steel us for the run to the championship, this series against the Bulls deflated us. Sure, we'd won it—barely—but our starters had played major minutes. In fact, I believe this series set the record for most minutes in a playoff series, with four overtime games, including double- and triple-OT tilts. It was a fast, physical series (that's playoff basketball), but so was the Atlanta series the year before.

What were the principal differences between the 2008 and the 2009 playoffs? Obviously, we were without KG, and when we learned he wasn't coming back it was a blow to our collective spirit. Whereas the year before we knew we were unbeatable if we were on our game, without the Big Ticket it just didn't seem like we had enough to run the gauntlet of Dwight Howard, LeBron James, and Kobe Bryant. Leon Powe was also out, meaning that our frontcourt was thin, and our frontcourt had anchored us on the defensive side of the ball since training camp in 2007.

Even with these obstacles, we still fought—and we took a talented Orlando Magic team with a prime Dwight Howard to seven games. We should have put them away in game six, but we didn't have enough gas in the tank to close it out. Many NBA playoff series come down to which team can turn it up one extra notch to pull out a close game, especially a close game that can end a series. The difference between a win and a loss in a game like game six against the Magic can be measured in a few key minutes, perhaps one run, even in a series of well-executed or poorly executed possessions.

I thought we were ready to come out at home in game seven versus the Magic and do our thing, but it wasn't our night. It had taken too much to get to that point. We were missing too much—were too thin— and just couldn't elevate to the level of basketball needed to win a decisive playoff game against a very talented basketball team with stars like Rashard Lewis and Dwight Howard.

It wasn't about effort, and it sure as hell wasn't about preparedness— Doc and Thibs always had us ready to go and in a position to win. Our team was just spent. We didn't have enough left to go the distance.

THE CENTER OF THE CIRCLE

The summer after our loss to the Magic, Vanity and I bought our first house, in the Houston area. We wanted to plant our roots in our home state of Texas, but I also knew I needed to stay away from Beaumont to avoid distractions. If we would have moved back to the 409, I would have been chilling and grilling every night with our family and old friends. Believe me, the Celtics training staff wouldn't have been happy about that, not after all the work those folks had put into getting my body into NBA shape. We had managed my diet and weight, and the hard daily work had paid off.

People might think that professional athletes get into shape and have a relatively easy time staying that way. The truth is that to be NBA-ready, especially for a guy my size and with my genes, you need to grind all year long, with diet, cardio, and strength work. For Father's Day that year, Vanity bought me my first boat, and it felt great to get back on the water and start fishing again after what seemed like many years away from it. I took my grandfather out on the boat, so we could spend time together like we had when I was growing up. Those are the moments, even more than anything on the basketball court, that are like gold, moments I'll have with me forever, now years after he's passed away.

A few weeks later, Vanity and I finally did it—we tied the knot, got married after being together more or less since the tenth grade. Our wedding took place at the Carlton Woods, a private golf club in the Houston area, near where we bought our house. The wedding was crazy. We had around eleven hundred guests. Many of my NBA guys were there, like Rondo, Stephen Jackson, and Ricky Davis. To my great surprise and pleasure, Celtics owners Wyc Grousbeck and Steve Pagliuca made the trip west for the festivities.

Before the ceremony, I was nervous, and tried to calm my nerves by sharing a few drinks in the clubhouse with the fellas. Vanity looked dazzling in her white gown and baby blue heels. We arrived for the ceremony in a horse-drawn carriage and were met there by the legendary local pastor John Adolph. You better believe that the reverend doctor spoke the gospel that day like none other, though I have to admit I was too damn nervous to take in what he was saying. I'd been brought up Catholic, but Rev. Adolph was just something special. After the service, we partied the whole day and into and through the night. We did it up so thoroughly that Vanity and I had to postpone our honeymoon. Two days later, we were still recovering. Now that's a real wedding.

The best man at my wedding was my grandfather, Raymond Lewis. There was no question in my mind that I'd ask him to do it. He'd been with me my whole life. In his own way, he'd given me everything he had to give, and I don't mean money or material things. The values that have enabled me to make it to the league, to survive and thrive in the league, the values that continue to guide me as I move on to other things—those core values come from him. In that sense, even if I didn't take any genes from him, even though he wasn't responsible for my nearly seven feet of height, he taught me to stand tall, to stand strong, to be a man. My grandfather was my best friend.

We had our same starting five back for a third straight year for the 2009–2010 NBA season: Rondo at the point, Ray and Paul on the wings, KG and me down low. On the bench in our second unit, we still had key contributors, like the defensive maestro Tony Allen and Big Baby, who'd come into his own during the previous season when filling in for KG.

The biggest change year-over-year had been the addition of Rasheed Wallace. 'Sheed had been one of my biggest rivals among big men in the Eastern Conference, but he quickly became an amazing teammate and friend. Not only did he bring us his incredible talent, still evident in this late stage of his career, and his ability to stretch the floor from the power forward or center position, but he also brought a championship mentality and his unique presence in the locker room. He was an instant fit with our culture, on and off the court.

Though we started off the season red hot, winning twenty of our first twenty-five games, our focus was on preparing for the playoffs. At this point in our run together, we were not concerned with seeding or home-court advantage. We knew if we made it to the playoffs with a healthy roster, unlike the previous year when we were down both KG and Leon, we would be set to make a serious push for our second title.

We didn't fear a single team in the league. We knew we were better than the Magic, even though they'd beaten us the year before in seven games. We knew we were better than LeBron and the Cavs. LeBron was special, but the organization couldn't get it together to build a team around him that would give him a serious shot at competing for a championship. Based on his will and immense abilities, LeBron pushed them as far as he could year after year, but he wasn't getting that team over our wall, not when we were healthy, and not once Tony Allen had come into his own on the defensive side of the ball.

The Celtics organization's experience with KG the previous year led to a shift in strategy. I won't say we were "game managing"—there was no possibility of "managing" KG in that sense—but Doc was intent on experimenting with different combinations and leaned more heavily on the second unit throughout the season. The result was that we finished the year with our lowest win total since Ray and KG joined the team: fifty. This meant that the path to another NBA Finals would have to go through both Orlando and Cleveland. It was a stiff challenge, but we were locked in and ready to roll.

We entered the playoffs as the number four seed, behind Cleveland at number one, Orlando at two, and those Hawks, now with Jamal Crawford added to the mix, at three. In the first round, we faced off against D-Wade and the Heat, but they didn't have nearly enough to hang with us. Our defensive intensity spiked up, and we shut the door on them in five games. Now, that's how a first-round series is supposed to go!

In the second round, we ran into a familiar opponent, LeBron and the Cavs. This time around, Cleveland had the home-court advantage. They came out and took care of business in game one. Game two was a different story. We were determined to play our style, meaning tenacious, hard-nosed defense, and we did just that, taking home-court with us as the series moved back to Boston. Even though we let the Cavs steal home-court back by playing an atrocious game three, we remained cool and confident about our chances. Our attitude proved justified, as we won three games in a row and closed out the series 4–2 with a home win at the Garden.

The Cav series launched us into the Eastern Conference Finals against the Magic. We were all set to get even with them for the previous year. We went down to Orlando and smacked them in the face, winning games one and two on the road. Ray was big-time in the first game, and Rondo and Paul turned it on in game two. We went north in complete control of the series.

Game three showcased one of our classic defensive efforts. The Magic couldn't get anything going against us from the tip. We held them to twelve first-quarter points and thirty-four for the half. We came out in the third and ran the lead up to thirty, walking away to an easy win. At 3–0, we were eyeing the sweep, knowing we would need everything we had to take on Kobe and the Lakers, who were dominating in great fashion in the West.

I'll give it to the Magic. They'd lost two home games and were down 3–0, and still they came out to play in game four. It was a chippy battle. Tempers were flaring all over the place. The Magic were playing with toughness and pride. They jumped out to an early lead, but we managed to play ourselves back into it, tying it up by the end of the fourth with a chance to win. Unfortunately, we didn't execute on the final possession, and the Magic, behind two three-pointers by Jameer Nelson, took the game in overtime.

This loss killed our momentum. We didn't show up for game five, which was uncharacteristic for us. Orlando blew us out, cutting their series deficit to 3–2. We gathered ourselves for game six, as a true championship-caliber team has to do. Locked in and ready, we won the game decisively and put the series to bed. As was often the case with us, our defense won it. We held Orlando under twenty-five points in every quarter. In the first and third, they managed only nineteen.

For the second time in three years, we were headed back to the NBA Finals, again to face Kobe Bryant, Pau Gasol, and the rest of the Los Angeles Lakers. The Lakers' frontcourt was big, long, and dominant. For years now, Pau Gasol had been one of the most skilled bigs in the game. Andrew Bynum was large and athletic. Lamar Odom added strength and length coming off the bench. In the backcourt, they had Kobe, of course, along with Derek Fisher and Ron Artest.

When the series opened in L.A., Kobe came out slashing, determined to get to the rim. He knew we'd prevented him from getting into the paint in 2008. We'd executed our plan brilliantly, making Kobe a jump shooter and limiting his effectiveness. It wouldn't be the same this time. Their adjustments paid off in game one. A bunch of our guys got in foul trouble early, and Kobe and company built a double-digit lead. With Ray on the bench for much of the third, we weren't able to make a sustained run. The Lakers went up 1–0.

We came out fired up and with great intensity for game two. We'd been outworked in game one—outrebounded and physically outplayed by the Lakers on both ends of the floor. Gasol had outdueled the Big Ticket, and that set the tone for the rest of us. Given the guys we had in that locker room, we were determined to change the narrative in game two.

The difference in our play from one game to another was clear. We were pressing and switching crisply on defense. Rondo, Paul, and Ray were preventing the Laker guards and wings from driving the lane, while KG and I were taking care of business in the paint. At the offensive end, Ray caught fire, hitting his first six threes. When Garnett got into foul trouble, Big Baby and 'Sheed filled in and played stout defense, clogging the lane and making life difficult for Gasol. When we think of NBA championships now, we tend to think of three-point shooting and scoring in general, but that series in 2010 was a battle in the paint. We evened up the series on the road and returned to Boston with home court in hand.

After a tough loss in Boston in game three, we squared the series again with a win in game four. Our bench unit sparked a late run. Big Baby alone carried us through much of the fourth quarter. He was a monster, hitting the offensive glass, finishing time after time with athletic moves at the rim, pushing the Lakers' big men out of the way with his wide, powerful body. Our backup point, Nate Robinson, came up huge, and Rasheed continued his stout defense on Gasol, making him battle for everything.

I was loving it, cheering the second unit on from the bench, rushing the court when play stopped to help a guy up, giving them the support they deserved. It was incredible to watch those guys clamp down on the Lakers' stars. Just think about this: game four of the NBA Finals, and a lineup of Glen Davis, Nate Robinson, Tony Allen, Ray Allen, and Rasheed Wallace put a beatdown on Kobe, Pau, Ron Artest, and the rest of the Lakers' starting five.

If you love basketball, go back and watch game five of that series. It was a classic. We blew open a close game in the third. Then Kobe Bryant exploded, scoring nineteen points in the quarter to keep the Lakers in it. When it came to the playoffs, it seemed like every time Kobe or LeBron would turn it up and start to play out of their minds, Paul would somehow find it within himself to match those megastars. Game five was no different. His twenty-seven points led us to the win and a 3–2 advantage as the series swung back to Los Angeles.

Game six of the 2010 NBA Finals was devastating for me—the worst basketball moment of my life. About midway through the first quarter, I went up for an offensive rebound. Andrew Bynum came over my back and committed a foul. As I came down, I felt a stabbing pain in my right knee. I knew immediately it was bad—really bad. It was series-ending bad, career-threatening bad. Before I knew what was happening, our trainers were on the floor. They got me stabilized and helped me to the locker room.

I'd had injuries before. In the 2008 series, I'd missed a game with a shoulder injury. But this one was different, and an MRI showed I'd torn up my knee real good. Just a few days later, I went under the knife. The surgery was successful, but I had a long recovery period in front of me. I was looking at six months of grueling daily rehab—and that was if everything went well.

Thankfully, and thanks to the medical and training staff in Boston, my recovery went about as well as it could have. For a guy like me, though, injuries like this are serious blows. It cost me some of my athleticism, and for a relatively unathletic player like myself, any loss of quickness or agility is huge. I don't think I ever returned to the form I was in before the injury. Though I'd learn ways to compensate for these setbacks, I can say this: any upward trajectory I'd had toward an All-Star Game came crashing down that day in L.A. The game itself was a blowout. It's painful to go back and watch it now, seeing how off the team was, how stagnant our play became. We didn't even manage to crack seventy points that night.

I was on the bench for game seven, wearing a green-and-white-striped dress shirt, Celtics colors. It felt awful not to have the uniform on, not to be out there with my boys, but at least I could cheer them on from the bench; you can't flip a switch and turn off the intensity you feel from playing in the NBA Finals. Rasheed Wallace took my place in the starting lineup next to KG, Paul, Ray, and Rondo.

If someone doubts my importance to the Celtics during the years of the Big Three, just tell them to go back and look at game seven of the 2010 finals, especially the opening minutes. By the nine-minute mark, Gasol already had five rebounds, and he and Andrew Bynum were absolutely dominating the paint. We had KG and 'Sheed, but they just weren't enough to clear out the Laker bigs. The Lakers had *ten offensive boards in the first half of the first quarter*! Given the nature of today's NBA, it is hard to imagine that apart from a couple of jumpers by Kobe and Fisher, all the Lakers' shots in the first quarter came in the paint.

Despite these huge challenges, our guys were battling—and we ended the first quarter with the lead. But we came out ice cold in the second. The Lakers, led by Ron Artest, came back to tie the game. We battled to regain the lead in what was shaping up to be another low-scoring affair. The dark spot for us was on the boards. The Lakers' bigs were dominating the glass. Gasol had ten rebounds in the first half alone. Kobe added seven, and if you add Bynum and Odom into the mix, you get a sense of how much the Lakers' size mattered in keeping the game within reach for them. Artest led the Lakers in scoring in the first half, with nearly all his points coming close to the hoop or from the foul line.

Our boys were scrapping in the third. Our defense was vicious. Rondo was rebounding, dishing, driving, and scoring at the hoop. At the eight-minute mark of the quarter, we'd pushed the lead to thirteen. The Lakers rallied behind Kobe, Gasol, and Lamar Odom. It was game seven. They were at home. They were not about to fold to our pressure. The defense on both sides was intense. On the offensive end, things just weren't falling for us. Ray had gone cold, missing shot after shot. Whether it was an open three or a mid-range jumper, everything seemed to come off the rim. The game went into the fourth with us hanging on to a slim lead.

From the start of the fourth, the Lakers' strategy was obvious. They were determined to pound the ball inside to their bigs. 'Sheed was hurting with a bad back. Big Baby was playing his heart out, but Gasol had a good five or six inches of height over him. It was absolute torture sitting on the bench during that fourth quarter, watching those guys battling inside, seeing how hard KG and the others were playing, as shot after shot clanged off the rim. Two of the deadliest and most clutch shooters the game has seen—Ray Allen and Paul Pierce—just couldn't buy a bucket. The combination was too much, and the Lakers gradually pulled even and then went ahead. We battled, and there was no lack of effort, no giving up, but it wasn't our day. The Lakers were bigger, stronger, taller, and on that day the better team. The title went to them.

Fans and members of the media have broken down that game seven in a thousand ways, but I have no doubt that if I'd been healthy we would have won it. The Lakers wouldn't have been able to dominate inside as they did. KG wouldn't have had to expend all of his energy on the defensive side of things and could have been more offensive-minded. He would have had way more in the tank heading down the stretch into the fourth quarter. As it was, he was absolutely spent. The Lakers' advantage on the glass would have been far less or nonexistent. On the offensive side, it's impossible to put an exact value on the type of hard screens I'd been setting to free up Ray or Paul for shots. Nothing came easy in game seven. The Lakers were playing tough defense, don't get me wrong, but our screening and movement without the basketball were not at our usual level.

In the chapter on fatherhood, I wrote about presence and absence, a circle defined by its nucleus, its center, and the relationship between the center and the curve. I'm not saying I was the entire nucleus of our 2010 team, but I was a key part of what made that group special. We played that game seven without a true center in more ways than one. There are times when absence can provoke a truly special, magical kind

of moment, one in which guys are somehow able to form the core anew
and pull out a victory against the odds. But that's not usually what happens. Usually, a circle without a center cannot hold its shape. It lacks
orientation. It lacks strength. It collapses under pressure.

This is what happened to our 2009 team against Orlando the previous year without KG. This is what happened in 2010 against the Lakers
without Big Perk. Little did I know as I watched the gruesome fourth
quarter unfold from the bench in the Staples Center on that June night
that I was seeing in front of me the end, for all intents and purposes, of
an era of Celtics basketball—and an end to the first half of my career.

DENVER, COLORADO

Let's take a seat in Tom Thibodeau's office and press fast forward on that
VCR. When we pull our fingers off the button, we find ourselves on February 24, 2011. I wake up in a Denver hotel room, the morning before a
game against the Nuggets. We're supposed to gather for a shoot-around
to get ready for the game that night. I'd fallen asleep with the television
on the night before, and when I woke up ESPN was running through the
sports news of the day. At first I think I'm imagining it, but then I start
to focus. The guy on television is saying my name. Then I hear him say
this line: "Boston Celtics center Kendrick Perkins has been traded to
the Oklahoma City Thunder for forward Jeff Green and center Nenad
Krstic." I look at my phone and see I've already missed a bunch of calls
from my agent, Bob Myers. When I call back and he picks up, he starts
right away telling me, "Yeah, Perk, you got traded. It's for the best. It's
a great situation for you."

"Naw, man, you got to call up Danny and call this off. We're going to
figure this out. We've got unfinished business here."

"Perk, it's over. Danny's going to be calling you. Don't worry. It's part of the business of basketball. I've got to go."

Bob hangs up. A few seconds later, Danny is calling.

"You can't break us up," I tell Danny. "We've got to finish this thing off. Call off the deal. We can figure out the rest in the off-season."

He pauses for a moment, then says, "Kendrick, I'm sorry. It's done. You're going to love Oklahoma City. Sam Presti is great. Scott Brooks is great. You'll be fine. This is a good move for you."

Danny might have been right, but in the moment I don't want to hear it—I *can't* hear it. It's like hearing I'm going to be separated from my brothers, my family.

When the fellas get back from shoot-around, I go by their rooms in the hotel one by one. Rondo is pissed, telling me the whole thing is fucked up, that management doesn't know what it's doing. I go to Ray's room. He's being firm, stoic. "Perk," he tells me in a very even, cool tone, "I appreciate you as a teammate, but this is part of the business." I didn't want to hear that again, not now. I go and see Paul. "Oh, man, big fella," he says, "it's been eight good years. I'm going to miss you. But look, you just got to keep pushing." I find Doc. He takes me into his room and asks me to sit down. We're talking for a good forty-five minutes in there. Finally, he says to me, "I know this thing is done, Perk, and you're heading out to OKC, but this trade is not going to change our relationship." I can see that he's tearing up, and I feel like I'm tearing up too. We embrace and then I'm on my way to my last stop: KG.

When I get inside his room and we start talking, KG breaks down. He falls to his knees. He's crying, and I'm on my knees and crying right along with him. He grabs me, presses his head to mine, and keeps repeating, yelling as only KG can, "What the fuck you mean, 'traded'? What the fuck you mean?" I don't know how long we stay like that—I think it was a long time—but when I rise from the floor and leave KG's room and close the door behind me, that's when I know, that's when I really feel it—it's the end of the line for me in Boston.

That evening before the game, we got together for one last round of cards. The mood was a strange combination of light and heavy. We were laughing, joking like we always did, sharing memories about the last years. I could tell right there that something bigger was ending. A team died when I was dealt to OKC, a team that had been to two NBA Finals in three years. The Celtics continued to have success for the next couple of seasons, but it was a different Celtics team. The guys went out that night and got blown out by Denver. Reporters told me afterward that the team had played with no life, no competitive fire.

It's difficult to tell before it happens when a circle will cave in, when the pressure beyond it will exceed the force emanating from within. It's difficult to tell what actually forms the nucleus of a team, what, in the end, holds a team together. It's an alchemy that very few owners, presidents, or general managers understand, and that's why so many of them get it wrong. They are looking to the right, and the truth passes them by on the left-hand side. They are busy crunching numbers when the key variables stand outside of their equations, variables even the most clever statistician hasn't managed to quantify—heart, toughness, brotherhood, love, and a collective will to win.

Much later, I learned that before he made the deal with Sam Presti to send me to OKC, Danny Ainge had called a meeting. At the meeting with Danny were Doc, Rondo, Paul, KG, and Ray Allen. At the time, because of my ACL tear, Danny had added Jermaine O'Neal and Shaq to the roster. The team was doing well, and Danny had his eye on the Miami Heat, like the rest of the basketball universe. Before the season, Pat Riley had formed what looked like an unbeatable team, adding the best player in the world, LeBron James, and perennial All-Star Chris Bosh to join with former finals' MVP Dwyane Wade. To compete with the Heat, Danny thought, the Celtics needed to get deeper at the wing position.

The other factor on the table was my contract. My agent, Bob Myers, and I had already turned down a four-year, $22 million extension, knowing that the going rate for a starting NBA center was between $9 and $15 million per year. Danny knew the Celtics didn't have the cap space to match the offers coming my way in free agency. If he waited until the end of the season, he was almost certain to lose me for nothing in return. Still, it was a question of this year, this team, and this season—and there was a championship run at stake.

During the meeting, Danny laid the issues on the table, the main feature being his desire to get back the wing player Jeff Green in order to be potentially more competitive with the Heat. Danny made it clear to the others that he wanted to go forward with the move on the table with OKC, but that he wanted the people at the meeting to vote on it. If the vote went against him, he told them, he'd cancel the deal.

KG spoke up first: "Fuck that shit. Keep Perk. I don't want to hear about that." Rondo agreed with the Big Ticket. "I'm riding with the big fella," he said. It went to Paul. He understood Danny's thinking. While he wanted to keep me, he was convinced the team needed more depth on the wing. He must have thought he saw his championship window closing. He told Danny to do the deal. Doc agreed with Paul. He didn't like it, but it was the business of basketball, and in his opinion, from a basketball perspective, it was the right thing to do. The tie-breaking vote went to Ray Allen. He didn't hesitate. "Let's do it," he said. The meeting was over, and with it my Celtics career.

I've always wondered if Danny or Doc thought again about that meeting after Miami beat them four games to one in the Eastern Conference semis a few months later and again the following year in seven. Perhaps they realized that they were never going to beat Miami on the wing. A team wasn't going to beat the Heat by being more like them. The Heat could be beaten only by a team playing its own game.

7

Protest

IT IS IMPOSSIBLE TO DENY THAT WE ARE LIVING THROUGH VERY TROUBLED TIMES REGARD- ing issues of race, equality, and social justice. To me, it feels worse now than ever before in my lifetime. During these last few years, the idea that the future is bound to be better than the past has been shattered. God only knows if this faith can be repaired. Belief, following Martin Luther King Jr., that "the arc of the moral universe is long, but it bends toward justice" has been deeply shaken, if not entirely swept away.

The legacies of the Civil Rights Movement are being dismantled as I write this. The movement's gains for the causes of justice and equality resulted from generations of struggle and protest, and now the work of those generations is being systematically undone in plain sight. The 2020 election, which expelled a racist President and checked the power of his white-supremacist supporters, might have been a turning of the tide against the politics of hate and division. On the other hand, the victory for decency might only be a moment of calm in the storm.

Has Ellison's nightmare of a raging mob turned from dream to reality? On January 6, 2021, as I watched a white-supremacist mob storm the U.S. Capitol Building, it sure seemed to me like that nightmare had come to life.

There is no waking up from this one, folks. The terror will not fade

away into the darkness and stillness of a Roman night, as it did for Ellison. It is here to stay, pressing against our chest. It is up to us to find
our way together, to hold firm against hate, injustice, and inequality.
We need to draw on our legacies of protest to fight for economic opportunity, human rights, and the dignity of all people.

ERASING PROTEST HISTORY

We need to take a step back to talk about history. I mean the "production of history," the stories we tell ourselves and each other to understand who and where we are and how we got to this point. When, at the
beginning of this book, I wrote about our need to turn around and look
back, I meant facing history, our own personal histories and the history of our society. We're living in a moment when the politics of this
storytelling are on center stage.

Shamefully, my home state of Texas has joined others to prevent a
true reckoning with the past. In the place of truth, Texas officials want
to give our children a set of recycled white-supremacist lies. But this
is no surprise, and in fact it has been this way since the beginning of
widespread public education in our country.

Against this, brave teachers, parents, and other activists are assert-
ing a harder, deeper, and more truthful story about the United States
and the world, one that busts up the very myths that have been supporting inequality in our society for generations. These brave folks are
being slandered in Texas and elsewhere as being biased or as bringing
ideology into the classroom. In fact, they are shining the light of truth
into spaces that have hardly seen a glimmer of it.

Who controls the historical story we tell ourselves and our children?
Until recently, control over the story of American history was dominated
by conservative members of the academic elite, educated at places like

Harvard, Columbia, Yale, and Princeton. For generations, these schools hardly admitted Black students, women, or students from other minority groups. In the late nineteenth century and the first decades of the twentieth, the white men trained in these environments produced a version of U.S. history that dominated most of the country's mainstream history textbooks until the 1980s. But that version of history continues to prevail in many respects to this day.

In terms of the experience of Black Americans, their story went as follows. Slaves accepted their position as slaves without much protest; there were only isolated, extraordinary moments of rebellion. Such revolts were either products of local circumstances and led by violent, unhinged men or were fueled by Northern white radicals like John Brown and other abolitionists. Slavery could be cruel, but cruelty was the exception rather than the norm. Most masters treated their slaves well, and in turn most slaves enjoyed good conditions on the plantations and in the domestic service of their masters.

In this version of the story, the Civil War was caused not primarily by slavery but by the desire of the people in the Southern states to protect their culture, their way of life, and their local power. That these factors—culture, economy, politics—were deeply entwined with slavery and racial hierarchy was hardly discussed. The North was the aggressor in this version of U.S. history, intent on exerting the wants and needs of the rising industrial and commercial economy over those of the agrarian South.

After the war, these historians argue, the North and the "federal government" attempted to destroy Southern life by imposing its values on the former Confederacy. Lincoln, in his Emancipation Proclamation, had set the stage for freeing the slaves, and now Congress, led by Northern "radicals," sought to impose racial democracy, integration, and economic redistribution on the conquered people. They argue that this project, called Reconstruction, was pushed by white Northern abolitionists. It was not, they believed, led by Black folk in the South, who were content (or even happy) to remain within the plantation system as it would be newly constituted through sharecropping and other hierarchical means. Most Black people preferred the racially hierarchical status quo.

This is why, when the federal government pulled the plug on Reconstruction in 1877, the whole thing fell apart. Not only was it corrupt and incompetently managed, but it also never had popular support.

The key architect of this version of history was the University of Michigan's Ulrich Bonnell Phillips, who summarized slavery as a mutually beneficial system, in which white masters and overseers took care of, and provided for, their mostly grateful slaves. The slaves, Phillips argued, were given the chance to improve their "notoriously primitive" natures by being under a plantation owner's civilizing hand. The ideas of men like Phillips, and others like William Archibald Dunning, shaped our country's understanding of its history until at least the 1960s, if not up to this day.

It's incredible to think about. We're talking about more than 150 years after the end of the Civil War and slavery, and still the dominant way of teaching and learning about our history has been a defense of Southern white-supremacist society based on racist views of Black people's inherent "natures" and their supposedly inferior cultural roots. Just consider the words of the historian and U.S. President Woodrow Wilson: "Domestic slaves," Wilson wrote, "were almost uniformly dealt with indulgently and even affectionately by their masters." On the issue of cruelty, Wilson asserted, "Such cases there may have been: they may even have been frequent; but they were in every sense exceptional, showing what the system could produce, rather than what it did produce as its characteristic spirit and method."

If you don't believe these ideas had real impact, think again. I'll stick to my home state of Texas to illustrate my point, though a similar story could be told about most other states. Throughout the 1960s, one of the main American history textbooks assigned to Texas eighth graders was *Our United States: A Bulwark of Freedom*. To paint a portrait of life in the antebellum South, the book presents a story of the fictional Idlewild Plantation, owned by Charles Austin. The scene of emancipation at Idlewild is disturbing. At one point in the story, Union soldiers show up at the plantation and declare their intentions to burn it to the ground. The following scene appears in the textbook (for real):

> The Austins and their house slaves carried out the few valuables they still possessed and some of their fine furniture. Around the corner came the other slaves—women, children, old folks, and a few young men—herded along by the squad of soldiers. The children were crying as they clung fearfully to their mothers. When the slaves caught sight of Mrs. Austin, they broke away from the soldiers, came to her, and crouched behind her as though asking for her protection.

Can you imagine what Black kids in the 1960s would have thought when reading this nonsense? Can you imagine *your kids* being forced to read this and taught that it is an accurate depiction of the way things were? It gets worse. A Union lieutenant then reads the Emancipation Proclamation to the group:

> To his surprise, the Austin slaves showed no joy over their new freedom. They stood still, eyeing the soldiers suspiciously. Finally Old Uncle Josephus stepped timidly forward.
>
> "Please sir," he said, cap in hand, "may we please go back to our work now?"

Throughout the 1970s, Texas changed its history textbooks multiple times. While the others didn't equal the racist preposterousness of

Our United States: A Bulwark of Freedom, they did echo in the main the line set by Phillips, Dunning, Wilson, and company. Authors continued to downplay the violence and horrors of the slave system. They claimed that slaves were a "great help" to the Confederacy during the Civil War. They asserted that after the war many slaves *wanted* to remain on the plantations to work for their former masters. They summarized share-cropping, like slavery, as a mutually beneficial partnership. Problems during Reconstruction were blamed on Black politicians and voters or white Northerners. Jim Crow laws were described as measures to lessen "trouble" between the races, its horrors either ignored or minimized. Images of white violence against Black people in the South were forbidden to appear in textbooks by state regulations. Disenfranchisement of Southern Black voters was hardly mentioned until it appeared as an issue in the 1950s in relation to the Civil Rights Movement.

When it came to the Civil Rights Movement, there was little mention of the fierce and violent white resistance to integration, even though most Texas schools were *still segregated* when kids were reading these books. The inclusion of the movement made little sense in the textbooks, since the realities of Jim Crow were never presented accurately and fully. As mainstream white society moved from open racism to the new color-blind racism of the 1970s, 1980s, and today, a massive whitewashing campaign began to use the Civil Rights Movement as a way of denying the continued relevance of racism in American society.

In sum, the portrait of our Black ancestors was devastating. They were presented as ignorant, incompetent, timid, corrupt, and by their very nature inferior to white people. Throughout these histories, it was the white citizen who organized and upheld the social order, while Black men and women were denied agency and humanity time and again. When Black history was included, it was commonly boxed off and separated from the main text. It was also nonpolitical—like George Washington Carver experimenting with the peanut.

THE STRUGGLE FOR THE TRUTH

If these whitewashed accounts of the history of slavery and Black life in the United States were dominant, the question becomes: how were they busted up? On one hand, sadly, they were never busted up. We are witnessing before our very eyes how racist arguments and assumptions—white-supremacist versions of our history—are being deployed and echoed to block progress toward freedom and equality and to support a racist, reactionary agenda. That's the first point. These stories are stubborn. The second point, just as important, is that these stories have been, and need to be, challenged through protest. Luckily, we have had people who were brave enough to discover and tell the truth, even if this meant their ideas were rejected by the status quo, even if it meant, in some cases, that telling the truth about American history could mean professional and personal hardship.

In the 1930s, two historians, W. E. B. Du Bois and Herbert Aptheker, laid siege to white-supremacist history. Du Bois and Aptheker told a new and better story. It went like this: protest by slaves and former slaves against the slave system and Jim Crow was constant. Slave revolts were not singular events but part of a tradition and culture of protest that began at the very beginnings of slavery and lasted throughout the Civil War. Reconstruction was not driven primarily by white Northerners but was *enacted* by Black men, women, and children throughout the South as they flooded into public life and schools and fought to secure a better future. This protest wasn't easy—the whole structure of Southern society was built around the fear of Black resistance and white violence in the service of preserving racial hierarchy.

W. E. B. Du Bois' attack on the prevailing white-supremacist versions of U.S. history was as brilliant as it was thorough. His ultimate agenda was not simply to dismantle the white-supremacist history that dominated American education—it was to dismantle and replace that history with a truer one that would advance the cause of racial justice.

It was this spirit of truth and justice that animated what is perhaps the single most important book on American history, Du Bois' *Black Reconstruction*. With *Black Reconstruction*, Du Bois shattered the entire construct that apologized for slavery and denigrated Black people during both their enslavement and their freedom. Nothing about that version of history, Du Bois demonstrated, was true. Slavery was inhuman, cruel, and physically and psychologically destructive. Free Black people, though held back by a lack of education and economic opportunity, were not lower down but inherently equal. When given access to land or education, they seized hold of these opportunities with incredible zeal. Reconstruction was an attempt, fought at every single turn by white power, by members of the newly emancipated Black community to participate at all levels of society and to advance their station by dint of work and talent.

In *Black Reconstruction*, Du Bois presented Black people and Black communities, for one of the first times in the telling of American history, as *agents of change*. He demanded that the humanity of the American Black community be central to American history. This revolution in the telling of American history might seem small to some of us today, but it was hugely important.

It was so massive, in fact, that the establishment could not tolerate it. Instead of being fundamentally reshaped by Du Bois' work, American historians cast it aside and tried to pretend it didn't exist. When the great John Hope Franklin and his coauthors attempted to highlight Du Bois' work in their groundbreaking textbook *Land of the Free* in 1966, white reactionaries used it as grounds to try to block the book's adoption in schools.

A few years after Du Bois' *Black Reconstruction* appeared, a second work delivered another broadside strike at the grand myths about slavery and

American history: Herbert Aptheker's *American Negro Slave Revolts*. Far from exceptional or rare, slave revolts, Aptheker demonstrated, were common. And not only common: slave dissent and unrest were *constant* features of American life. Contrary to what Phillips, Wilson, and others of their ilk would have us believe, there was no state of peace between slaveholders and overseers and slaves. If any kind of "peace" existed, it was the type created by a system of violence and control dedicated to keeping the slaves down. Fear of slave unrest and the corresponding desire for domination lay beneath the entire social structure of slave society.

It was this fear and active oppression of slaves, who were in a constant state of revolt and protest, that accounts for the ideological fervor of white supremacy, the brutal labor conditions, and the legal and policing apparatuses. It is to Aptheker's enduring credit that he produced the first systematic, documented history of Black protest in America.

The reaction to Aptheker's work was even more hostile than to Du Bois' narrative-shattering *Black Reconstruction*. The topic of slave revolts and Black rebellion made white historians very nervous, especially in the Jim Crow era. Aptheker was also a member of the Communist Party of the United States, and the typical character assassination Communist Party members suffered ensued, discrediting his work and preventing him from teaching.

What's incredibly disturbing about the politics surrounding these two books is that it would take another thirty years after their publication for their arguments to gain traction. It was only in the 1960s, with grassroots pressure by activists, especially supporters of Black Power, that these ideas were forced out of the shadows of white-supremacist history. Even then, though Du Bois' and Aptheker's ideas started to change the way professional historians approached American history, they did not penetrate the American mainstream.

Honest education in Black history is critically important for our country. The NBA brotherhood has made it a priority to promote Black history, but there is still much work to be done. We are only at the very beginning of our journey. It is vital for our children, if they are to grow up in a society that pushes back against and rejects white supremacy, that we build on the legacies of Du Bois and Aptheker in the pursuit of truth. This is a huge part of today's protest agenda, especially as state after state, including my home state of Texas, tries to demonize this history in a naked attempt to return us to history as it was written in the shadow of Jim Crow. This was a history—make no mistake—that denied Black people agency and as a result denied Black people humanity and dignity. No thanks! It's hard to say it better than Aptheker, writing in 1937:

> John Brown's idea that slavery was war had considerable concrete justification. During slavery the South was a dictatorial oligarchy which terrorized the slaves and suppressed their frequent insubordination and revolts. The fear of such rebelliousness was a persistent factor in the life of the South which has too long been overlooked by social historians. The facts presented here certainly refute the stereotype of a docile Negro slave; the American Negro consistently and courageously struggled against slavery in every possible way and he must continue in this tradition if he is to break down the barriers of discrimination today.

As Aptheker proved, the main opponents of slavery in the United States were not the Northern white liberal abolitionists that historians most often highlight. The main opponents of slavery were the slaves themselves, who risked their lives and those of their loved ones by standing up to their oppressors. When slave revolts were put down, when plots were uncovered by plantation owners or others, punishments were severe. Gruesome public executions of suspected conspirators graphically displayed what was at stake in fighting back against white-supremacist power. It was with incredible bravery and resolution about the justice of their cause that these condemned Black men and Black women went to their deaths. They are the martyrs in a quest for justice that still has not been fulfilled. We owe it to their memory to get the job done.

Ask yourself: why has this war against the slave system by the slaves themselves been ignored in our classrooms? Why, more than eighty years after Du Bois and Aptheker gave us their magnificent work, do we continue to tell the same story of white Northern abolitionists and a President who emancipated the slaves? Why has there not been room for the true story of Black protest and its centrality in American history?

As W. E. B. Du Bois vividly captures, the end of Reconstruction was a travesty for Black Americans, allowing the slave-era system to be rebuilt on the same foundation of white-supremacist racism. Police, prison guards and wardens, state troopers, rangers, and vigilantes combined to form the foot soldiers of white terrorism that propped up racist regimes in state after state.

As under slavery, Black folk during Jim Crow did not passively accept this status quo. In countless ways, Black individuals and communities pushed back against the structures of oppression, whether it meant trying to acquire land, opening a business, or violating the social norms imposed on them by Jim Crow society. This protest took various forms, like Black community organization, the formation of voluntary associations, the development of educational institutions like Black schools and colleges, Black athletic leagues, and the publication of Black newspapers, journals, and magazines.

THE LONG HISTORY OF BLACK POWER

There is a long list of great, heroic opposition to Jim Crow. Organizations like the NAACP formed to push the cause of freedom. Individuals like Ida B. Wells and Frederick Douglass campaigned against lynching and the denial of Black people's human and civil rights.

The most profound "event" of protest against the racial caste system in the South, however, occurred among the common folk. It was the common Black folk who together launched the greatest movement against injustice in the history of the United States. It was called the Great Migration. Black men, women, and children protested by the millions by leaving everything behind to try to build new lives beyond the rural South.

The Great Migration set the stage for the Civil Rights Movement in many important ways. The greatly expanded Black communities in the North would organize to push for civil and human rights both in the increasingly intolerant North and in the Jim Crow South. Memory of Southern oppression animated Black activists whose families had made the momentous journey in the decades before.

We've had many examples in previous chapters of Black leaders whose parents had gone from the South to the North during the Great Migration—Bill Russell, Kareem Abdul-Jabbar, Richard Wright, and James Baldwin. The list could go on and on. The Great Migration fostered the Harlem Renaissance and the rise of jazz music. Its greatest protest legacy was Black Power. We can point to the example of Huey Newton, cofounder of the Black Panther Party, who came, like Bill Russell, from Monroe, Louisiana, and moved, like Russell, to Oakland, California, when his parents, like Russell's, found jobs in the defense industry during World War II. The parents of Chicago's Black Panther leader Fred Hampton were also migrants from the Bayou State.

Black Power combined the desire to overcome the racial tyranny of Southern Jim Crow with the direct protest of the virulent racism Black communities faced in Northern cities. In traditional accounts of U.S. history, much has been made of tension and antagonism between what is deemed the nonviolent Civil Rights Movement, led by Martin Luther King Jr., and "militant" Black Power, most associated with Malcolm X. Like other historical simplifications, this easy and clear division needs

to be set aside. It is largely a product of the white imagination and mis-
leading voices in the media. The truth is that the Civil Rights Movement
and Black Power were so deeply intertwined that they formed a single,
broader protest movement: the Black freedom struggle.

The media and political campaign against Black Power was part of a
highly racialized politics of backlash against the goals and aspirations of
the Black freedom struggle—including those of the Civil Rights Movement. We continue to live with this backlash today. The idea that the
Black Panther Party, and the Black Power movement in general, was a
cult of violence became a rallying cry among both liberal and conservative white folk. The truth is that Black Power is not—and never was—a
movement based on violence. Far from it. Like civil rights, Black Power
was a movement of peace, equality, and human dignity.

Take, for example, the famous event of the Panthers showing up in
Sacramento at California's State Capitol Building. They came dressed in
their typical black leather clothes. More significantly, the thirty participating Panthers, including the leader, Bobby Seale, came fully armed,
carrying (legally registered) loaded rifles and pistols into the building.
While the Panthers were making a symbolic show of force, they had
no intentions of acting violently. They filed into the capitol building in
an orderly and relaxed fashion. They submitted peacefully and without struggle to police, surrendering their weapons and submitting to
searches and arrest.

This was not violent revolt by any stretch. Rather, it was a piece of
guerrilla street theater meant to demonstrate powerful and prideful
Black presence, as well as resistance to California's racist policing and
its hypocritical enforcement of its gun laws. The key moment of the performance had nothing to do with guns or violence. It came when Bobby
Seale commanded the media's attention and issued a statement con-
demning past and present American racism. It's important to go back
and hear these words:

Statement of the Black Panther Party for Self-Defense calls on the American people in general and the black people in particular to take full note of the racist California legislature aimed at keeping the black people disarmed and powerless at the very same time that racist police agencies throughout the country are intensifying the terror and repression of black people . . . The enslavement of black people from the very beginning of this country, the genocide practiced on the American Indians and the confining of the survivors on reservations, the savage lynching of thousands of black men and women, the dropping of atomic bombs on Hiroshima and Nagasaki, and now the cowardly massacre in Vietnam, all testify to the fact that towards people of color the racist power structure of America has but one policy: repression, genocide, terror, and the big stick. Black people have begged, prayed, petitioned, demonstrated, and everything else to get the racist power structure of America to right the wrongs which have historically been perpetuated against black people. All of these efforts have been answered by more repression, deceit, and hypocrisy. As the aggression of the racist American Government escalates in Vietnam, the Police Agencies of America escalate the repression of black people throughout the ghettos of America. Vicious police dogs, cattle prods and increased patrols have become familiar sights in black communities. City Hall turns a deaf ear to the pleas of black people for relief from this increasing terror. The Black Panther Party for Self-Defense believes that the time has come for black people to arm themselves against this terror before it is too late. A people who have suffered so much for so long at the hands of a racist society must draw the line somewhere. We believe that black communities of America must rise up as one man to halt the progression of a trend that leads inevitably to their total destruction.

Ironically, the Republican governor of California, Ronald Reagan, addressed the press after the Panthers left the capitol and told reporters,

"There's no reason why on the street today a citizen should be carrying loaded weapons," adding, "Americans don't go around carrying guns with the idea of using them to influence other Americans." Reagan, not surprisingly, missed the Panthers' central point—Americans, in the form of the police, were already on the streets with loaded weapons, and they were using them to "influence" (meaning intimidate and terrorize) other Americans—Black Americans. The Panthers' aim was not violent revolution but the demonstration of inequality and governmental hypocrisy.

It is useful to compare the Panthers' peaceful act of guerrilla theater with the violent white-supremacist mob that attacked the U.S. Capitol Building on January 6, 2021. Unlike the Panthers, the people on January 6 did not come to the Capitol for symbolic protest. Unlike the Panthers, they beat, injured, and killed police officers. Unlike the Panthers, the rioters on January 6 smashed and looted the seat of the U.S. government. The Panthers had prepared an articulate and powerful statement of protest, delivered by Seale to the media during the direct action. The white-supremacist mob of January 6 had no statement. Like the mob in Ellison's dream, it was a wild frenzy of hate and violence.

The mass politics of hate and violence have played a large role in American history, but this is not what the Black Panthers or the Black Power movement was about. Violence and the politics of hate was what the Panthers and other Black freedom fighters were battling against.

What were the aims of the Black Power movement? Inspiringly, if also tragically, they were similar to the goals of today's protest movements. The Panthers' "Ten-Point Program" called for economic justice, jobs, reparations, decent housing, educational reform, universal health care, the end to police brutality, the end to wars of aggression, and penal and judicial reform. Community organization and activism were at the heart of the Panthers' agenda and the agenda of Black Power more generally.

This is a legacy that is still going strong in Black communities throughout America, one that my NBA brothers and WNBA sisters are deeply invested in. Youth programs, sports camps, schools, job training, poverty relief, food assistance, free health care—Black Power aimed to address the fundamental issues of Black lives, with dignity, opportunity, and equality as its guiding principles.

Black Power confronted many of the foundational myths that supported white supremacy, and it formulated powerful critiques. We've already seen how Black Power challenged stereotypes about the "Black Family" and the "Black Father." Black Power sought to insert Black history into what was still a predominantly white historical narrative, making sure the arguments made decades before by Du Bois, Aptheker, and many others would start to see the light of day. Black Power asserted the reality of slavery and shined a light on slave resistance and revolt. Black Power told the Black perspective on Jim Crow, Reconstruction, the Great Migration, and spoke the truth about Black urban life in the North. Black Power presented a new and empowering understanding of Black culture in America, including its African roots—a strong rebuke of notions that slaves and former slaves lacked cultural heritage.

Black Power athletes focused the nation's attention on injustice, on the devastating war in Vietnam, and on collegiate and professional exploitation of, and discrimination against, Black athletes. In colleges and universities throughout the country, Black Power demanded and achieved Black Studies programs, overcoming stiff opposition through student activism. Young people were demanding a more just and better future, as they are today.

The process of caricaturing and demeaning the Black Power movement was part of the mobilization of backlash against the Civil Rights Movement and against the expansion of government aid to the poor. The acceptable freedom struggle, according to the white majority, was one that demanded only civil rights. The "bad" part of the freedom struggle was represented by groups that remained dissatisfied with the accomplishments of the mid-1960s civil rights legislation. These groups demanded economic justice, the transformation of everyday living conditions, and human rights. They asserted the legitimacy of Black voices and Black agency in all areas of human activity—from the Olympic Games to the lecture hall, from the boxing ring to the boardroom.

Black Power got crushed in the media, which was more than willing to go along with the FBI and other groups to label the Panthers domestic terrorists. Such demonization provided fuel for city, state, and federal agencies to target Black urban populations in the name of crime prevention. The criminalization of Blackness has a very long history, but the intensity and aggressiveness of the police assault on Black communities in the 1980s and the 1990s was truly astounding.

Many voices of dissent rang out during these decades, but few were listened to. White moderates and even many white liberals joined with conservatives to leave American cities for the suburbs, where the only connection they maintained to Kenneth Clark's "dark ghetto" was their shared media-constructed vision of nightmarish gang violence and crack cocaine. Those "invisible walls" were growing higher and higher, thicker and thicker, year after year. Far from a time of progress, these were decades of reactionary regression.

Facing political defeat at the hands of Ronald Reagan, a media landscape that declared the Civil Rights Movement over and done, a deteriorating economic situation, and the cataclysmic consequences of the "war on drugs," Black communities throughout the United States faced dire circumstances.

Who tells this story best? It was certainly not coming from mainstream politicians or television broadcasters, most of whom were happy enough to throw gasoline on the fire. It was not coming from celebrities. It was no longer coming from Black athletes, as it had in the past.

Black protest, Black Power, the Black freedom struggle found its clearest voice in music. Hip-hop and rap artists picked up the torch of the Black freedom struggle and kept the protest tradition alive by telling stories "polite society" didn't want to hear. They told the story of urban poverty to an increasingly suburban nation. They told the truth about the brutality of policing to a nation obsessed with "law and order." It's no wonder that one of the things Democrats and Republicans found common ground on in the 1980s and 1990s was sticking warning labels on rap and hip-hop albums, giving license to mega-corporations like Walmart to refuse to carry the "offending" content.

PROTEST TODAY

On July 13, 2013, a Florida jury found defendant George Zimmerman not guilty of the charges of murdering seventeen-year-old high school student Trayvon Martin as Martin was on his way home from a trip to the local convenience store in Sanford to buy snacks before watching the NBA All-Star Game. The jury's acquittal of Zimmerman inspired writer Alicia Garza to include the phrase "Black lives matter" in a heartfelt post on her social media page. From a statement, the phrase "Black lives matter" became a hashtag: #Blacklivesmatter. From a hashtag, the phrase grew into a powerful movement. The Black Lives Matter movement would become one of the largest social justice movements in the history of our country. It continued to grow through grassroots organizing and digital sharing, especially in response to other police killings of Black people.

On August 9, 2014, in Ferguson, Missouri, a suburb of St. Louis, a city police officer shot and killed an eighteen-year-old Black man named Michael Brown. Ferguson's Black community reacted to Michael Brown's killing by calling for the arrest of the officer who'd fired the gun. People took to the streets to demonstrate against this latest example of police brutality. As the protests continued, they started to grow and attract supporters throughout the St. Louis area and across the country, many of whom were connecting this moment with the Black Lives Matter movement.

When people started digging deeper into the policing situation in Ferguson, the case became even more disturbing. The killing of Michael Brown was part of the Ferguson police's systemic racism. Though Ferguson was 68 percent Black, only four of its fifty-four police officers were persons of color. Black residents of Ferguson made up an astounding 93 percent of arrests in the city.

When five members of the St. Louis Rams football team protested systemic racism and police brutality in Ferguson by giving the "Hands up, don't shoot" gesture before a game against the Raiders, the St. Louis Police Department responded with threats. Utilizing the very language of racial division that had created the Ferguson context in the first place, the St. Louis police called protesters "thugs" and called for the Black athletes to be "disciplined" by the franchise and the league. This just made the Rams players' point: rather than look in the mirror and deal with the racism in its midst, the police in St. Louis and Ferguson lashed out.

Ferguson's police department responded to the protests by taking to the streets in full military-grade gear, backed up by urban warfare–style tanks. Images from Ferguson showed to the world that America's local police forces were equipped for war conditions, and the war they were fighting was against their own communities—communities of color. The killing of Michael Brown did not result in charges being brought against the officer, another example of white violence against Black people going unpunished. Justice was again denied, to the family of Michael Brown and to all of us.

Black Lives Matter is a shared way of expressing the latest movement in the quest for justice among a wide range of people and groups. It is a movement both digital and physical, a social media movement and a movement of street-based protest. In 2020, after the murder of George Floyd, it became part of a larger political movement to defeat a dangerous and racist President.

Despite the defeat of a racist President, 2020 was far from a thorough victory—and the gains made did not come easily. As in the 1960s and throughout earlier phases of the Black freedom struggle, powerful interests, especially in the media, sought to distort and falsify the movement's essence. Black Lives Matter's demand for substantial police reform ran into a wall of opposition.

Despite the momentum gained from the protests in the summer of 2020 as people across the country and the world reacted with both shock and hope, the push for reform seems to have stalled. George Floyd's murderer has been brought to justice, but the unjust system itself has not gone anywhere. Racist backlash, like before, is galvanizing large parts of our country. The historical story—pioneered by Du Bois and Aptheker, championed and expanded by Black Power, and reinvigorated by the Black Lives Matter movement—faces strong opposition in states throughout our country. At stake in this fight is whether our kids learn the truth about our country and its past or a myth—and a myth is another way of saying, in this context, a lie.

If Black Lives Matter went viral and helped inspire a movement of mass protest for social justice, so, too, did the forces against it. Are we facing the last stand of the white-supremacist backlash that has played such a major role in U.S. history since the Civil War, or is this only the beginning of a dark chapter in our history, in which racial hierarchies are deepened, inequalities are expanded, and hatred and fear of difference reign?

JANUARY 6, 2021, AND THE DAY AFTER

Like many of you, I was at home watching television when a mob, organized by the President of the United States, stormed the U.S. Capitol Building. The people breached the security perimeter and occupied
our seat of government, interrupting the vote that was happening in
Congress to certify the election of Joe Biden and Kamala Harris as the
next President and vice president of the United States. Members of the
House of Representatives and the Senate were forced to evacuate their
chambers and were rushed by security to safe rooms to avoid being
taken and possibly killed by the crowd. Violent, life-threatening chants
and shouts resounded through the mob. They were aimed at members
of both parties, including the sitting vice president.

The moment might have been confusing, but many things about the
scene I was watching were totally clear. This was a white crowd. Thousands of white Americans had come together with violent intentions
to prevent a peaceful functioning of government and transfer of power
from one administration to another. The people in the mob went there
specifically to block the will of the American voters, who had risen by
the tens of millions to defeat the incumbent.

From his reaction to neo-Nazi marches in Charlottesville to calling for the support of right-wing militias from the debate stage, the
President was actively defending, encouraging, and supporting white-
supremacist groups. We remember when he referred to neo-Nazis, their
arms raised in the Hitler salute, as "good people." We remember when
he demonized Black communities like Baltimore, a community that
basketball star Carmelo Anthony has recently written about so power-
fully, and countries with Black populations.

This was a moment long in the making, stretching back even before
2008 when Barack Obama was elected President. The right-wing reac-

tion to President Obama, though, requires special attention. It was intense. Let me tell you this: it was deeply and personally felt throughout the Black community. Certain media outlets worked hard from the day he won in 2008 to fan the flames of racial division in our country. They played on prejudice. They worked to provoke and deepen people's fears.

The attempt to undermine President Obama's legitimacy through the ridiculous "birther" movement was a racist call to oppose the country's first Black President. Claims of voter fraud, not surprisingly, came from these white reactionary communities and spokespeople and targeted communities of color, whether they were composed of "illegal immigrants," falsely accused of fraudulent voting, or Black urban areas. The attempts were nothing more or less than what they have always been: white power seeking to subjugate Black people and other minorities.

Nobody is fooled by this, especially in our Black community. We saw it coming. We see it in our neighbors, who are getting ginned up with hate, searching for meaning and identity in this latest version of American racism. But even though we saw it coming and can see clearly what it is, when I sat there watching the mob enter the Capitol and occupy offices and the Senate chamber, I have to admit I was in a state of shock and panic.

I got up and started pacing around the house. I was nervous, agitated. By now, Vanity and the kids had come into the room and were seeing what was going on. My two older boys, Ken and Stone, could tell, I think, that something really strange and bad was happening. How to address it? How could I find the words to explain this situation to two young boys ages fourteen and nine?

At that moment, the full scope of what I was seeing dawned on me. If this had been a Black crowd, I said to them, the police would not have hesitated. They would have opened fire, and we would be watching a bloodbath. There's no way in hell, I said, our government would allow itself to be threatened by thousands of Black men and women storming the Capitol; there's just no way. The hypocrisy was breathtaking—the literal acting out of white privilege before our eyes. If President Obama were in the White House, I said to Vanity and the kids, they'd be leading him out of the White House right now in handcuffs on his way to standing trial for treason.

Eventually, the kids and Vanity went to bed. But I couldn't sleep. I tried to calm myself down, but my mind kept racing. During the previous years in Texas, I'd been seeing more and more disturbing behavior. People were acting in threatening, aggressive ways. Pickup trucks with the red flags of the President flew with images of AK-47s printed on them. If this maelstrom of violence could happen at the U.S. Capitol, I thought, who knows what could go on elsewhere in America, to anyone, at any time? I'm big into accountability, as anyone who watches me on television or listens to me on podcasts knows. January 6 showed that the lack of accountability in our country reached all the way up to the very top. How do we, as a society, carry on with that knowledge?

The next day, I went on ESPN to do my shows. The topic of the day, of course, wasn't basketball, but the scenes we'd witnessed the day before. The producers wanted us to voice our thoughts on what had happened and about how the NBA community was responding.

This wasn't the first time I had addressed political questions on the air as a basketball analyst. Through the spring and summer of 2020, following George Floyd's murder and continuing through the NBA Bubble and the boycotts there over the shooting of Jacob Blake, social justice issues had been front and center. I've always had strong stances on issues of social and racial justice.

You have to keep in mind that these were not abstract issues for me. These were connected to my daily life. They were my lived reality, especially during my first eighteen years when I grew up in poverty in a mostly poor Black community. Unlike many others who were engaging in social and racial justice issues for the first time, we in the Black community have been pushing for justice and equality just about every day of our lives. What was new to me in 2020 was that I had a platform to speak directly and publicly to millions of Americans. I had been hired to talk about the game of basketball, and suddenly basketball was politics.

My transition from talking about sports to addressing our problems with social justice was important. I knew I needed to do my best to get it right. It wouldn't be enough for me to go on the air and pop off with my raw feelings and frustrations. I had this platform now, and I wanted to learn to use it effectively. I wanted to show respect to my audience by putting in the work and the thought to help make an impact and to contribute to the movement for change.

I had some amazing people to lean on in this process. Vanity was instrumental in helping me hone my statements to be as true and as powerful as possible. I'd reach out to Rich Gray, my creative and business advisor, and run through what I planned to say. At times, I sought out the counsel and wisdom of people in the industry I deeply respect (my new elders), like Stephen A. Smith or Marcus Spears, and they'd always be there to give me guidance. Just like in my first months in Boston, I had the good sense and the humility to listen to and absorb what they were saying to me.

At the same time as I was finding my public voice on politics and social justice, it was becoming clear to me that issues of racism were entering a new phase. Racism was not new in 2020. Everyone knows this. It has four hundred years of history behind it. What was new—or, rather, a return to the old—was that everything was coming out into the open. Certain people stopped feeling the need to conceal their true beliefs. I could take a look at my neighbors in Texas and say, "Okay, now at least I know exactly what I'm dealing with." When they reacted to the results of the 2020 election by scaling back voting rights, banning critical race theory, and allowing the open carry of guns, we in the

Black community saw it clearly for what it was. It is the latest offensive launched by white power.

Let's be clear what, exactly, we're dealing with. The push for racial equality, the Black Lives Matter movement, and the work of my friends LeBron James and Stephen Jackson are up against the powerful opposition of people who either want to deny that racism exists to perpetuate the status quo or who are actively devoted to the racial caste system. How do we overcome this powerful opposition to justice? What do we do to make our world better, to make it more equal, more just, for people of all communities?

At the heart of our movement, I think, must be a commitment to daily work. Maybe it's the Catholic schoolboy talking—and it's certainly connected to the way my grandparents raised me—but I was brought up to believe that good work should be done out of the spotlight. Human nature makes us try to act our best when we're standing in front of a camera, or when we're projecting an image through social media. What really matters, though, is the good work we do when the phone is off (or at least in our pocket) and the video camera isn't rolling. This is not the time to turn away from our individual and collective responsibilities. It's not the moment to disparage others or settle scores. It's the time to step up and be the best versions of ourselves. My grandfather would always tell me that acts of charity are between you, the person you're helping, and God. Let's remember, whether it's Christianity, Judaism, Islam, or something else, God loves generosity toward those less fortunate and despises selfishness and greed.

The other part of creating a better future is by educating ourselves and others, and then speaking out from a position of truth. Truth isn't just sitting out there in the open. We have to actively search for it. This means questioning and often abandoning some of the most comfortable and important stories we tell about ourselves, our society, and our country. Many of these stories were ones we learned as children—and so they might feel true to us, even if they are not. Truer, better versions of history are often more difficult and complex, messier, and harder to make complete sense of, harder to process.

Nothing is more important for our kids than this search for truth and our refusal to accept anything less. Over these past years, our society has so devalued truth and assaulted knowledge that our kids must at times feel out at sea or in the darkness. We cannot leave them like this, abandoned in that moral void. It is our job, collectively, to shine the spotlight and guide them safely back to shore.

This will not be an easy process, and the forces on the other side are hell-bent on preventing the truth from spreading. We can't be hesitant or restrained about getting it out there. It will take all of us speaking out, thinking critically, educating ourselves, and educating others, across every racial or religious or national boundary.

My hope is that this book will be one brick in the wall of truth and knowledge. Others will lay a brick on one side, then on the other, then others will set their bricks on top of mine, as I have done on those below, and in this way, we will raise our house.

I remember another day: January 20, 2009. On this day, a man named Barack Obama was inaugurated as the President of the United States, the country's first Black President. For the whole year leading up to that day, my Celtics brothers and I had been obsessively following the campaign and election. There were days in the locker room during our championship run through the playoffs when it seemed like basketball didn't exist. We'd be sitting around talking about Obama and his speeches, in awe of his eloquence and intellect. There was immense pride among us, as Black men, when we saw him rise and meet every challenge with dignity and his unmatched grace.

I can tell you, these conversations weren't happening only in the

Celtics locker room. They were happening throughout the league. They were happening in every basketball locker room in this country where Black boys and young Black men gathered to play and compete. To this day, I would love to have the chance to shake President Obama's hand. He wasn't perfect; he made mistakes, as we all do. But he achieved something much more valuable than a single policy. He pointed in the direction of a better future. He taught us that more was possible than what we had previously imagined.

No single person can carry that weight alone—not even Barack Obama. The forces of reaction and hate came after him with everything they had. They might have done huge damage to our country, but they have not destroyed our sweet hope for a more just and better world. This yearning is the core of our protest. It is stronger than ever. Tomorrow will be our day.

8

Young Guns

FROM BRAHMIN BOSTON TO THE WILD WEST—AT TWENTY-SIX YEARS OLD I ARRIVED IN Oklahoma City as an old sheriff among a pack of young guns. As a Celtic, I had always hated going to Oklahoma City to play. We'd say to each other on our way out there, "Let's hurry up and get out of this truck stop–ass city." In the days after the trade, I kept telling myself I was going to Oklahoma, but I just couldn't make myself really believe it. Oklahoma? What? I'm a Texas boy, and for a Texan to move to Oklahoma is something like moving from the pros down to the minor leagues. Whenever I'd think about it, the main thought that kept coming to me was this: what the hell is happening to my life?

Talking with Vanity about the move to OKC was one of the toughest things I've ever done. We were kids when we first moved in together in Boston. We'd grown up there. She'd made some of the most important relationships of her life there. Women like Ray Allen's wife, Shannon, became mentors to Vanity and lifelong friends. It killed me that while I had to head straight for OKC from Denver, Vanity was left to pack up our house in Boston alone. I'd never again step foot in that town house, which over the years, and especially with Vanity and Little Ken, had become my first adult home.

When I arrived in Oklahoma City, I went straight to the Thunder's practice facility, which was located at the time in a converted skating rink. I'd watched the Thunder play in the playoffs the previous year against the Lakers. I knew they had a good young core of guys who'd pushed the Lakers to six games. But Kobe, Pau, and company had been too big and too experienced for those young fellas.

The talent was undeniable. For three straight years, the Thunder had owned a top-four draft pick, and whereas most organizations would have jumped out of their seats to get at least one of the three right, Sam Presti and his team had hit home runs with each selection.

In 2007, with the second pick in the draft, the then–Seattle Super-Sonics (before the franchise moved to Oklahoma) took Kevin Durant. If you remember, it was the Celtics' missing out on Durant that became the catalyst for Danny Ainge to pursue deals for Ray Allen and Kevin Garnett—it's amazing how things are connected. The next year, Presti used the team's first selection to pull the trigger on a UCLA guard named Russell Westbrook. If that wasn't enough good fortune, the organization grabbed the virtually unknown Serge Ibaka toward the end of round one with pick twenty-four. Completing what has to be the best streak of first-round picks in NBA history, the Thunder took "The Beard," James Harden, with the third overall pick in 2009.

On that first day, though I knew the team had talent in bunches, I had absolutely no idea what to expect from the guys or the situation in general. The players weren't around when I got to the facility. The night before, they'd played the second of back-to-back games on the road against the Orlando Magic, and they were on their way home. The first people I met when I got to OKC were Donnie Strack and Joe Sharpe of the team's athletic staff. After chatting with those folks, I went and sat down with Sam Presti and Troy Weaver, the primary architects of this young Thunder roster; it had been Weaver who had pushed the case for the team to take Russell Westbrook in the draft.

Weaver and Presti gave me a great welcome. They were telling me, "Perk, we're really excited to have you here. You're going to love it." It was a quiet day there, so they told me to take a walk around and meet everyone in the organization. I did, and then went back to the athletic and medical team and had my physical. I wanted to get all of that out of the way so I could focus on meeting the players the following day.

In Boston, our team never practiced after back-to-back road games. When I got to the facility the next day, I was surprised to learn that everyone was gearing up for practice.

"Hey, Perk," someone said to me, "Scott Brooks is waiting for you in his office. He wants to holler at you before we get going."

Doc Rivers had already preached to me about how great a guy Coach Brooks was and that I was going to love him, but, as always, I had to wait and judge for myself. I went and sat down with him.

"What's up, man? We're happy to have you here, Perk. We think you're going to have a huge impact. But Perk, it's a lot different here than what you experienced in Boston. We call this Oklahoma U."

"What the fuck you mean you call this Oklahoma U?"

"You'll see when practice starts, Perk, but these fucking guys just love to play basketball."

After my meeting with Coach Brooks, I went to meet the guys. I was still working my way back from injury at the time and wasn't suiting up for practice, but I gabbed with them as they were getting ready to take the floor—Eric Maynor, Kevin Durant, James Harden, Serge Ibaka, Daequon Cook, Russell Westbrook. I saw the veteran Nick Collison stretching out and thought, Okay, they're coming off a back-to-back, I guess it's going to be a light practice.

The next thing I knew, practice was going, and it was intense. After a while, Brooks yelled out to the guys and asked if they wanted to scrimmage. The answer was uniform: "Hell yeah!" The game began, and those guys started playing some of the hardest basketball I've seen. Right then, sitting and watching that first scrimmage from the sidelines, I realized that I'd just walked into a gold mine.

And this wasn't even the most impressive thing about that first day. After what had been one of the most competitive practice scrimmages I've ever seen, many of the guys stayed after practice to get in extra time doing individual drills. I looked at one end of the court, and there was Kevin Durant going through a set of drills on how to beat double- and triple-teams. On the other end, I was seeing James Harden, still in his second year, putting time in with assistant coach Rex Kalamian. He was working on coming off dribble handoffs and stepping back into threes.

Picture it. I'm sitting there watching my first OKC practice. I'm seeing a bunch of guys who were still incredibly young. Durant and Westbrook were twenty-two, Harden and Ibaka twenty-one. At twenty-six, Thabo Sefolosha was one of the oldest guys on the court. But despite their youth, these guys were *working*.

The next day was a game day in OKC. I didn't suit up yet and had a seat next to Mo Peterson when the lights came on and the crowd got roaring. I remember Mo leaned over and whispered to me, "Get ready for this, Perk, those little guys be hoopin'." The arena was packed. The crowd was going fucking crazy, like it was a late-series playoff game, not a regular-season game in early March.

The team came out ready to play. Sefolosha was locking up on defense and shooting the passing lanes. Durant and Harden were pulling up from all over the place and draining threes. Westbrook was slashing, playing some of the fastest and most fearless basketball I have witnessed to this day, not a step slower than Derrick Rose before Rose's injuries—blazing fast.

Right then, sitting on the bench and watching that first OKC game, I instantly put Boston behind me. That was the past. This new generation of players was the future—the shooting, the speed, the athleticism were on a different level. I also understood why I was there and what I needed to do. This time, I didn't need Danny, Doc, or KG to tell me my role. I recognized it on my own, and with that I had graduated from one stage of my NBA career to another. What I understood was that I was no longer just a student of the game. I would have to do some teaching at Oklahoma U, and I'm not talking only about basketball.

This group of young guys loved the game of basketball more than any other team I've ever played for. That's why from that first practice to my first game in the starting lineup a few weeks later, I couldn't wait to get on the court with them. The atmosphere was electric. The play was fast.

At the same time, they were nowhere near as close and cohesive as the team I'd just left in Boston. Those Celtics teams had been family, even during the first years when we were losing. Over the previous three and a half years, Rondo, KG, Ray, Paul, the others, and I had become brothers. There were tensions and conflicts along the way, but because we were so close we could speak openly about anything and resolve conflicts between ourselves without the coach's or organization's involvement. There was no issue or problem so big that it pulled us apart. On the road, we were always hanging out together. At home, we'd constantly be at each other's places. On the court, there was no ego—no sense of the importance of the individual stat sheet. This type of team chemistry had not yet taken hold at Oklahoma U.

CHEMISTRY LESSONS

I get it: it's not fair to compare our 2008 Celtics team, a roster of seasoned veterans, most of whom had been around the block at least a few times, with the bunch of gunslingers in OKC. Many of them had only recently come into the league, and they were more or less mirroring the behavior they saw around them. On the other hand, I could tell pretty quickly that the lack of cohesion was a problem. You don't get that perfect on-court harmony and chemistry, no matter how much talent you've got on the floor, without feelings of trust, loyalty, and a desire to put the team—and that means, at times, the needs of others—above yourself. In this case, the young superstars-in-the-making were each surrounded by their own group of friends and family. It was clear when it came to closeness and loyalty, the guys' first priority was their group and only after that the team.

When we went on the road, the players' friends traveled with us. When I saw that, I said to myself, Oh, hell no, we're not going to do this. I started to emphasize the need to come together as a unit. I got everyone together in a group chat, and when we'd reach our hotel I'd send out an announcement about a team dinner that night, or I'd let everyone know we'd be playing cards in my suite. I told them that when we were on the road, they had to leave their friends out of it. This wasn't about their friends or family members. It had nothing to do with who they were or what they were doing. It was about pushing the guys on the team to spend time with each other, without a lot of outside noise. It was about the guys getting to know each other on a deeper level.

I heard there had been issues between some of them before I got there. I didn't care about any of that. What I knew, what I could see as clear as day, was that the only way we were going to get where we wanted to go (and that was the peak of the NBA mountain) was to take the path as a team. After I took this step to close our circle and form a true team concept, I established myself as a leader in the locker room.

A team doesn't build its core and come together overnight. I had to put in work both on and off the court, on the individual and the group levels, to make my case for this type of philosophy. Part of my team-building campaign was to sit down with the guys one-on-one. During my first couple of weeks in Oklahoma City, I went to each player's house by myself. It wasn't just to have a conversation with them. I wanted to see for myself what was going on in their houses. You can tell a lot about a guy by seeing how he's living and whom he's living with. I'm not talking about judging people. I wanted to understand as much about them as I could in order to figure out how best to reach them. I wanted to see how I might help them out, if they needed anything, whether it be emotionally, psychologically, or about basketball.

I found about what I had expected to find. KD had his brother and his boys. James had four or five of his L.A. friends, and so on. I had no problem with this. Everyone I know, inside or outside of professional basketball, has something like an inner circle of friends and family. That's good, especially when you have a brother or a group of guys who love and support you, like I did in Boston with my crew from Beaumont—George Davis, Dab, Vanity, and others.

I don't want to get into any talk of the guys having a "posse" or any of that nonsense. There are two reasons why it mattered that KD, James, and Russ each had his own group. The first reason is simply that the more people you have in the mix, the more chances there are for misunderstandings and conflicts. Even if the players themselves might have been cool with each other, if someone's friend is having it out with someone's brother, for example, the players can't help but be dragged in.

The second reason is just as simple. If these inner worlds became too tight, there was no space, no opening, for the team concept. Those guys could feel pulled between one center of gravity and another, and the natural pull from family and friends was, of course, much stronger. I knew if I wanted to help build the type of team dynamic that would get us to the next level, the guys' groups would also have to buy in.

When we first got to OKC, Vanity and I rented a small town house, and we made a point of inviting over not only my teammates, but their friends and families, too, so that the whole big crowd of us could get on the same page and share a meal. It was a safe space for everyone to talk and chill. I don't think Vanity ever did more cooking than in those OKC years!

Over time, I grew close to the guys on that OKC team and formed some of the most important friendships of my life. At times, it wasn't an easy process, but it was worth it. The stars on that team were all alpha males, each a future superstar and league MVP. At the time I arrived, though, that story was still in the future. James and Russ hadn't made an All-Star team. KD wasn't yet NBA scoring champion. It's normal that players with this amount of talent, as young as they were, would be striving after individual goals and accolades. They had people around them who were fiercely loyal to their individual careers on and off the court. Often, the team came second. I knew those individual goals weren't going away. Team goals would have to coexist with them and, when possible, supersede them.

Kevin Durant was the first OKC player to reach out to me after the trade. This meant a lot to me, because I knew that the deal had sent his close childhood friend Jeff Green out of town—and I knew from Boston how it felt to have these relationships ripped apart by the business of basketball. For me, this spoke volumes about the type of guy KD was. I could tell from our first conversation that he was genuine, that he wasn't putting on any act or playing any games, that he was just being himself.

It was also clear right away that his love of the game of basketball was equal to or greater than that of anyone I'd ever played with. KD lived the game—watched it, studied it, and pushed himself constantly to be better. Many nights over the next few years would find us on the phone into the early morning hours chopping up games and breaking down situations, figuring out what we could do better, thinking through together what was going on with our team. Or we'd meet at his house or mine, watch basketball or football games together, and just chill.

My Boston days had been amazing, but it felt different to emerge as a leader in Oklahoma City. I knew that, besides the team's need for a defensive presence on the low block, leadership was one of the central reasons Troy Weaver and Sam Presti had traded for me. At the same time, when you're dealing with the game of basketball, words will carry you only so far as a leader and an elder statesman. These were hardworking dudes, and if I was going to gain and maintain their respect, if I was to continue to have their ear, I'd have to show them I was committed to putting in the work.

I made a point of showing up first every day in the locker room. I was always one of the last guys to leave. I busted my ass in practice like I was still an eighteen-year-old rookie fighting to make it. After a time, I earned the job of giving the guys the pregame speech before we took the court. It was a huge honor and responsibility.

I have to give Coach Brooks a lot of credit. He stepped back and provided the space for my voice to emerge in that locker room. He recognized what I was bringing to the group in terms of experience in a championship, in Hall of Fame culture. He knew I was all about winning and that I'd been able to put my ego aside to a great extent in Boston to focus on the team game. In film sessions, he didn't mind if I interrupted him and asked him to run something back so I could let the fellas know what I was seeing.

Coach Brooks and I shared a passion for defense. He appreciated when I'd get on some of the younger guys for not doing what needed to be done on that side of the ball. Ironically, though he coached three of the greatest scorers ever to lace up basketball shoes, Scott Brooks didn't give a damn about offense. He was a defensive-minded guy. It wasn't at the maniacal level of Thibs, of course, but Brooks knew that to win a championship a team needed to win those 90–85 type of games. Those games—the games you have to grind out possession by possession, not the ones when you explode for 120 points—are what decide a close series.

The other way I led was to demand that the young guys act with a level of respect in everything they did around the organization. One day, not long after the trade, I saw Serge Ibaka come directly from a workout and lie down on the massage table in the training room without showering first. This really set me off. The main reason it bothered me was that I found it disrespectful to our massage therapist, Ms. Val, or Mama Val, as we called her. It was also showing no thought toward the guys on the team who'd have to come in behind him for the next massage. It wasn't a matter of rudeness or intentional disrespect on Serge's part. I think it was a kind of carelessness and inattentiveness that comes with being young.

Serge didn't react well when I got on him that day, but I knew I'd have to stand strong and make my point to show everyone on the team that I wouldn't back down when I believed in something. Thankfully, the argument with Serge didn't get physical, though it might have come close. My point was made: show respect to yourself, your teammates, and every other member of the organization who is coming to work, many of whom were coming to work to take care of us players.

No organization will function well if a culture of respect and dignity isn't established and upheld. This can't be done by the executives. It has to come from the ground up, from each member of the organization taking responsibility and holding others accountable for their behavior and their work. This type of thinking was drilled into me early on in life by my grandfather. It was one of the most valuable lessons he taught me. I think it's gotten me further in life than just about anything else.

Happily, my relationship with Serge wasn't permanently damaged by the massage-room dustup. At the time, Serge was taking off each day to have his English lessons, and the only one on the team he was really talking to and connecting with was Thabo Sefolosha, who, like Serge, spoke many languages. Thabo was from Switzerland. His mother was a Swiss artist, his father a South African musician. Thabo spoke English and Italian, and he shared the common language of French with Serge.

It was great that Serge had Thabo there, but the language barrier did create some distance between him and the rest of the guys. They were probably too young and too busy to really think about how they should try to get over or around this cultural divide.

I made it a point to spend as much time as I could with Serge. When we were on the road, I insisted that he come out to eat with me, and I checked in with him to see what he was up to. A team isn't just a collection of guys. It's a collection of guys with complex lives and even more complex histories. Each player, coach, member of the front office, and trainer has a story and is coming into the organization with a unique perspective. Part of being a leader in that OKC locker room was trying my best to learn these stories. I wanted to be able to pay my respects to the experiences people brought with them. To know where they were at, I had to know where they'd been.

Serge Ibaka was a special case. His athleticism was unreal. I'd never seen a guy of his size move like Serge could move. The closest similarity might be to a young KG, but KG wasn't the jumper Serge was. Through my friendship with Serge, a whole world opened up to me that I hadn't known much about. He came from the city of Brazzaville, the capital of the Republic of the Congo. I learned that, like me, Serge had lost his mother at a young age. His father, a former member of the national basketball team, spent years in jail as a political prisoner when Serge was still a boy. I know something about having horrible uncles, but Serge's uncles outdid mine. They put him out into the streets when he was still a kid, and he had to survive by begging and doing anything else he could.

Beyond these incredible personal hardships, there were tragedies of national proportions. The Republic of the Congo was in the midst of a brutal civil war, the center of which was Brazzaville. For Serge, war wasn't something on television or in the movies—it was part of his everyday life. The sounds of guns and bombs were constant, so much so that people started to refer to it as "music." During the fighting, large sections of Brazzaville were destroyed.

As Serge demonstrates, the NBA has grown over the last decades into a truly global league. With players like Serge, the spotlight can fall on other parts of the world, other cultures and experiences. This is an amazing aspect of the league today. It allows us to share stories that broaden the public's understanding of the world, stories that will help our fans and ourselves see how the world is not only a collection of different countries and peoples—it is also one world stitched tightly together.

This is especially important for the league's young fans. They are invited by players like Serge to travel in their imaginations. They can follow Serge to the mouth of the Congo River, or to South Africa, where Thabo and his brother do charity work. They can wander to Athens, Greece, to try to see and feel the way life might have been for a young Giannis Antetokounmpo, whose family emigrated from Lagos, Nigeria, to Europe.

There is so much to be gained by opening ourselves up to knowledge of other peoples and places, knowledge that takes us far beyond the game of basketball. Thabo's father, for example, was a Black musician from South Africa who grew up under the apartheid regime. Serge is a survivor of a civil war in the Republic of the Congo that had its roots in European imperialism.

Just as history is alive in our country, playing out every day in our minds and across our bodies, so, too, is it present in every place on the globe—in many cases, like in the Republic of the Congo or South Africa or the United States, creating conditions of poverty and hardship. That Serge Ibaka made it from the streets of Brazzaville to play in the NBA with the Oklahoma City Thunder is as close to a miracle as we will find in the world. Even with his success, he has kept a close connection to his family and culture in his home country, especially with his grandmother, another thing a boy from Beaumont and a boy from Brazzaville have in common.

It was a group of strong, proud, and at times stubborn guys. There were occasions when it would take me literally banging on Russell Westbrook's door to get him to come and talk to me. I'm glad I did. Every dinner Vanity and I hosted, every meal on the road with Serge or the other guys, every trip to the casino card tables with Russ to quench our thirst for poker, every late night workout session—all of the energy created by these experiences eventually found its way back onto the court, and when it did, we were rolling.

In 2011, the year I arrived, we entered the playoffs with fifty-five wins. We took care of business in the first round, putting the Denver Nuggets away in five games. The next round was a battle with the Memphis Grizzlies. We took the series in seven hard-fought games. We met Dirk Nowitzki and the Dallas Mavericks in the Western Conference Finals.

Dirk, Jason Kidd, and crew were more experienced and tested than we were. This is exactly what I've been talking about. A team might be able to outscore its opponent in a shootout or two during a seven-game series, but when it comes down to it, the question is always this: which team is going to win those dogfights? What team has the emotional and psychological strength as a unit to scrap out close win after close win? In game three of the Dallas series, for example, with it evened up at one game apiece—and we'd just taken one of two in Dallas—the Mavs were able to beat us scoring only 93 points, Dirk only 18. And we lost the game even though KD and Russ got theirs, ending the game with 24 and 30, respectively.

Those headline numbers don't tell us much. Our ball movement wasn't good enough. KD and Russ were forced into hard shots. James never got going. Could we win a game like that despite shooting poorly from three-point-land? Despite the tenacious defense being played on the other side? It wasn't our year. Courtesy of the Mavs, our summer vacation started earlier than we would have liked.

A SHOWDOWN WITH THE KING

By the time the 2011–2012 season got off to its late start, following the end of the labor dispute between the league and the players' association, our team had figured out a few things. On defense, we would rotate me onto the opposing team's strongest offensive player on the low block, whether it was a center or a power forward. This left Serge free to roam the paint and do what he did best: block shots. His shot-blocking abilities were crazy—some years he was averaging three a game. I remember one game when Serge posted the first triple-double of his career. It was for points, rebounds, and something like eleven blocks!

With Serge roaming and blocking shots; Thabo, one of the best wing defenders in the league, locking up on the outside; and KD and Russ giving more on the defensive side of the ball, we were suddenly a problem for the rest of the league. On the offensive side of things, we were elite, just as you'd expect with three of the most gifted offensive players of all time. Still, we needed to get even better, because come playoff time things get tougher. I encouraged KD and Russ to get Serge involved in the offense early in games; I was noticing how his defense would elevate to new heights when he made a few shots in the first quarter or two.

The playoffs in 2012 opened with something like a mini-revenge tour. We met the Mavs in round one and swept them. We won the first three games by double digits and then finished them off in Dallas with Mavs owner, Mark Cuban, looking on. It always felt good to me personally to come back to Texas and get a big win.

In round two, we had the Lakers. They'd beaten the Thunder in the playoffs the season before I got to OKC, the year Kobe and company had beaten my Celtics team in seven in the NBA Finals. But 2012 witnessed a changing of the guard in the NBA. The decade and a half of Laker dominance had come to an end. We knocked them out in five games, winning game one by close to thirty points.

Another Western Conference powerhouse, the San Antonio Spurs, were waiting for us in the conference finals. This was a very good team—one of those Gregg Popovich teams that always played better than they looked on paper. Tim Duncan was getting up there in age, but he was still a force on the low block. Added to Duncan, they had Tony Parker, Kawhi Leonard, and Manu Ginobili. It was a hell of a basketball team. And you better be sure Pop had his guys ready to play from the jump.

It was one of those made-for-Hollywood matchups, and the script seemed to write itself. We had way more talent than the Spurs, but San Antonio had its legendary "system" and a group of players with deep experience who bought into that system 100 percent. Everyone on that team knew his role and put the team above his individual goals. In this way, it was the purest possible team against what people were calling a collection of individual stars. We all know how this story usually ends, and it isn't with the hotshot young guys winning.

The first two games of the series just reinforced this story. San Antonio came out to play and won both games on their home court. For us, everything was riding on game three. If we lost that game, I don't think there's any way we would have been able to dig ourselves out of a 0–3 hole, not against that team. This was the conference championship, not the regular season, and the media chatter was exploding.

The main focus, as it usually was, was on Russ and how he chose to play the point guard position. The attacks were fierce. People came down on him for shooting too much, not distributing, not creating offense for his teammates, and, primarily, not deferring to KD. All too often, people said, Russ would end up taking an out-of-control shot, especially at key moments in the game. This criticism was a prelude of things to come.

In game three, we turned the tables on the Spurs. Russ dished out nine assists. Serge scored fourteen. James Harden added fifteen off the bench. I pulled down eight boards and had three blocks. A huge second quarter blew the game open, and we were right back in the series with a true team win. This kind of game—a Spurs-style win—lit our fuse. We came back to life, and it felt like we were rolling downhill in the series after game three. By game six, with us up 3–2, KD had one of his epic playoff performances, scoring thirty-four on better than 50 percent shooting and adding fourteen boards. It was more than enough to close out the series and stamp our ticket to the 2012 NBA Finals.

This was my third trip to the finals in five years—not bad. And it was a matchup for the ages. No, it wasn't the storied rivalry of Celtics-Lakers. It was the beginning of a new rivalry in the NBA. I'm talking about the battle between two of the greatest players ever to play the game of basketball, Kevin Durant and LeBron James. Here we had the new version of Russell versus Wilt, Larry versus Magic.

At the time, I have to admit, I didn't realize how special or significant this series was. Our opponent was the Miami Heat, the "super-team" of LeBron James, Dwyane Wade, and my old high school rival from Texas, Chris Bosh. Added to the Heat's stars was a group of fantastic and experienced role players like Mike Miller and Shane Battier, and the dynamic young talent of Mario Chalmers.

Despite the talent we were facing, I can honestly say we were the better, more talented team. People forget, but the Heat barely made it out of the Eastern Conference that year, and it is likely that they would have been beaten by the Celtics if both of Boston's big men and Rondo hadn't gotten hurt. Even with the injuries, it had taken heroics by LeBron to pull the Heat out of a 3–2 series deficit to win the conference finals in seven games.

Our OKC team, on the other hand, was heading into the finals coming off four straight wins against the mighty Spurs. We were younger than the Heat. We were faster. We had better shooting. We had a deeper bench. We had more presence in the paint, better shot-blocking. When we were on our game, our defense was better than Miami's.

If all this is true, why didn't we win the series? How did LeBron and those boys snatch our rings away?

At the start of the series, things looked good for us. We had home-court advantage and were looking to take the first two games in OKC in front of our amazing fans. In game one, we weathered an early Heat run, battled back, and won in pretty decisive fashion. By the middle of the second quarter, we had the game under control. This was a boost to our confidence, which seemed to be growing by the minute.

Game two was huge in this series. Again, as in game one, the Heat jumped out to an early lead, pushing it to twelve after one. We didn't fold. We kept fighting, but nothing we threw at them got them out of their game. In the fourth, we were finally able to make a serious run and cut the Heat's lead to three. Miami responded and pushed it back up to seven. KD drove the lane on our next possession to bring it back down to five. We got a steal and swung the ball over to KD on the break. He drilled a three—a typical icy KD big shot—making it 98–96, Miami. The Heat decided to run the clock on their next possession, forcing LeBron to heave up a three. It came off the rim, and Thabo grabbed the board.

Coach Brooks called a time-out and drew up a play to get KD the ball on the low block directly off the inbound pass, knowing that Miami would be doing everything to prevent us from having an open look at a three-pointer, which would have won the game. The play worked perfectly. KD got a high-quality shot close to the basket over the shorter LeBron James. Maybe he rushed it. Maybe there was contact on KD's arm. The shot came off the rim. LeBron hauled in the rebound and sealed the game at the line.

You would think that the combined effect of these two games would have increased our confidence. We won one game after a slow start. We almost stole game two. That game two loss, though, shook us. The media criticism of Russ started to pick up again, this time with an intensity only possible during an NBA Finals, when the spotlight is white-hot and not going anywhere. The issues were the same—a supposed lack of distribution, too much dribbling, not going to KD enough, and so on. From where I stood, I thought Russ had played two pretty incredible games of basketball. It seemed that the more he did, the better he played—and in game four of the series he would be utterly brilliant—the more the media was all over him, picking him and his game apart. As I said, Russ could be a stubborn motherfucker. He wasn't changing his approach to the game because of anyone talking, and thank God for that.

At the same time, the outside noise was affecting the team. It was throwing off our chemistry just a little bit, and in the NBA Finals "a little bit" can mean everything. Games two and three came down to the final possessions with the Heat clinging to small leads. We had chances in both games to pull even or go ahead, but we came up short. Mental mistakes and poor execution at key moments did us in. Victory in game four again eluded us, and Miami pushed the lead in the series to 3–1.

Maybe a more steeled veteran team could have regrouped after what had been three tough losses. That team might have been able to take one game on the road and then move back home with a puncher's chance to win in seven. We didn't have it. We lacked the knockout gear, or the will or determination to grind out a win against LeBron, D-Wade, and their squad. The Heat weren't playing flawless basketball by any stretch of the imagination, but they were staying within their game plan and making us play hard on every possession. When Mike Miller caught fire in game five, it was over. Their role players and second unit had been outstanding—Battier, Chalmers, and Miller hitting clutch shot after clutch shot. The Heat took the series 4–1. It must have been the closest five-game NBA Finals in history.

Blame for the loss, as far as the media was concerned, fell heaviest on Russell Westbrook. Magic Johnson had come out in the middle of the series to claim that Russell Westbrook "was the worst point guard in a championship finals" he'd ever seen. Others piled on him for his foul at the end of game four, when Russ hadn't been aware of rules related to the shot clock after a jump ball. The foul ended any chance we had to even the series and, in the minds of many, erased his truly spectacular performance, shooting twenty out of thirty-two from the field over the first forty-seven minutes and thirty seconds of the game. There is no way we would have been competitive in game four without Russ. He carried us at times, making shot after shot, finishing drive after drive to keep us close.

I couldn't believe what Magic and others were saying. I kept thinking: what are these people talking about? Have they lost their damn minds? Russ was a scoring point guard, and it could be that the old guard of the NBA had trouble dealing with it. Now in his fourth year, Russ had made huge strides. In my opinion, the heat he was taking had more to do with the greatness of KD than anything Russ was doing. KD's style and attitude were so smooth, so pure, that it shaped the way the media looked at Russ. The media couldn't accept his style, especially since it cut against the grain of so many of the league's greatest point guards, guys like John Stockton or Magic himself. Russell Westbrook played with a different type of passion and aggression, a different spirit, an edge and an intensity rarely seen on the basketball court or anywhere else in life.

What I love, though, is that Russ refused to change his game. He knew that what he was doing was special, and eventually he earned the respect he deserved. It finally took the great Kobe Bryant to come out and bless Russ—telling the world that he had the "Mamba mentality," which he did—for the basketball world to come around.

In short, the conversation about Russell Westbrook costing us the finals was total bullshit. He had balled his ass off for the entire series. Nonetheless, the talk served to cover up the more significant mystery. And that was this: what the hell happened to James Harden in the NBA Finals? James came into the playoffs after a hell of a year. He had many huge games for us during the season and was the offensive anchor on our second unit, though nobody thought of James as anything less than an NBA starting-caliber player. In the early rounds of the playoffs, especially in the Western Conference Finals against the Spurs, he'd been huge. He was a key reason we were able to put the 0–2 deficit in the rear-view mirror and whip off four straight wins.

In the finals against the Heat, Harden's quality of play fell off a cliff. Though he had a moment here or there of Hardenesque brilliance, they were few and far between, and most of the time he was ineffective—sloppy on offense and a liability on defense. This was hard for me to watch. Since arriving in OKC, I'd become a great admirer of James' game. James put more work into his game than just about anyone. Like KD and Russ, James loved to hoop. He stayed late. He studied the game. In those early years of his NBA career, his learning curve was out of this world. By 2012, his third year, it was clear that he was on his way to being a special player, though perhaps not yet the franchise cornerstone and megastar he'd become.

People in the media have been talking about James and his performances in the playoffs for a decade. I don't buy any of the talk about him not being able to handle the pressure at big moments—and a lot of this conversation ultimately connects back to him not showing up to ball in the 2012 finals, the only time in his career (as I write this) that he's found himself on the game's biggest stage. It happened to be an epic confrontation between us and the LeBron-led Heat. This was a legacy match, there's no doubt about it. The fallout from the series has in many ways shaped the subsequent careers of the biggest stars of this generation: LeBron, D-Wade, KD, Russ, and James.

To this day, I don't have a definitive answer to questions about James' play in finals. My read of the situation is that the city of Miami got the best of him in 2012—and by "city of Miami," I don't mean the Miami Heat players or the fan base inside the arena. It wasn't the pressure of the finals. It wasn't what the Heat defense was throwing at him. It was the city of Miami and its siren song that took his legs away, affecting his speed, quickness, and ability to drive to the hoop or knock down shots from distance.

THE DYNASTY THAT NEVER WAS

In the summer of 2012, in the aftermath of our loss to the Heat, if you would have asked anyone around the organization or the NBA about the future of the Oklahoma City Thunder, that person would probably have told you that we were on the verge of a dynasty. If you then told that person that our Thunder team would eventually break up without a single ring, that person would have looked at you like you were fucking crazy. Our stars were under twenty-four. Thabo and I were in our mid-twenties—I was finishing the first year of my new four-year contract. It seemed like we had many years left together to play winning basketball.

Not only did we not win a championship, but we never made it back to the NBA Finals.

Our failure to win a ring during my four years in OKC can't be blamed on management. The combination of some of the best basketball and management minds in the business had built a powerhouse from the ground up. Troy Weaver, Joe Sharpe, Donnie Strack, Sam Presti, and Clay Bennett had done it the right way. Their draft success is now a thing of legend. It began, as I said, with KD, Russ, Serge, and James—and it continued with Reggie Jackson and Steven Adams. They moved us out of the old rink and into one of the best practice facilities in the NBA. They made sure we had everything we needed to succeed at our highest level. We had top-notch diet and nutrition experts, the best trainers, sleep therapists—everything you can imagine.

The organization wasn't concerned just with our bodies. They took a complete approach to health: mind, body, and soul. As a result of this, I lost weight and increased my quickness and speed getting up and down the floor. I needed to keep up with Russ and those boys, and in any case the NBA game was evolving and becoming much faster. Getting lighter was also key to maintaining my health, especially coming off the ACL tear. This is one of the reasons I'm concerned about Zion Williamson. I, more than anyone, know what it's like to battle with weight gain as an NBA player. And I know from experience that being lighter is important for staying injury-free.

The truth is, when you're talking about an NBA championship, an organization and a team can do everything right—from the draft to the trainers, coaches, contracts, etc.—and still have the ultimate prize elude them. By the fall of 2012, it was clear that James wasn't going to pick up his one-year option and stay with the Thunder. That summer, he'd been to London as a member of the U.S. Olympic team, along with KD and Russ. Stars from around the league were in his ear, telling him he needed to get to a place where he could be the man, and they were exactly right. There was nothing Sam Presti could do but deal him. On the eve of the season, we learned that James Harden was headed to Houston.

Despite losing Harden, we won sixty games in 2012–2013. We had the number one offense in the league, and our defense continued to improve remarkably; we ended the regular season ranked fourth in the league on that side of the ball. Unfortunately, we lost Russ to injury late in the season and had to go into the playoffs without him.

KD stepped up to the challenge, as he always does, and put up monster numbers. He led us past James and the Rockets in six. In the next round, the Memphis Grizzlies put the clamps on us. After averaging around 110 points per game in the regular season, we didn't crack 100 in a single game of that series. Twice we didn't even hit 90. We lost in five.

The year after that, 2013–2014, we made another run to the conference finals. This time the Spurs were ready and waiting for us. In their four wins, they seemed unstoppable, and though we were hitting shots and executing well, it wasn't enough. For another year, we were sent home before reaching the finals.

The following season, my last in OKC, injuries devastated us. KD went under the knife twice that season and played only twenty-seven games. Russ also missed a chunk of the season, with a right hand fracture. I'd fallen out of the starting lineup, replaced by Steven Adams. The team added the big man Enes Kanter as well, signaling that my time in OKC was coming to an end. As 2014 rolled into 2015, I was traded for the second time in my career, landing, after the Utah Jazz bought out my contract, with LeBron James, Kyrie Irving, and the Cleveland Cavaliers. It was time to gear up for another run at the title, this time playing with, not against, the best player in the world.

NOTES FROM LAWRENCE, KANSAS

One summer morning during my OKC years, I woke up in Lawrence, Kansas. I had arrived the night before to start a monthlong program recommended by the Thunder's management. Increasingly, I was struggling to control my anger. The Thunder's staff had watched my number of technical fouls spike. Tensions with teammates and off-court incidents were becoming more common.

I know I play the game with a mean game face , but in the past I'd always been able to separate the world on the court from the world beyond the out-of-bounds lines. I wasn't the type of guy who brought frustrations home to my friends and family. Over the previous months, I was experiencing something I'd never felt before. I was in a rage basically all the time. I wasn't controlling it; the wild and intense emotions had their grip on me, and it didn't look like they were ready to let go.

James Baldwin once famously said, "To be a Negro in this country and to be relatively conscious is to be in a state of rage almost all of the time." While on some level rage might be clarifying, its unpredictability and intensity cause damage to its host and the people around him. My rage wasn't just on the periphery of my life and selfhood. It was inside my core, and because it went deep, I knew that it was threatening who I was and everything I had, everything I hated and everything I loved. It was a problem.

Rage, by its very nature, is irrational, even if it connects at times to many "rational" thoughts. There didn't seem to be one specific reason why I found myself in this state. On the basketball side, I was dealing with a lot. You have to keep in mind that I had been hoopin' my entire life. When I was a Celtic, I knew my role, and I learned over the years how to put my personal ambitions aside; I understood it was necessary if I was going to get any real game minutes, especially as a starter on a championship team.

During my first years in OKC, I continued to embrace my role, and added leadership responsibilities to it. The problem was that even though I was doing my thing—playing hard, leading, staying in the best shape of my life—my numbers were falling. If I would get up six or seven shots a game in Boston for eight or ten points, I was down to two or three shots per game in OKC and four or five points. In Boston, Rondo would look for me under the hoop on drive-and-dish plays. KG was a master at passing out of double-teams on the elbow or the low block. These shots dried up on the Thunder, and I was limited to put-backs on the offensive glass or a rare post-up.

On the defensive side, I was battling like always, but because I was always matching up against the other team's premier low-post scorer in order to allow Serge the freedom to roam and block shots, I found that my rebounding numbers were also taking a hit.

In other words, I couldn't get it out of my mind that what should have been my peak NBA years were being squandered. Added to that, I was becoming increasingly concerned that these falling numbers would impact my next deal. The rise of social media during these years only exacerbated things. As a relative latecomer to social media, I couldn't believe at first how much talk was going on about my game. People felt like they could say just about anything they wanted about me, and let me tell you, there was some crazy shit.

All through my life, I'd felt like I could get a handle on pretty much any situation I found myself in and figure it out; but for some reason, at this moment, things just seemed like they were slipping out of my control. On and off the court, I became a firecracker, ready to pop off at any time, the slightest provocation enough to light my fuse. I must have been searching for something, something I wasn't even aware of needing, because I started to go out more than I had in the past. I started drinking way too much.

Hovering above this was my grandfather's death. Losing him was like losing a father, a best friend, a mentor, an elder, and a focal point of my entire life. He passed away in 2013, the day after my twenty-ninth birthday. He was seventy-eight years old. He'd been sick for three or four years before he passed, struggling with dementia, Alzheimer's, and Parkinson's disease. I'm sure many people reading this have been through it—watching the person you love the most getting sicker and sicker, knowing it's only going to get worse. It was devastating to see him like that. He'd been a big guy all his life, but toward the end he barely weighed eighty-five pounds.

I asked my grandparents to move up to Oklahoma City to be closer to me, but my grandfather wouldn't hear of it. He wanted to be home in Beaumont, in his community. I took some time away from the season when he died. Even though I knew it was coming, it hit me hard. I was losing the most important person in my life, the man who did more than anyone to build the core of who I am.

I was grieving and at the same time trying to carry on without him. When his spirit left us, it punched a hole right through me. I've talked a lot about the center of a circle, the presence or core that is strong enough to hold the shape together, whether it's the circle of the self, the family, or the team. It's really hard to say what exactly gives a core its strength, but it's as clear as day when that strength is gone and its power is emptied out. That's when the whole structure falls apart. My grandfather was the man who centered me. He was my compass through this wilderness of life. What would hold me together without my core? What would hold my family together if I didn't get myself right? These were painful thoughts, disturbing realities I needed to face.

It had been my choice to come to Kansas. It had to be my choice or nothing good would have come of it. Deeper down, I must have sensed it would have been hard to find the path out of these dark woods on my own. How could I take the first step, and then the next, to walk on out of there if I didn't know the right direction?

The program was a combination of individual and group sessions. Though some of the techniques and discussions in the one-on-ones were helpful, what really made the difference for me was listening to other people's stories in the group meetings. The people in the group came from all over the country. Many of them were successful professionals, some of them surgeons and other doctors, people who were dealing with life and death on a daily basis, working long hours and sacrificing time with family and kids to get their jobs done.

It wasn't any particular story that made the difference. It was a kind of slow pressure created by hearing one after another, putting myself in other people's shoes, imagining the struggles they were facing on a daily basis.

At some point that summer, it just seemed like a door in my mind opened. I could look through it and see my own life on the other side—and it looked pretty damn good to me. I was standing there in the darkness, but across the threshold in the light was the life of an NBA basketball player making millions of dollars a year with a beautiful wife and great kids. Whatever had brought me into the darkness—frustration, anger, insecurity, disappointment, past trauma—seemed to fade into the background or to disappear altogether when that clarifying light shined through.

I'd been wasting my time, I told myself, reacting to everyone and everything, trying to seize hold and control what was ultimately impossible for me to control. I'd lost focus on what was real and important. God had blessed me, and here I was trippin'.

But it wasn't just thoughts like this that mattered. Overcoming my anger wasn't a rational process. It required me to open myself up, listen, take in the emotional and psychological realities of the people around me, and then to feel as deeply as possible the truth flood into me. When a truth like that comes pouring in, the anger gets washed away.

9

The Age of LeBron

DID THE "AGE OF LEBRON" BEGIN WHEN LEBRON JAMES ENTERED THE LEAGUE AS THE number one draft pick in 2003? No. Did it begin when he won his first MVP award in 2009, or his second in 2010, or his third in 2012, or maybe his fourth in 2013? No. No. No. And still no. Did the Age of LeBron begin when The King made his "decision" to leave Cleveland for Miami, where he won the first two of his four championship rings? No, not then either. We'll see in the following pages that what marks the dawn of the Age of LeBron is something altogether different, and much bigger than basketball.

The Age of LeBron has witnessed important and fascinating changes in sports and society, and, of course at the nexus of the two. When it's all over and the Age of LeBron gives way to what will inevitably follow, people will look back on this era as one of the most significant periods in the history of American sports, if not the most significant, especially if we're talking about the power and the voice of Black athletes. LeBron himself, whether it's ten or twenty years from now, will stand with Bill Russell and Muhammad Ali on the summit of greatness, far above the rest of the basketball elite, including Magic Johnson and Michael Jordan. He will stand with Russell and Ali not primarily because of his unbelievable accomplishments as a player but for what he has done beyond the hardcourt—beyond the arenas and their JumboTrons across America and the world.

To fully take stock of the Age of LeBron, we need to get a sense of what came before it. Most of this history is well known, but it is often misrepresented and misunderstood. I have already talked about how our collective storytelling works to define us as individuals and groups, specifically how the histories of Black people in America have been misrepresented for many generations. These faulty stories, whether they were about the realities and legacies of slavery or the Black Power movement, have worked to the advantage of the powerful and to the detriment of those with less wealth and influence.

The American sports story is no different. It has been dominated by a combination of white media executives, mostly white journalists, and white fans who clamor for an understanding of sports that feels uplifting and nonpolitical. The American sports story, like most American stories, is typically about progress and good overcoming evil. It is about merit and talent winning out. But there's a lot more to it than that.

BROOKLYN, NEW YORK, 1947

The familiar story about Black athletes and American professional sports runs along the following lines. At the advent of mass spectator sports like baseball and boxing, Black athletes were barred from competing together or against white athletes. Over time, certain athletes, like the boxer Joe Louis, who became heavyweight champion in 1937, or the track star Jesse Owens, who won four gold medals in the 1936 Berlin Olympics, were able to break through the color barrier to display their incredible talents against the best white competition. These athletes were, and still are, seen as pioneers, both for their athletic accomplishments and for the impact their performances had on American sports and culture.

The individual assault on the color barrier in sports had its most famous moment in 1947, when Jackie Robinson became the first Black
baseball player to ink a Major League Baseball contract, signing up to play
for the Brooklyn Dodgers. Robinson's entry into Major League Baseball
marked the beginning of a new era for American professional sports. The
Black ballplayers who followed Robinson—Willie Mays, Hank Aaron,
Ernie Banks, and countless others—would be some of the best the game
has ever seen. By the 1950s, other sports leagues would follow MLB's
lead. I've already talked about Bill Russell's impact on the NBA and the
entire sports world, beginning with his dominance of college basketball for the University of San Francisco and continuing in the NBA as
a Boston Celtic.

For boundary breakers like Robinson and Russell, there was no sep-
aration of sports and politics. In Jim Crow America—and I'm talking
about the North and South, East and West—everything a Black athlete
did on the diamond, in the ring, and on the gridiron or the hardcourt
was, by its very nature, a political act, an act of defiance, resistance, and
affirmation. An athlete's presence in what were only a short time before
segregated spaces made his "play" deeply political and meaningful—
and every athlete in Russell's or Robinson's day knew it.

Black athletes understood very well and *very personally* that what
they were doing was challenging social norms and hierarchies. The intensity of the resistance to their presence in formerly white-only spaces
was fierce, and often violent. I'm not talking only about the raw, immediate reaction to Jackie Robinson. Don't get me wrong, the opposition
to Robinson and other trailblazers was enormous, but this focus on the
specific moment of integration—Brooklyn, 1947—obscures the more
important fact: the struggle to integrate all levels of American sport
was long and grueling, lasting not seasons and years but decades.

Let's take college basketball as an example. The modern era of NCAA
basketball began in 1939 with the advent of the NCAA's postseason

national tournament. By the 1950s, Black basketball players were earning spots on teams in the northern and western parts of the country. Like Russell, they were quickly becoming some of the top players in the college game. Russell and K. C. Jones dominated while at San Francisco. Wilt Chamberlain starred at the University of Kansas. Oscar Robertson averaged almost thirty-four points a game over his three-year career at the University of Cincinnati.

Throughout the South, however, things were very different. In 1956, Louisiana passed a law barring white and Black athletes from competing against each other in sports. Not to be outdone, the University of Mississippi declared its intentions to withdraw from any contest that might compel its all-white rosters to square off against even a single Black player. In 1962, now a decade and a half after Jackie Robinson's debut in Brooklyn, Mississippi State University finished the year tied with the University of Kentucky for the Southeastern Conference (SEC) basketball title but refused to enter its team in the NCAA tournament to avoid competing against Black players from other schools.

The fabled program of Coach Adolph Rupp at the University of Kentucky took the floor for the national championship game in 1966 with an all-white team, facing off against Texas Western. Texas Western, unlike the Kentucky Wildcats, had pushed to integrate its basketball team in the wake of *Brown v. Board*. This 1966 championship game, for the first time ever, pitted an all-white starting five against an all-Black lineup. Texas Western carried the day, winning 72–65. It was an important milestone in the history of the Black athlete, nearly two decades after Robinson's MLB debut.

One might think that Texas Western's historic championship run would quickly change the face of college sports. Think again. In 1968, the writer Jack Olsen went to Texas Western, which had changed its name to the University of Texas at El Paso (UTEP), to report for *Sports Illustrated* on the status of its Black student-athletes. What he discovered was simply appalling: an athletic program and university administration rife with racism, white coaches' and administrators' obsession with preventing interracial dating, social segregation on campus, a pattern of broken educational promises, and, in some cases, severe economic hardship in the college's Black athletic community. When UTEP's track team boycotted a meet to protest this racial oppression, its members were kicked off the team and lost their scholarships.

Beyond Texas Western, change came slowly. Vanderbilt University would become the first SEC school to successfully recruit a Black basketball player when it signed Perry Wallace in 1966. It took another two years for a second Black player to make it into the SEC, Auburn's Henry Harris. Rupp's Kentucky team didn't sign its first Black player until 1971. In and out of the stadiums and arenas, the barrier-breaking Black athletes—from Robinson to Perry Wallace—faced opposition, discrimination, threats, and hardships. Jackie Robinson was not the end of segregation. His was the beginning of the integration story and the fight for equality in sports.

Professional and collegiate sports are big business, and on the level of the business of sports, Jackie Robinson and the courageous and talented athletes who came after him had little impact, sadly. As is well documented, the integration of Major League Baseball took the best talent from Negro League clubhouses, but it did nothing to integrate baseball's management and ownership structure. Basketball, which was quickly becoming a predominantly Black professional and collegiate sport, likewise fielded nearly all-white coaching staffs and front offices, men working beneath a completely white cadre of owners.

In fact, the first Black majority owner of a major professional sports franchise in the United States was Robert Johnson, who purchased a majority stake in the NBA's Charlotte Bobcats *in 2003*. There is currently only one Black majority owner in the NBA—Charlotte's Michael

Jordan. No other American professional sports team, whether in the NHL, NFL, or MLB, has ever had a Black majority owner.

Black athletes' political activism was at its high-water mark in the late 1960s. Who can forget the image of Tommie Smith and John Carlos standing on the medal platform in Mexico City after winning gold and bronze medals for their country in the 1968 Olympic Games, their black-gloved fists raised proudly in the air while "The Star-Spangled Banner" played? In that famous photograph, we can see Smith, Carlos, and the white Australian silver medalist Peter Norman wearing the badge of the Olympic Project for Human Rights (OPHR), a protest group led by the activist and sociologist Harry Edwards.

Smith and Carlos performed a great act in Mexico City, one that commanded the world's attention for the cause of freedom, justice, and equality. It would be a mistake to see their act in isolation from the deeper context. This moment of symbolic protest had been cultivated for decades in and beyond the institutions and structures of American sports, amateur and professional. There is no Mexico City moment without Dr. Harry Edwards, and no Harry Edwards without the countless acts of courage and dissent that over generations broke down the barriers to spaces of competition: segregated gyms, white-only locker rooms, discriminating private clubs, courses, courts, and on and on.

This was the landscape of American sports that had to be conquered quite literally one space at a time. Clichés like "sports are a meritocracy" don't hold up when we look at the historical record. If Black athletes wanted to compete on anything close to a level playing field, they had to work twice as hard, be twice as good, and overcome an untold number of obstacles just to get there.

One might think that when Smith and Carlos raised their fists as a sign of human rights, it would have marked a new era of justice and equality for Black athletes. Here, however, the story becomes complicated.

The typical telling of what we might call the "Jackie Robinson story" is an uplifting one of right prevailing over wrong, justice over injustice, integration over segregation. But it is commonly assumed, incorrectly, that the Jackie Robinson moment led to a flood of integration across American professional sports. In fact, Robinson made only a small, albeit important, crack in the dam. To this one significant crack thousands or even hundreds of thousands of others would need to be added before the dam would break. Parts of this very same dam stand today, mainly blocking the flow of Black talent into the business side of sports.

The socially engaged, politically outspoken Black athlete faced a hurricane of criticism in the aftermath of the Mexico City Olympic Games in 1968. Media outlets and journalists were determined to read Smith and Carlos' gesture as a threatening symbol of the potential violence of the Black Power movement, and the Black Panther Party specifically. Although the salute had absolutely nothing to do with violence, Smith and Carlos were ostracized from competitive track and field in the United States and were both financially ruined. The salute, far from being a symbol of violence, revealed a symbolic dedication to justice, equality, human rights, and the OPHR's push to exclude the racist regimes of South Africa and Rhodesia from Olympic competition.

The entertainment and information gatekeepers were intent on pushing back against, even crushing, what Edwards termed "the revolt of the Black athlete" as part of the broader campaign against Black Power and the expansion of the civil rights agenda. Dissent against this system came with real-life costs and risks for the individuals involved. Even Peter Norman, who simply stood on the platform wearing the OPHR's badge in support of Smith and Carlos, paid a heavy price for his embrace of equality and justice. Norman was severely criticized at home in Australia and was prevented from competing in the 1972 Munich games.

We have a bad habit in our society of viewing historical developments as if they were inevitable. The radicalization of the 1960s, many people claim, led to the relatively apolitical 1970s, which, in turn, gave us the materialistic, "greed is good" 1980s. In the realm of sports history, specifically with regard to the Black athlete, it is often argued that there is a reverse correlation between monetary success and political activism. The more money a player makes, so the conventional wisdom goes, the less he engages with the key economic, cultural, and political issues of the day. There is some truth to this, but I think it is time we started to talk about what has happened to the "revolt of the Black athlete" in different terms, through a different, better lens.

Any reasonable account of what's happened to the political activism of Black athletes from the 1970s until very recently needs to begin by addressing our broader culture. Though the media and much of our society today might look back and celebrate the courage of Smith and Carlos, at the time—and for a long time afterward—this defining moment of postwar Olympic history was met with open hostility. This was an era in which the vast majority of media contributors and sports journalists—local and national—were white men. The vast majority of spectators at professional sports events were white. Across the country, in newspaper after newspaper, on television and radio, the message to Black athletes was clear: keep "politics" out of sports—or, more accurately, the message beneath the simplistic idea of keeping politics out of sports was that Black athletes should not use their positions as emerging celebrities to challenge the racist status quo.

While the media was campaigning for Black athletes to "shut up and play," the platform for professional athletes across America's major sports leagues was growing larger. Television deals, especially with the advent of cable television, pumped hundreds of millions of new dollars into the NFL, MLB, and NBA. After various challenges to the leagues' contractual systems, players could become "free agents," attracting larger contracts and more media attention, especially if they made a leap to a big media market like Los Angeles or New York. With the rise in sports viewership, corporations jumped in and began recruiting athletes to advertise and endorse their products. Athletes were turning from stars into celebrities, whose images could be successfully sold for thousands, and soon millions, of dollars. For some athletes, the money flowing to them from corporations would exceed their income from their teams.

MICHAEL JORDAN: MAN, BRAND, ICON, SPECTACLE, LEGEND

If Jackie Robinson has come to represent the integration of sports and the age of the political athlete, then the iconic celebrity athlete, the nonpolitical athlete, is without doubt Michael Jordan. Michael Jordan wasn't just an athlete, and he wasn't just a symbol—he was a phenomenon, a complex image, a spectacle, the components of which came together to form a global brand with unprecedented marketing power. From the mid-1980s to the "Last Dance" in 1998, Jordan's final season with the Chicago Bulls, the NBA's global television viewership grew to over 750 million fans. This exponential growth in viewership meant that the league brought in more money than ever before, and this meant that NBA players' salaries, which in the early 1980s topped out at $1 million per year, grew into the tens of millions.

Beyond the court, the Jordan phenomenon reaped enormous profits as a vehicle for advertisers. We're not talking about millions here but billions, as Michael Jordan became the face of shoes, sports drinks, hamburgers, underwear, breakfast cereal, and many other products. The central beneficiary of the Jordan brand was the sneaker and sports apparel company Nike, which Jordan's image almost single-handedly transformed into a global corporate behemoth. Other corporations followed in Nike's footsteps, cutting huge checks to cash in on people's desire to "be like Mike."

There is no shortage of people writing about how Black athletes in the 1980s and 1990s fell silent on social and political issues as money from the leagues and corporations flowed to them. Black athletes, it is often said, turned their backs on the tradition of Robinson, Russell, and Harry Edwards and surrendered the fight for social and racial justice. Following the lead of O. J. Simpson and others in the 1970s, a depoliticized Black athlete became the norm in the 1980s and 1990s, writers like Howard Bryant tell us, eventually becoming part of, or contributing to, so-called post-racial America.

The most famous piece of evidence for this post-racial or "color-blind" turn in the status of celebrity Black athletes is provided by Michael Jordan: his statement "Republicans buy sneakers too" was spoken in response to his rationale behind refusing to endorse North Carolina's Democratic Senate candidate Harvey Gantt, a civil rights leader, in his race against the notorious racist Jesse Helms (Helms, the incumbent, went on to win). In the same vein, Tiger Woods, perhaps the second-most-famous athlete of color in the United States, went on *The Oprah Winfrey Show* and refused to identify himself as Black.

It's true that Black athletes from the 1970s until recent times were not following in the direct footsteps of Robinson, Russell, Smith, and Carlos. Luminaries like Harry Edwards believed that Black athletes had lost their message and voice as huge money from salaries and endorsement deals drowned out a more radical ideology. To tell the story like this, however, is to place the blame on the Black athletes—the victims of racism, not its perpetrators. It also ignores many additional factors, like the role of the media in the "depoliticizing" of sports.

After the 1968 Olympic Games, and gathering steam in the 1970s, the American media grew increasingly hostile to anything in the sports world it deemed political. By then, the media had declared the civil rights era over, and Black Power, as I have already discussed, was defined as violent and bad. Sports had been integrated, at least at the level of the players, which was more than good enough for the media. "Meritocracy," according to most sports writers, had been achieved—and salaries had spiked. It was time, the media told us, for Black athletes to "shut up and play."

During this period, if a player spoke out, he was criticized for not appreciating what "had been given to him." Old discussions about Black athletes possessing natural physical attributes that gave them advantages over "hardworking" white competitors returned to prominence in discussions of Black achievement. They were used to qualify or lessen Black success while glorifying white athletic accomplishments.

This is the bottom line: in Reagan's America, there could not have been a political Michael Jordan in the same way we had a political Bill Russell. Russell faced enormous opposition to his political statements, but he was also buoyed by the broader movement for civil rights, integration, and desegregation. By the 1980s, the sports media had turned its back on these issues, to say nothing of economic and racial justice. Instead, the media policed the national discussion, making sure to amplify and support Reagan's demonization of the "ghetto," his brutal war on the poor, his racist appeals to suburban white folk, and his attacks on the legacies of Black Power.

In this context, there existed no reality in which Michael Jordan could have been Jackie Robinson 2.0. There was no chance for a political "Jumpman," no chance that a political Jordan could have told America to "be like Mike." In any battle between Michael Jordan and Ronald Reagan, the media would have flocked to Reagan's side. Jordan wouldn't have had a chance.

Michael Jordan brought the whole package together, crossing nearly every boundary one could cross in the domain of marketing and image construction. He was the ultimate winner, the greatest-ever individual performer, the model athlete, the perfect physical specimen. As serious and focused as he was on the court, battling the "Bad Boys" in Detroit, overcoming the legacies of Bird and Magic, he could be comedic and even childish off the court, especially when messing around with Bugs Bunny and those folks.

Jordan was the symbol of the urban blacktop, brilliantly captured (or constructed) by the filmmaker Spike Lee in those unforgettable early Nike ads. At the same time, Lee and Jordan's "urban blacktop," filmed in black-and-white, was not too urban—it was an environment (usually containing only Jordan and Lee) safe for the sporting dreams of America's suburban white kids. That Jordan was becoming the ultimate commercial symbol is best signified by the nickname given to him by Lee's alter ego, Mars Blackmon—"Money."

For Jordan to be "Air Jordan," an image needed to be created in line with the times he played. To argue that Michael Joran should have carried the torch from Jackie Robinson seems naïve to me. This was a fundamentally different time. It was not Michael Jordan who massively expanded Nixon's "war on drugs." It was President Ronald Reagan. It was not Michael Jordan who signed into law the devastating 1994 Crime Bill. That was President Bill Clinton. It was not Michael Jordan who beat Rodney King in the streets of Los Angeles. Those were members of the Los Angeles Police Department. It was not Michael Jordan who acquitted those officers. That was a majority-white jury from Ventura County. Michael Jordan did not create or support racist sports journalists. He did not invent the media's racist narratives that filled the headlines and the television airwaves day after day. What he did do was dominate the sport of basketball for over a decade.

Michael Jordan's star power began to fundamentally transform the balance of power between the league owners and the players. He broke barrier after barrier for Black celebrity athletes and businessmen, to the extent that he was able to become the single Black owner of an American sports franchise. Ask yourself: should Michael Jordan have given up the endorsements and business opportunities available to him to take political stands on issues of specific importance to the Black community?

And if he had no endorsements, if he wasn't an icon, would anyone have cared what he said?

Though these are complex and deeply felt issues, and though I respect those who see it another way, I believe that the debate surrounding Michael Jordan and politics is misplaced. Jordan did what he did—and what he did was incredible. To ask him to also be the heir to Jackie Robinson is asking too damn much. He showed the country and the world that a Black athlete could rise to become a billionaire and team owner. He showed the country and the world that a Black athlete could be the face of a global brand. Was it Michael Jordan's responsibility to do all of this and also to be a leader of the Black freedom struggle?

This last question gets me to my biggest point, the point about responsibility. The 1980s and 1990s witnessed the escalation of the "war on drugs" and the assault against Black communities throughout the country. If Michael Jordan should have confronted this reality, so should many others have. Above all, in the world of sports, it is time to start asking about the responsibility of white athletes to stand with their Black teammates.

As Black athletes, we face the struggle for social justice every day of our lives—and we have faced it since the day we were born. We bear the responsibility all the time. It falls squarely on our shoulders—and we carry it within us beyond view of the television cameras.

Where, in the long and glorious history of Black athletes standing up for our dignity, do we find similar stories of white athletes leading the charge toward equality and justice? Who among MLB players in 1947 or in the years before was publicly calling for a Black player to join his clubhouse? Which white college basketball players throughout the South were fighting for integrated football or basketball teams in the post–Brown v. Board SEC? Which white athletes stood side by side with Muhammad Ali in his protest against American racism and the Vietnam War? How many stories do you know of white athletes challenging oppression and discrimination? Is there a white athlete out there in the long history of our country whose name could stand with Russell, Ali, Kareem, and Robinson as a champion for justice?

The answer is no. There is not a single one. The problem isn't—and has never been—that Black athletes have been apolitical. It is impossible for a Black man in this country to be apolitical. The problem is that until very recently *only* Black athletes have fought for equality and justice. White teammates, coaches, owners, and executives have stood on the sidelines, fingers in the wind—or worse.

Ever since Bill Russell took the NBA by storm in the mid-1950s, the league has had a troubled and complex relationship to Blackness—and by "the league" I mean ownership and the commissioner's office. I also mean the mostly white journalists—local and national—who have covered the league over the previous seventy years. I also mean the corporate sponsors who pour hundreds of millions of dollars into the league's coffers each year. I also mean the NBA fan base, especially the predominantly white crowds that fill the arenas around the country night after night, year after year.

Not least thanks to the extraordinary play of Michael Jordan—and a supporting cast of other superstars like Karl Malone, Patrick Ewing, Clyde Drexler, Charles Barkley, and Hakeem Olajuwon—David Stern was able to see the NBA grow into an international sensation. Salary caps and drug testing worked to calm fears of Black success and Black deviance. NBA players avoided politics and controversy, and not a single NBA great of the Magic and Jordan era became a figurehead of the social justice movement. No Black player took on and challenged Ronald Reagan's racist policies, George H. W. Bush's war in the Middle East, or Bill Clinton's expansion of the "law and order" regime. The combined power of the commissioner's office and white-dominated media was a potent force, strong enough to silence an entire league of Black millionaires.

If you don't believe me, just look at the exception to the rule, former Bulls guard Craig Hodges. He performed the politest act of resistance one can imagine when he delivered a letter of grievance to President George H. W. Bush during the team's visit to the White House after winning the 1992 NBA championship. Afterward, Hodges was cut from the team and then blacklisted throughout the league. He never found a roster spot in the NBA again. He was a Colin Kaepernick before his time.

YOUNG AND BLACK IN THE NBA

I've known LeBron James since we were kids, long before the 2003 NBA draft when we entered the league together. Let me just say this from the outset: there has been no other athlete in the history of sports who had the amount of pressure on him that LeBron James has carried since he was sixteen years old. And nobody has handled this pressure better than The King. Just take a look at the *Sports Illustrated* cover from February 18, 2002. There you'll find LeBron James with a basketball in his hand. He is wearing his green headband and his high school basketball jersey. His arm is stretched out toward the camera. It's his junior year. The caption, printed in glowing block letters and underlined in red, reads: THE CHOSEN ONE.

The first time I played against LeBron was in the eighth grade. When we reached our senior year in high school, we briefly overlapped on the same AAU team, the legendary Oakland Soldiers. Our first game together took place in Houston, not far from my hometown of Beaumont. The team's starters included LeBron, Leon Powe, and me. We were facing off against an Atlanta team with Josh Smith and Dwight Howard. We absolutely destroyed them, LeBron finishing the game with close to sixty points. The Soldiers team might have been a short-lived experiment, but my friendship with LeBron continued to develop through ABCD

(Academic Betterment and Career Development) Camp, the McDonald's All-American Game, and into the pros.

When LeBron and I entered the league in 2003, we were coming into a world still very much under the watchful eye of David Stern, a group of white owners, and a largely white media corps. None of these entities had much sympathy or tolerance for dissent or even for expressions of individuality that cut against the conformist norms of the day. Black players in the NBA knew we had to walk a fine line, one that allowed us to try to stay true to ourselves and our communities while at the same time operating inside the parameters set by Stern and the league.

People have criticized NBA guys during that time for steering clear of political expression, but you have to take into account our situation. We were young—some of us very young. Most of us had come from backgrounds of poverty, often extreme poverty. When we got into the league, we encountered an atmosphere of pressure to not speak out on issues of racial and social justice, to be silent about what could be controversial topics. Veteran players would warn all newcomers. "Hey, man," they'd tell us—and I was told this on many occasions—"you'd better leave that alone. You're best off not speaking on that." What was unspoken but deeply felt in locker rooms across the league was the looming threat that speaking out on sensitive issues would be bad for a guy's career, maybe even an existential threat to it.

Since the day he took over the commissionership in 1984 (and even before), David Stern was hyperfocused on the image of the league. Guys who posed a threat to the NBA image could be gone from teams without another team picking up their contract, and it wasn't because they couldn't play basketball at the highest level. If the league's office and the owners were the ultimate judges of a player's image and behavior, the sports media and the media in general could be called the "image police."

The local sports media—and I'm talking here about sports talk radio, local television, and the local newspaper sports beat guys—were

decisively pro-league and strongly anti-player. Reporters and other talk-
ers were always ready for anything bad to happen to a player so they
could be the first to write or speak about it. They viewed Black players
who made a ton of money as open targets. Stories about Black players who were young, rich, and "out of control" were always in demand.
Some guys even had private detectives trailing them. Whether they
came from the media or elsewhere is anyone's guess.

Around 2003, the media's assault on the image of its young players
was particularly vicious—and it would get even worse over the following couple of seasons. This was especially the case when it came to guys
like me who entered the league directly from high school, making the
"bad" (code: Black) decision to forgo college. In the white fantasy, college represented the good, right, responsible track. Going pro directly
to the NBA from high school indicated that we somehow didn't value
education, were too focused on money, or had an inflated ego.

The high school–to–pro phenomenon was relatively new. KG had broken the barrier when he came into the NBA as the fifth overall pick in
the 1995 draft. The Garnett pick typified the attitude toward the high
school–to–pro player at the time. Kevin McHale and the Timberwolves
made the pick, but of course the stories surrounding it were not only
about Garnett's dominant play or his fit with the pro game; the main
focus of story after story was on Garnett's background, psychology,
maturity, and "readiness" to exist as an adult without supervision—as
if he hadn't spent the last year taking care of himself and his sister as
a high school kid new to the city of Chicago. By age nineteen, Garnett
had already overcome more challenges than many sportswriters face
in a lifetime.

Between 1995 and 2004, there were thirty-eight guys drafted into
the NBA directly from high school. The sheer amount of hostility directed against us was shocking. The media piled on just about every insult
you could imagine. Regularly, we were called "immature" and "undisci-

plined." If a guy had tattoos or cornrows, he was labeled a troublemaker, at times even a gang member. The media was throwing around terms like "angry young man" and "thug" left and right, seemingly without thinking about how loaded this kind of language was.

It was racism as "common sense." If a guy had any sort of problem, if he showed emotion on the court or off, if he was at times angry or frustrated with himself or others, the media would be all over him, talking about his "upbringing," mentioning how he'd been raised by a "single mother," lamenting that he didn't have the grounding experience of being under the guiding hand of a sagacious (and usually white) college coach like Roy Williams or Mike Krzyzewski. To be better, the white establishment thought, meant to be "disciplined" and "controlled" by the white power structure. It was stereotype layered upon stereotype. It was lazy thinking, and a big part of our problem in this country is our collective willingness to tolerate this laziness instead of doing the work to push beyond it.

In retrospect, the media's obsessive attack on the high school–to–pro players looks outrageous and ridiculous. Many of those thirty-eight picks are now or soon will be in the NBA Hall of Fame. A dream team could be assembled from the list that would rival any other in NBA history: Kevin Garnett, Kobe Bryant, LeBron James, Tracy McGrady, Jermaine O'Neal, Rashard Lewis, Dwight Howard, and so on.

We were young Black men who were making it in America. Like I said, Black success can be a very scary thing to many people in our society. The high school–to–pro era coincided with other transformations in American culture. Different styles began to filter into the mainstream. It wasn't just the long, baggy shorts (Michael Jordan had worn long shorts); it was the tattoos, the body piercings, the clothes, and the hairstyles that signified a new and different generation, and with this new generation, a new mentality.

These styles were not confined to Black America. There were millions of suburban white teenagers getting tattoos. If a Black player showed up with a tattoo, though, he wasn't "experimenting" or "searching for an identity"; he was deviant, a troublemaker. He upset the corporate sponsors, now used to what they considered the "clean" image of Michael Jordan.

On the other hand, corporations saw the writing on the wall—or in the marketing numbers. This is why we got the contradictory impulses of Black styles becoming massively popular while still being defined as "ghetto" or dangerous. Think about this one: in the year 2000, we have the release of Allen Iverson's signature Reebok "The Answer IV"—a legendary shoe—and at the same time we have the NBA airbrushing Iverson's tattoos from the cover photo of *HOOP* magazine!

The shifting culture and styles and the increase in high school–to–pro players coincided with a decline in NBA television ratings in the early 2000s. The media was quick to define this decline as a "crisis," and the crisis was blamed on players for being too young and, though not explicitly stated, too Black. As salaries escalated in line with the budget of the league, players became "lazy," in the eyes of the media, or "spoiled"—a perennial media favorite. Commentators claimed we played an undisciplined brand of basketball and that we lacked fundamentals. This entire conversation—blaming and scapegoating young Black athletes—did nothing to clarify the reality of what was going on during those years. The truth about NBA ratings lay elsewhere.

It is no surprise that the decline in the NBA's television ratings came after the end of the Chicago Bulls' dynasty and Michael Jordan's retirement from the league (before he returned to play for the Washington Wizards). When the Jordan Bulls broke apart, so did the only NBA franchise with a truly national (and international) following. Fans across the country and the world would turn up or tune in to watch the Bulls play. The viewership numbers Jordan's teams attracted were nothing short of phenomenal. This was doubly the case when he would face off against his longtime rivals: Patrick Ewing, Karl Malone and John Stock-ton, Clyde "the Glide" Drexler, Sir Charles Barkley, Shawn Kemp and Gary Payton, and Reggie Miller.

Close to thirty-six million people watched Jordan's final game as a Bull. The year after Jordan left, despite the New York Knicks and the country's largest media market representing the East in the finals, viewership dropped by nearly 50 percent. Though the Lakers with Kobe and Shaq brought the numbers back up a bit in 2000 and 2001, a non-competitive contest between the Lakers and an outmatched Nets team produced low ratings the following year. Ratings fell again when those same Nets lost to the San Antonio Spurs in a matchup of two small-market teams without a true celebrity megastar.

There was no way the ratings for the NBA were going to hold up in the post-Jordan era. Ratings climbed in years when major-market teams faced off against each other, declined again when smaller-market teams won their conference championships. Competitive contests, especially if a series went seven games, would pull up the ratings, but between 1999 and 2009 only one series went seven, and many of them lasted five games or less.

To all of these basketball-related reasons, I could add many other important factors, like the expansion of cable television, but I think I've made the basic point. The quality of NBA play was not falling, and a "lack of fundamentals" was not causing people to turn away from the game. Players' behavior—their acting "too Black"—was not alienat-ing fans, at least not until the media created and hyped this idea in the public imagination.

In November 2004, the whole issue came to a head. The media had been demeaning NBA players for years, calling us thugs and gangsters, saying we were immature and undisciplined, lazy and spoiled, and claim-ing that fans were turning against us because we lacked fundamentals and didn't know how to play the game "correctly."

Tellingly, the criticism came from both Black and white reporters. This doesn't make it true, and it doesn't mean it wasn't infused with racial stereotypes and racist meanings. What it means is that it had become so common as to *seem like* a neutral, race-blind position. It was anything but. The attacks were the latest example of wave after wave, century after century, of attacking young Black men. It was fear of Black success. It was a rejection of Black culture, of hip-hop styles and rap music, which since the 1980s had been coded in the white imagination as deviant and dangerous.

On November 22, 2004, an on-court altercation between the Indiana Pacers' Ron Artest and the Detroit Pistons' Ben Wallace turned into a physical conflict between Artest and other members of the Pacers' team and its fans at Detroit's arena, the Palace of Auburn Hills. The so-called "Palace Brawl" or "Malice at the Palace" is famous. In the aftermath of the conflict, Pacers players Ron Artest, Jermaine O'Neal, and Stephen Jackson were suspended from the league, at a cost of millions of dollars for each player.

The firestorm in the media was unrelenting. The whole suitcase of insults was hurled at them—and not only at them personally, but at an entire generation of players: Black players. We were suddenly a league of violent criminals and hip-hop gang members—or, to translate, young, out-of-control Black men with money, which made it all the worse, according to the talking heads.

David Stern reacted quickly to the media commentary, and punishment for the players came swiftly. Stern followed up the suspensions and fines by issuing a series of new rules aimed at policing players' behavior and polishing the image of the NBA. The first rule to come down wasn't a surprise: there were to be no more high school–to–pro players entering the league. The second rule, or rather set of rules, was the NBA's new dress code: no more hip-hop or identifiably Black fashion. Players had to start looking "respectable," meaning that they had to conform to the standards of white professionalism. Craig Hodges knew a thing or two about the NBA's fashion police. During his 1992 visit to the White House, he'd had the audacity to wear a dashiki and had paid the price for appearing "too Black" in white-dominated society.

Stern, acting on the advice of Republican strategist Matthew Dowd, went beyond the mandate that players wear "business attire." Attached to the code was a host of prohibited items, including throwback jerseys, chains and other jewelry like pendants and medallions, sunglasses worn indoors, hoodies, and headphones. If Stern had once washed away what he and others perceived as the stain of Blackness in the 1980s and 1990s, he was now intent on another deep "cleaning" in the wake of the Palace Brawl.

As players in 2004, we saw something different from what Stern saw in the tape of the events in Detroit. What we saw was certainly nothing close to the story the media was telling in the days and weeks after the conflict. The media's version went something like this: an out-of-control Black man named Ron Artest, full of rage, charged like an animal into the stands to fulfill his inner need for violence.

I remember getting off the plane in Boston that night and watching the replay of the events with Paul Pierce. What we were seeing was an on-court situation that we've lived through hundreds or even thousands of times. Two guys, Ron Artest and Ben Wallace, got heated at the end of a rivalry game. As usual, other guys stepped in to prevent the heat from turning into fire. Guys like Reggie Miller and others seemingly had the situation under control. Artest and Wallace were separated, and Artest went, however oddly, to lie down on the scorer's table to calm himself and regain his composure.

It was at this point, with the situation under control on the floor, that a Detroit fan, a middle-aged white man, threw his beer from the stands and hit Artest in the face. This was an unprovoked assault, let's make no mistake; the man who threw the beer eventually faced criminal charges.

Artest went into the stands after the man in response to this assault, and whether right or wrong, he was defending himself against that aggression.

This is an important point, but in our culture we tend to think that when a Black man faces physical aggression and an attack on his body, he should "act like Martin Luther King Jr." and accept the violence. Little do most people know how long King and others *trained* so that they could maintain their composure under physical duress. Stephen Jackson followed Artest into the stands. Why? Because Jackson saw that Artest was under attack on all sides from the Detroit fans.

Go watch the tape. It's clear. Jackson and others like Jermaine O'Neal were fighting to get Artest out of harm's way, not to fulfill some deep desire for violence. The fact that his older brother had died from injuries sustained when he was jumped on the streets must have increased Stephen Jackson's sense of urgency when he saw the fans mobbing Artest.

What followed when the players returned to the court was truly amazing and frightening. Thousands of Detroit fans seemed to think they now had permission to do whatever they wanted. They started to throw what they could find down on the Pacer players: cups of beer, bottles, food, and even a chair, which injured multiple people.

If two or three Pacers could be labeled as "out of control," the same must be said for the thousands of fans, the vast majority of whom were far away from the altercations. These people were not responding to any threat. They weren't trying to help a teammate. Given the opportunity, the perceived "permission," the fans embraced the chance to go on the attack.

When, during the game, Bill Walton called the events a "low moment in NBA history," he was talking mostly about the fans' behavior, not the players'. Mike Breen, the game's announcer, though coached not to give his opinions, was unable to contain himself, exclaiming, as stuff came raining down on Indiana's players, coaches, and staff, "What a disgraceful showing from the Pistons' fans here."

In the aftermath, blame quickly shifted away from the fans to Artest, Jackson, and O'Neal. Players throughout the league were highly distressed by this. It was as if the league and the media saw us as nothing but animals in the zoo—giraffes and elephants on display for the paying crowds. I can't recall a single mention by league officials of the horrendous behavior of those thousands of people in Detroit who thought they could throw things at the "animals" and that these animals would remain docile in our cages on the court.

Stern's reaction to the brawl might have been praised in the media and applauded in the corporate boardrooms, but it was despised by us players. We couldn't stand David Stern after that, and we knew that behind Stern stood a group of racist owners like Donald Sterling, ready to do what they could to blame and denigrate us if they thought it would be good for their investment.

Certain guys who made a lot of money were ready to accept the fines from the league to continue wearing what they wanted. Allen Iverson wasn't changing his look because David Stern wanted to attract more red state white viewers upon the advice of Matthew Dowd. For us younger players just starting out on our rookie deals, we didn't have a choice. Not only was the monetary penalty significant for us, but more serious was the risk to our reputations around the league. Once a player was labeled a bad seed, it was very hard for him to come back from it. Jermaine O'Neal and Stephen Jackson can tell you a little something about that. They have been dealing with the fallout from November 2004 for close to twenty years.

Stern's attempt to "cleanse" the NBA's image by blaming and disciplining the league's Black players was absolutely loaded with racism, whether Stern himself was conscious of it or not. It played on stereotypes and racist narratives about Black male youths that stretch back generations. It fed into white suburban fears of Black urban culture.

From our point of view as players, not only were we subject to insults and attacks, we were blocked from calling the situation what it was. If someone said the dress code was racist, the league and the media would be sure to slap him back, calling him ignorant or saying he was just "playing the race card." If the media called us thugs and criminals—as they did over and over—there was nothing racist about it, so they claimed; they were just "reporting facts." The truth was the opposite, and the players had it right. The dress code, the banning of high school athletes, the media's reaction to the Palace Brawl and to players' transgressions— these policies and stories were steeped in the long history of racism in this country.

Behind racist policies, narratives, or statements is not always, and perhaps not even that often, an individual who is motivated by racial hatred toward Black people or another minority group. Often, racism is used as a way of maintaining the structures that benefit one group over another, and I'm talking here about money and power.

The complicity of the media in the commissioner's image-cleaning project put them squarely on the side of white ownership and the league's corporate sponsors and against the players. In an era of rapid growth in NBA revenue, only players' salaries received media attention and criticism. The media seemed to care less about the owners' profits, not to mention the rising team valuations that now reach into the billions of dollars. The same reporters who complained about our greed if we held out or sought a contract extension would lavish praise on an owner's skillful investments and financial moves.

Even a guy as thoughtful as David Halberstam got it mixed up when he wrote about Scottie Pippen's reaction to general manager Jerry Krause in the summer before the Bulls' final championship run. Halberstam said that Pippen complained that Krause's messages to him were racist.

"More likely," Halberstam corrected the Bulls' star without any proof, "they were . . . just the clumsy work of an executive who had no reservoir of trust with a great and quite sensitive player." In other words, according to Halberstam, it was Pippen who was "misinterpreting." It was Pippen who was "sensitive"—so sensitive, it was implied, that he saw racism where there was none. Krause, on the other hand, was forgiven—he was just "clumsy," as if being clumsy and being racist are mutually exclusive.

The deeper truth of the matter is that Krause and Bulls owner Jerry Reinsdorf had Pippen locked into one of the most exploitative sports contracts in the history of American professional athletics. Reinsdorf was banking tens of millions of dollars a year on Pippen's back, and paying the future Hall of Famer, in comparison, next to nothing. Whether Krause's specific statements to Pippen were racist or not, the entire context of the Pippen-Bulls relationship was deeply racist: white ownership exploiting Black labor.

The issues here go way beyond individuals, beyond David Stern or Jerry Krause. They are at the intersection of race, wealth, and power.

When I entered the NBA with LeBron James in 2003, it was a league of contrasts and contradictions. It was a league of Black players and white owners (as it still is). It was a league that wanted to appeal to the "hip-hop generation" but was terrified of being identified with the "ghetto." It was a league of young, exciting talent with a media out for the blood of Black youth. It was a league and media that complained about the excessiveness of player salaries while owners became unfathomably rich and corporate sponsors raked in huge profits. It was a league that thought it had transcended race with the global iconic figure of Michael Jordan only to find itself again and again thinking it needed to placate its white, red state fans.

In short, the post-Jordan NBA needed a new identity, a new torchbearer to pick up Jordan's legacy and carry it into a new age. That person would be LeBron James—and once LeBron picked up the torch, the league would never be the same.

THE AGE OF LEBRON

LeBron James played the first seven years of his career with the Cleveland Cavaliers. During this span, he averaged close to thirty points a night. In five of those seven years, he led the Cavs to the playoffs, once to the NBA Finals. As I've described in previous chapters, our Celtics team had epic series after epic series against LeBron and the Cavs. In the end, he just didn't have enough around him to seriously compete for a ring.

He might not have accomplished the ultimate goal during those years, but LeBron's impact on the Cavs franchise is truly astounding. The season before LeBron arrived from high school, the Cavs had a dismal 17–65 record. LeBron's rookie season, the team improved to 35–47. The year after that, they won more games than they lost. By 2008–2009, the year KG went down, LeBron's squad won sixty-six games. When LeBron left for Miami, the decline was fast and furious. In 2010–2011, the Cavs were right back where they began in 2002 at 19–63.

LeBron was only twenty-six years old when he made his "decision" to take his talents to South Beach. By then, he was without a doubt the most dominant force in basketball. He understood better than any of us the situation he found himself in. The Cavs were not making moves to put the necessary pieces around their star to make a serious run at a title. They were a good team—and with LeBron they could, on a given night, be an excellent team. As long as there was a Big Three in Boston and powerhouses out west, he and his teams in Cleveland had no real chance.

LeBron could tell that his interests and those of Dan Gilbert, the Cavs' owner, diverged. Gilbert might have paid LeBron's NBA salary, but LeBron James was raking in money for the organization, for the league, and even for the city of Cleveland. Under the circumstances, it would have taken Gilbert spending on another star, maybe two, to make the Cavs competitive. But why spend when one star, LeBron, already brought in the goods?

LeBron's decision to leave Cleveland for Miami and to team up with Dwyane Wade and former Toronto Raptor Chris Bosh dramatically shifted the balance of power in the NBA and changed the way players around the league, especially superstars, thought about free agency and the trajectories of their careers. There have been many key moments in the long story of player empowerment, but I'd argue with anyone that LeBron's move to Miami, and his role in building that roster, was one of the most significant. It sent a clear signal to owners that players were ready to take control over their careers and futures, especially if a franchise's management hadn't lived up to expectations.

Reactions to LeBron's move to Miami were harsh, which is unsurprising given the landscape of the media at the time. Dan Gilbert penned his famous letter full of absurd and childish accusations and claims, including the playground-level taunt that LeBron was a "Benedict Arnold" to the city of Cleveland. Instead, Gilbert should have been explaining to Cavs fans how he and management had failed them (and failed LeBron). Then he should have thanked LeBron James profusely for lifting his organization to heights it had never before achieved, bringing pride and economic vitality to the Cavaliers and to the city itself.

As a player and a rival, I can't say I was pleased by the news of LeBron's decision, knowing his new team would be a formidable opponent and the new favorites to win the Eastern Conference Championship. Eventually, the formation of his team in Miami would lead to the trade that sent me to Oklahoma City for Jeff Green. Still, I had to appreciate what LeBron had done. Power had always resided with ownership in the

NBA, even in Jordan's day. Now power was seemingly being wielded by a player, albeit no ordinary one.

LeBron's move to Miami was both a basketball and a business decision, and a very good one on both accounts. We know what it led to on the court: two championships in four years, and four straight trips to the NBA Finals. On the business side, LeBron's move to a bigger and more glamorous market, combined with his leading his team to the title, served to expand his profile and magnify his endorsement presence. It was this power, this magnified presence—and to magnify the presence of The Chosen One is no small feat—that created the platform for LeBron to create the most important piece of his legacy by far: his role as a leader off the court.

I can remember it like it was yesterday. On March 23, 2012, I saw an unforgettable image. It was the entire Miami Heat team, LeBron included, wearing black hoodies with the Heat logo on the front. The team had the hoodies pulled up over their heads. It was difficult to tell who was who. The guys' hands were buried in the front pockets of the hoodies. Their heads were bent down in a pose of solemnity and respect for a young man named Trayvon Martin, who had been shot and killed by a self-proclaimed "neighborhood watchman" in Sanford, Florida, on the night of the 2012 NBA All-Star Game. A series of hashtags led off LeBron's tweet to the world: #WeAreTrayvonMartin #Hoodies #Stereotyped #WeWantJustice.

The photograph is arresting and powerful. The guys are standing in front of an eerie orange background. You can't help but feel the seriousness and heaviness of the moment: the senselessness of Trayvon's death, the failure of justice in allowing his killer to walk free, the powerlessness that we feel when confronting the depth and stubbornness of racism in this country.

A boy had walked to the store to buy snacks for the All-Star Game and never returned. This is a family's nightmare, a parent's worst fear, a communal trauma, and a national disgrace. There is nothing that can set this right again. A young man was lost before he had a chance to live a full life, cut down when a toxic blend of stereotypes, fears, and racist laws came together one night in Florida in a storm that consumed him.

No photograph and certainly no tweet—not even a million tweets to a billion followers—will right the scales of justice in the case of Trayvon Martin. Where was Trayvon Martin's right to "life, liberty, and the pursuit of happiness"? President Obama was exactly right when he said that if he had a son he would look like Trayvon. Trayvon Martin represents each one of our sons—and when he was killed, a member of our family died, too. LeBron and the rest of the Heat team took an important first step in recognizing that the death of Trayvon Martin was a tragedy for the entire Black community and for American society in general. It was the first step in LeBron's search for his voice in our collective struggle for equality and freedom.

In this sense, LeBron's eight preceding years in the NBA were a prologue. The Age of LeBron began on March 23, 2012.

What did LeBron's tweeting of this photograph really mean? Let me try to define it for you from the perspective of a former NBA player who lived through these years in the league. Part of the game as a sports celebrity is to be broadly liked, and the model for developing the broadest possible appeal is Michael Jordan. There have been others—Iverson, Garnett, Kobe—but a true heir to Jordan's legacy had to aspire to universal appeal. James was the closest approximation to Jordan in terms of the sheer dominance of his play. With the tweet of that photograph and the message it contained, LeBron was telling the world that he was no longer chasing Jordan's shadow. He was going his own way. He was going to fight for something that he believed in more than his own image.

LeBron took this risk—and you better believe it was a risk—by going around traditional media. He didn't hold a press conference, release a statement, or sit for an interview. He went right to his followers on social media, and through them, directly to the public. By bypassing the media, LeBron was sending a message: his views, his opinions, his *narratives* were not going to be filtered through the mostly white journalists who'd erected an industry on the back of telling his story. He, LeBron James, would start to tell his own story. He would speak first and the members of the media would have to react to him, instead of the other way around.

LeBron announced to the world with that tweet that henceforth he would define himself, and that a large part of that self-definition would be his fight for social justice and racial equality. With that tweet, LeBron James and the other members of the Miami Heat threw down a challenge to professional athletes around the country: are you going to stay on the sidelines or are you ready to enter the game? It's amazing to see, nearly ten years later as I write this, how many people, including myself, have taken up this call and followed The King into the fray.

In 2012, there was no guarantee that LeBron James could succeed where a generation before him had failed in injecting a political consciousness into sports and overcoming an often conservative and racist media environment while holding on to one's broad-based popularity and corporate sponsors. Remember, this was a year before the formation of Black Lives Matter. It was years before Colin Kaepernick took a knee in protest. It was eight years before the worldwide reaction to George Floyd's murder.

I doubt LeBron's turn to activism would have succeeded without three important differences between 2012 and the Jordan era. The first difference, as I've just described, was the power of social media, which was still relatively young at the time LeBron posted his tweet. Social media allowed for direct public expression. The second difference was that LeBron immediately got the support of other players around the league, not only members of the Miami Heat like Dwyane Wade but guys from around the nation, including other superstars. The players, largely with one voice, stood up and threw our collective weight behind LeBron's message. The third big difference was the culture of the league itself, meaning the culture of the NBA commissioner's office. David Stern might have included a ban on hoodies in his dress code, but you better believe he wasn't going to come out and say anything against LeBron's photo.

In 2014, David Stern—the Jordan-era commissioner—retired and passed the commissioner's reins to his longtime protégé, Adam Silver. Silver quickly and decisively proved to be his own man. He was tested early on in his tenure when audio of then Los Angeles Clippers owner Donald Sterling making racist comments went public. Silver acted quickly to fine Sterling and to ban him from participating in NBA activities for life. A lifetime ban from the NBA was the strongest possible rebuke and condemnation, and we, as players and Black men, were impressed and immensely proud of Adam Silver's resolve and clarity.

But Silver wasn't done. His ultimate goal, which he accomplished again with great force and speed, was to compel the Sterlings to sell the Clippers. I would have loved to see another Black owner emerge to take control of the franchise, but it was not to be. Still, new Clippers owner Steve Ballmer is a dramatic improvement over Donald Sterling.

There is no doubt in my mind that Adam Silver's reaction to Donald Sterling was related to the growing power of NBA players and their increasing public engagement with issues of social and racial justice. I'm not saying that Adam Silver acted under duress or that LeBron or anyone else had to force his hand. Adam Silver is a great man, and I believe he did the right thing because he knew it was the right thing to do.

On the other hand, I don't think he would have been able to garner the support of the NBA owners to oust one of their own had it not been for the ways power had realigned in the league in the Age of LeBron. Donald Sterling's removal was one of the most important events in the history of American professional sports. Adam Silver deserves immense credit, but it is vital for us to remember that he didn't act alone or in a vacuum. The act of banishment was the result of hundreds or thousands of voices speaking up in concert—from Magic Johnson to Gregg Popovich to LeBron James to Charles Barkley and Shaquille O'Neal.

The presidential campaign in 2016 turned up the temperature on America's professional Black athletes. Vicious and racist rhetoric against Colin Kaepernick was escalating and resounding through the sports media, especially sports radio, and across cable news and social media. It seemed like every time Kaepernick took a knee, he brought the entire white media establishment down on his back. As a result, a large majority of white people in the United States disapproved of his symbolic act of protest against police brutality.

The National Football League, the most powerful professional sports league in the country, came out against one of its own. Money and fear were once again more powerful than truth and justice. Commissioner Roger Goodell proved beyond a shadow of a doubt that he does not possess the courage or moral compass of Adam Silver. The Kaepernick story was the type of story the American media knew how to cover, meaning they knew how to crush nonconformity and dissent and to twist the meaning of Kaepernick's protest from one about racial justice to one about "patriotism." The media took its side in the culture war, or to put it more bluntly, in the war being waged on Blackness in our country. It's no wonder we ended up with the result we did in 2016. We were a country of too many Goodells and not enough Silvers.

The attack on Blackness in the wake of Colin Kaepernick's peaceful and respectful act of protest and the frenzied, white-supremacist reaction to the presidency of Barack Obama posed what in decades past might have been existential threats to the NBA. David Stern had built the NBA on the premise that its excellence and market savvy would be able to overcome the image of basketball as a Black sport. His goal was to make a Black league less Black, not in terms of the players on the court—that ship had sailed long ago—but in its image and reputation.

Adam Silver moved the league in a new direction. The Donald Sterlings of the world were in retreat. As our country faced the strongest backlash against Blackness and minority rights in a generation, it was the NBA of LeBron James and Adam Silver that led the fight for justice.

The Age of LeBron isn't only about LeBron James, though I think it's fair to say he has shaped the league more than any other single player since Michael Jordan. From the moment he inked his first shoe deal with Nike at the age of eighteen, LeBron set a new standard for the size and length of rookie endorsements. When he went to Miami, he blazed the trail for other players to take their careers into their own hands, a move many players in previous generations had been hesitant to do given the owners' power and the monopolies of professional sports leagues. When LeBron returned to Cleveland after four years in the Florida sun, he demonstrated how much we players care about our roots, how much we love our communities, and how much we are prepared to give back. When LeBron and the Heat stood up for Trayvon Martin, they signaled that the days of the media and the league pressing us into silence were over. When LeBron stood toe-to-toe with a racist President of the United States, he showed us that we, too, needn't fear, that we didn't have to back down to anyone as long as we had the truth on our side. The forces of reactionary politics and culture, and the language of white supremacy, were not going to intimidate us.

The Age of LeBron became the age of all of us: the Age of Kendrick Perkins, the Age of Kyle Korver and Kevin Durant and Russell Westbrook and Jaylen Brown.

Before I get carried away, I need to offer some words of caution. Though LeBron has led the way to the next stage of player empowerment and has changed the culture of the NBA, work on these issues is far from complete. Racial and gender imbalances pervade all levels of individual franchise and league management, from a lack of women as NBA head coaches to the dominance of white men in positions of power in league offices and throughout the teams' front offices—to say nothing of the lack of diversity among owners.

Kevin Garnett's failure to obtain a majority stake in the Timberwolves is a great example of the invisible barriers still in our way. Players might make a lot of money, and they might have more control now than ever before over the trajectories of their careers, but those gains are delicate and could erode quickly as circumstances shift. The NBA players and owners are in an evolving relationship of relative power, and there is absolutely no guarantee, as the results of the 2011 lockout show, that players will always have the upper hand. It is not even clear to me that the players have the upper hand right now.

Another thing: the solidarity and clarity of purpose of NBA players in the 2020 Bubble, building from the league-wide reactions to George Floyd's murder, were a high point of player activism, even by standards set in the 1960s. Many guys spoke out and acted in a godly fashion in response to this ugly and disgraceful act of police violence. As Black men and women in America, we've seen this situation many times before. There is an outpouring of grief, anger, and commitment among thoughtful people in our country. This is usually followed by a strong reaction in the other direction.

A certain portion of white America is attempting to protect the racist status quo. They want nothing more than to break our will to dissent. The responsibility for withstanding and overcoming this reactionary wave is not LeBron James' responsibility. It is not my responsibility, or the responsibility of Black athletes in this country. All of us, of whatever race or creed, must link arms and form an impenetrable wall against this storm. It's time for us to hold the line.

While we hold this line, we need to do our work to sink the still-shallow roots of social justice deeper, especially among the members of the generation who are right now rising into social and political consciousness: our kids. The days of Black athletes "sticking to sports" or "shutting up and playing" have come to an end. It's not enough for us just to tweet and post. It's not enough to repeat a slogan or add a hashtag. It's not even enough to give money to causes we believe in, even if those acts are important and can change lives—just look at the impact of LeBron's I Promise School in Akron. We need to do all of this and more.

It is vital, if we are to act with power and knowledge and with justice on our side, that we understand our present and past in the deepest way possible. It is vital that we act out of truth. Truth matters, and we cannot surrender our truth to people who peddle lies in the service of hate and inequality. That's been going on in our country for far too long. Only truth will take us to justice. Only on truth's pathway will we reach goodness and godliness. The Gospel of John got it right: *The truth will set you free.*

10

Twilight, Purgatory, Dawn

TWILIGHT

I HAD A DECISION TO MAKE. AFTER THE THUNDER TRADED ME TO UTAH, THE JAZZ BOUGHT out my contract. For the first time in my career, I was a free agent. Three offers came in quickly. The first was from defensive guru Tom Thibodeau. He knew my value on that end of the court and was looking to bolster his defense as the head coach of the Chicago Bulls. The Bulls had a nice combination of young players like Jimmy Butler and great vets like Pau Gasol. It was a tempting situation, but at the same time I knew the Bulls had no chance of coming out of the East, and at that point in my career I wanted to compete for a ring.

Another offer sat on the table from the West Coast. My greatest basketball mentor, Doc Rivers, was now coaching the L.A. Clippers, and Doc wanted to bring me on for what he expected to be a deep playoff run. The Clippers were stacked with talent: Chris Paul, Blake Griffin, DeAndre Jordan, and J. J. Reddick, just to name a few of their bigger stars. With this roster and Doc at the helm, the Clippers had a real chance to come out of the West and win it all.

Only one situation could have convinced me to turn down Doc's offer, and that was the third opportunity I had in front of me. The Cleveland Cavaliers were looking to bring me in. After decades of going up against LeBron James, from our AAU rivalry of the Houston Hoops versus the Ohio Shooting Stars to series after series, year after year, in the NBA playoffs, I now had a chance to play beside him. He'd gone back to Cleveland with one thought in mind. He wanted to bring a championship to those long-suffering fans, fans who'd lived through "the fumble" and "the drive" and hundreds or thousands of other disappointments, large and small. After the Red Sox and the Cubs had finally vanquished their demons, the Cleveland curse was the last major sports curse left. LeBron was on a mission to break it. Ty Lue's presence on the coaching staff sealed it for me.

I arrived in Cleveland in March 2015 and found LeBron James at the peak of his game. This LeBron James, not the Miami version, was the most dominant basketball player in the history of the game. He was locked in like I'd never seen him, making even KG's intensity look mild.

It was an amazing experience for me to join LeBron and the Cavs for those months, primarily because I got to see for myself, up close, how LeBron worked. To say that LeBron was "locked in" or to use any other phrase like that can only be an understatement. He was beyond all sports language and postgame-interview cliché. LeBron's mission to win a championship brought a different type of energy to this team. It was a kind of tenacity I'd never felt before. There was a certain look in LeBron's eye during our run. It was as if he were staring out into the future, his gaze locked on the distant goal. Nothing could pull him from it. The desire to complete the mission brought out a kind of total commitment in LeBron of both mind and body.

For most of us, we can want something badly and still have no realistic shot at getting it. For LeBron James, as it was for Michael Jordan, the sheer power of the desire seemed to bring any possible outcome within reach.

On and off the court, LeBron led by example. If I'd get to the facility an hour early for a pre-practice workout, I'd find LeBron already finishing up his weight training and getting ready to start his second session.

If I'd get there two hours early, he'd still somehow beat me there. No matter how hard the rest of us worked, LeBron worked harder. His game, already outrageously good, seemed to be growing before our eyes.

In my first call with LeBron after I'd signed the deal, he'd said to me, "Welcome to the family." When I walked into the Cavs locker room for the first time, I was embraced by all the guys, including LeBron, Kyrie Irving, and Kevin Love. It was a close unit, and LeBron was in full leadership mode. The younger guys, Kyrie included, seemed genuinely happy to be learning from him and playing alongside him. During my time in Cleveland, there wasn't any tension between LeBron and Kyrie, and in general the rock-solid team dynamic was reminiscent of my Boston years.

I'd been friends with Bron for a long time before I joined the Cavs in 2015. After I got there, our relationship off the court went to another level. We were both married to our high school sweethearts and had kids. Our wives became close friends. He welcomed me with open arms into his house, where we'd watch and break down games together. It was an incredible experience to see how his mind took in and analyzed the game of basketball. There is probably not a single human being who has ever lived who understands the game better than LeBron James. This time with LeBron and the deepening of our friendship, more than anything else, was the best part of my stay in Cleveland. We realized we were kindred spirits. We shared a similar worldview about life, on and off the court.

On the court, the Cavs had depth in the paint with Timofey Mozgov and a young Tristan Thompson. I knew going into my time in Cleveland that game minutes would be hard to come by. Over the years in Boston and Oklahoma City, I'd grown used to starting and playing between twenty and thirty minutes a night. To adapt to my new role with the Cavs, I had to shift my mindset. It was a new and different role. I was brought in to be a mentor to the other big men on playing playoff-style basketball. I was brought in to be a veteran presence in the locker room during a long, grueling playoff run.

Having version 3.0 of LeBron was certainly a distinct advantage entering the postseason, but you have to remember that Kevin Love and Kyrie Irving hadn't yet played in a single playoff game.

When I lay it out like this for people to read, it makes it seem like the transition from being an NBA starting center to taking on a mentorship and leadership role was simple and easy. On some level it was, but it still required a tremendous amount of emotional and psychological wrestling with myself. It was hard to push down my pride and to accept the limits of where I was at. Nobody was going to feel sorry for me. I knew that right outside the locker room there was a long line of young, talented, hungry guys just waiting to grab one of these coveted 450 NBA roster spots.

I wasn't about to let my pride cost me mine. It took self-control and discipline, and I called on many of the lessons and strategies I'd taken with me from my stay in Kansas. To put it another way, reality was punching me in the face, and I could either engage in a fight I had no chance of winning, or I could embrace it and roll with The King on another title run. The choice to "turn the other cheek" was obvious, and once I made peace with it, I found pleasure and fulfillment in this new role.

Late in the season, Kevin Love went down with an injury that would keep him out for the playoffs. Even without him, we played our way out of the Eastern Conference and into the NBA Finals. We'd swept the Celtics in the first round. In the second round, we'd taken out Thibs and the Bulls in six. Then we destroyed the Atlanta Hawks in four games to win the conference. In that series, LeBron averaged over thirty points, eleven rebounds, and nine assists per game. As I said, during these years in Cleveland he was at the pinnacle of his powers.

In the NBA Finals, we ran into the Golden State Warriors. They were coming off an incredible regular season. They had the number one offense in the NBA, powered by the backcourt of Steph Curry and Klay Thompson. They had a rock-solid defense, anchored by Draymond Green. They'd rolled to the NBA Finals, dispatching the Houston Rockets in five games in the Western Conference Finals. This was the matchup the world had been waiting all year to see.

As I've said before, though from the perspective of the opposing huddle, when a team with LeBron James enters a seven-game series, it always feels like it has a chance to win it, no matter what the other variables might be. I think we had a pretty damn good shot at winning that series. In fact, I think we would have won it—maybe even in six—if Kyrie hadn't gotten injured in game one. Without Kyrie and Kevin Love, we didn't have enough offensive firepower to hang with the Warriors through a long series.

But before we jump too far ahead, consider this. After losing game one in overtime, we took game two in Oakland to tie it up and steal home-court advantage. LeBron led all scorers on both sides with thirty-nine points. He led all rebounders on both sides with sixteen boards. He led all players in assists (yes, on both sides) with eleven, which doubled the highest assist-getter on Golden State. He did it again in game three, this time pouring in forty points on his way to leading us to a win and a 2–1 series lead. This was as far as he could take us, however, and despite LeBron's absolutely monster performances in games five and six, we didn't win another game. The Warriors, with a 4–2 series victory, were NBA champions.

You can't tell me, though, that if we'd had Kyrie and Kevin the series wouldn't have at least gone seven. And you would have a very hard time convincing me that if we were fully loaded and LeBron was playing at the level he was playing, we would have lost a decisive showdown. But in the end, this is NBA basketball—results matter, not hypotheticals. The rest is for commentators and fans to chew on in the years to come.

I have to give it to the Warriors. They stayed in their game. They hit big shots, especially Andre Iguodala. Ty Lue had set our defensive game plan specifically to funnel the ball to Iguodala and to keep it out of Curry's and Thompson's hands. If we were going to go down, Lue thought, let Iguodala beat us. He did, and he won finals MVP for his performance.

If our run to the finals proved something beyond the toughness and talent of the Warriors and beyond LeBron's unreal will to win, it was that the man sitting next to Coach David Blatt needed to be elevated to the top job. I'm talking about Ty Lue. I have nothing against David Blatt, but he just wasn't ready. At crucial moments in the playoffs, he seemed to get nervous and couldn't figure out the right move. It was Ty Lue who was always stepping in to make the necessary adjustments.

The following year, the year I moved on to the Pelicans, Ty Lue and LeBron James—now with Kyrie healthy and balling—would come back from being down 3–1 to those same Warriors to win the NBA championship in seven games. This was one of the greatest accomplishments in sports history, and it is only now, years later, that Ty Lue is starting to get the recognition he deserves.

Fans and the media have caught on to the fact that Ty Lue is a brilliant game planner and makes fantastic in-series adjustments. His skill was on full display during the Clippers' 2021 playoff run to the Western Conference Finals without Kawhi Leonard. This has always been Ty Lue. He was doing the same work for us in 2015 as an assistant coach. When he took over the head coaching job the following year, I had no doubt he'd be great.

Part of coaching a championship-level team is being able to manage some of the world's largest egos. Ty Lue had learned this side of the business as a player. He'd played alongside Shaq and Kobe during the Lakers' championship runs in 2000 and 2001. He was on the Washington Wizards team when Michael Jordan returned to the game. In Orlando, he played with Tracy McGrady. In other words, Ty Lue saw greatness up close. He was also coached by some of the best in basketball, like Phil Jackson and Doc Rivers.

By the time he took over for David Blatt at the start of the 2015–2016 season, Ty Lue had assembled the pieces necessary to be one of the next generation's elite NBA head coaches. Yes, he could create excellent defensive schemes. Yes, he was a master at making adjustments. Most important, he knew what it took to build a team dynamic without alienating any individual player. In professional basketball, as in all high-level sports, these psychological dimensions shouldn't be underestimated. It's how Phil Jackson accomplished what he did. It's how Doc Rivers brought Boston its seventeenth title. It's how Ty Lue helped LeBron, Kyrie, and the rest of the Cavs vanquish the Cleveland curse.

The end of certain phases of our lives can be painful, these last years stretching out and often marred by disappointments and frustrations. After the finals against the Warriors, I signed a one-year deal with the New Orleans Pelicans. Pelican management was interested in me primarily to provide locker room leadership and mentorship to the franchise's young superstar, Anthony Davis. The opportunity to work with AD was exciting, and this aspect of the move didn't disappoint.

On the other hand, as I got set to head down to New Orleans, people were telling me to be careful about Dell Demps, the Pelicans' general manager. I didn't take it seriously at the time. In hindsight, I should have been listening very closely. The way Demps handled my situation was far below the level of professionalism I'd grown accustomed to in Boston and Oklahoma City with Danny Ainge and Sam Presti.

In general, the three organizations I'd played for before the Pelicans had treated me well. Most important from a player's perspective, the front offices had been straight with me. Of course, there are flaws in everything—that's natural—and all people make mistakes from time to time, but then there are guys who lie and work against a player's interests.

In my case, I learned that midway through the 2015–2016 season both the Cavs and the Thunder were looking to deal for me as they got ready to make their playoff runs. The opportunity for me in either direction was fantastic. In Cleveland, I would have again joined Bron and Kyrie in their successful quest for the championship. In Oklahoma City, I would have been a part of the last year of the Russ-and-KD era. Either way, it was a dream scenario. The only reason to stay in New Orleans, and the only reason for the organization not to deal me, would have been if they wanted to keep me around on another contract for the following year or two.

I went to meet with Demps to discuss the options on the table. He assured me that management and ownership were committed to me. He said they wanted me to end my career as a Pelican, and that they were intending to offer me a two-year deal at the end of the season. Unwisely, I took Dell at his word, not knowing, despite the advice I'd been given, that his word was worthless.

No trade went through, and I waited all summer long for Dell to call me with news of the new contract. No call came. Finally, only weeks before training camp, he called and told me that he was "moving in a different direction." He said he'd been wanting to reach out to me for a while, but he'd been "too busy." By this time, free agency was for all intents and purposes over and most NBA rosters were full. I was left blowing in the wind.

When I was playing, I can remember former players coming around and telling us to enjoy every moment of the game because you never know when it's going to end. They said the end comes quickly, and it catches most guys unprepared. They said you never know when it'll be the last time you take the court. I would always blow off this kind of talk. I had a lot left, I'd tell myself; at the very least I had a couple more solid years, and for a while I was right, but then at some point I was wrong.

I could feel the changes happening around me—the changes in the game, the style of play; the changes in my body—but I couldn't quite make myself believe them. Then it happened, just as those older guys had warned it would. My agent started striking out in his entreaties to teams. My phone stopped ringing. It was over—but I couldn't admit it.

I picked up the phone myself when my agent couldn't bring me anything and started to make calls to my guys around the league. Nothing worked, and the first NBA season in thirteen years rolled by without Big Perk. As the following season approached, it looked like I would get the final spot on the Cavs bench, but then they made a deal for Dwyane Wade and the opportunity closed. Ty Lue convinced me to do a stint for the Cavs' G League affiliate, the Canton Charge, to stay in shape and ready, so that he could call me up as soon as he had the chance. What choice did I have?

PURGATORY

If there's such a thing as purgatory in the basketball universe, it has got to be the NBA G League. Every soul there is looking for his ticket to heaven; almost everyone is going in the opposite direction. Moving down to the G League was the hardest thing I ever had to do in my basketball career. It was humbling—but again, like so many times in my career, I was able to put destructive pride aside and do what was best for my career. At the time, what was best for me was to stay in shape and be ready for another shot at an NBA roster.

A transition from the NBA to the G League is jarring, but at the same time people might not realize just how good the G League is. The guys who are playing there have enormous talent, and they are some of the hardest-working players in the basketball world. The Canton Charge's coaching staff—Nate Reinking, Sam Jones, Melvin Ely—knew the game inside and out.

While people in the NBA talk about careers in years, the guys in the Canton locker room would have given anything for a ten-day NBA contract, for just a single chance to prove themselves. They were young and hungry. I remember one time when we were playing a game in the Cavs' arena while they were on a road trip. The Charge players were ecstatic just to be in an NBA locker room—taking selfies, posting on social media, in awe of the glimmers of NBA life.

The visit to the Cavs' arena was a stark contrast to the everyday realities of G League life. Our practice facility was a neighborhood church, where we were just one of the organizations with a set practice time. We'd be out there practicing, and I'd be looking through the windows into the little fitness center next to the court where twenty grannies were busy doing yoga. We'd need to vacate the court when our allotted time was up to make way for the eleven-and-under schoolkids filing onto the court after the final-period bell.

The travel conditions to and from games certainly weren't anything like NBA travel. It was a series of six- or twelve-hour bus rides and budget flights that seemed to take ten hours to get from Canton to Fort Wayne, Indiana, to face off against the Fort Wayne Mad Ants. One time, we traveled down to Florida. We left at five in the morning and arrived at seven at night. Then there was the utterly miserable Maine hotel the team had booked for us. It was the only time I couldn't take it and went and found myself a proper place to stay. At all other times, I wanted to stick with the team. Whether that meant being cramped up in coach or staying at the roadside dive motel, I did it.

The G League might have been humbling, but I have to say it was an amazing experience to play there for a few months. It taught me a lot about how the basketball world works, how to think about and cherish the memories of my time in the NBA. I made some great friends. Guys looked to me for advice and called on me for support. People might not realize this, but many players in the G League could go overseas and make ten times the money. They stay in the league because it gives them the best shot at getting called up to the NBA. It's a league of dreamers, and for that reason alone, you gotta love it.

On the last day of the regular season, the Cavs called me up for their playoff run. It would be my final NBA contract, though at the time I wouldn't have believed that. The Cavs had won the Eastern Conference the year before, and we made it back to the finals again in 2018, this time without Kyrie Irving, who'd been traded to the Celtics.

We needed seven games to get through both Indiana and Boston on our way to another face-off against the Golden State Warriors. Minus Kyrie, and with KD in his second season with the Warriors, the cliff was too steep. We battled in game one, pushing it to overtime, but the combined power of KD, Steph, Klay Thompson, and the rest of that crew was way too much. They swept the series.

I knew in my heart that this run, my fifth trip to the NBA Finals, was my curtain call. For the first time since I can remember, I was facing the reality of a life without basketball.

"Without basketball"—it sounds simple. It was anything but simple. Losing basketball was losing my entire way of life. It was losing a culture, a family, an energy and intensity, a routine, a status, and an identity.

I wasn't angry about it. There was no bitterness. I knew the game had given me everything it had to give, and it had given me more than I would have dreamed. I didn't hold anyone else responsible. I didn't even hold myself responsible. I'd stayed in shape and had done everything I could think of doing to keep it going. What I was feeling wasn't anger or regret—it was depression.

I could feel the depression creeping in on me as time went by. It was getting worse day by day, as my life's structure started to fray and crumble. Then, suddenly, it was bad. If before I had been obsessed with the daily basketball highlights on *SportsCenter*, now I couldn't bear to watch any sports at all. If the kids had on a game or highlights, I couldn't handle it and made them switch the channel. I refused to leave the house, and at home I couldn't get myself to do anything. In the morning, I'd get out of bed and move to the sofa. Then I wouldn't move again for the rest of the day.

My relationship with Vanity was getting strained. She wasn't used to me being around the house all the time doing nothing, and I wasn't used to it either. At first she thought I was being lazy, and I didn't have it in me to open up and explain to her what was really going on.

Over the years in the NBA, I'd missed out on so much with the kids, and now that I had all the time in the world, I wasn't able to appreciate it. I couldn't be with them in the moment.

My body was transitioning to life beyond the grueling regime of a professional sports career. People might not realize how difficult the physical transition from playing professional sports to retirement can be. The injuries that a player endures over the course of a long career leave scars, and the damage that's done to knees, elbows, ankles, wrists, fingers, feet, and shoulders can't be undone. Once the body falls out of shape, it's hard to stop the spiral, especially when depression presses down on the mind.

In the year after I retired, I gained close to two hundred pounds, putting my health and life at serious risk. This was my present, and under these circumstances, after having lived the game of basketball for the previous quarter of a century, from youth basketball to the NBA, it was impossible to imagine a future. The future wasn't cloudy—it was as dark as night.

When life shatters, how do we put the pieces back together? I wish there was an easy answer to this question. There isn't, as many people in our society know from firsthand experience. Depression is serious business.

DAWN

As my NBA career was winding down, my two older boys, Ken and Stone, had started playing youth basketball. Even though I was struggling with depression, it was a relief to go and watch their games. It connected me to basketball in a new way—as a parent and fan. At first, I was doing the typical "coaching" from the sidelines—you can imagine how that went. Then it occurred to me that the people organizing the kids' AAU program had a huge amount going on. I went to see if they'd have any interest in letting me coach one of the teams. They were glad to have the help, and soon I was coaching Stone's squad.

They were an amazing group of kids. They worked hard. They were there to have fun, and they played the game the right way, meaning playing as a team. No matter what I was going through before or after practice, it was impossible to be depressed while working with those kids.

After my NBA career ended, my kids and the kids on my team brought me back to my youth and my pure love for the game of basketball. I found new energy in the time spent coaching my team. I loved how hungry the kids were to learn the game. They listened to what I was telling them and soaked in the knowledge. They responded on the court by executing the lessons they were learning—and they had a great time doing it. For me, making connections with the kids was the best feeling in the world.

In this way, I started to feel rejuvenated. My attention was pulled away from my own issues. It was better spent trying to nourish others.

It was during these months that I came back to an idea I'd flirted with for the previous couple of seasons—that after all was said and done with my playing career, I'd try to become the next Big Man head coach of an NBA team. With Steve Kerr and Steve Nash, with Doc and Ty Lue, we have plenty of former point guards at the head of the bench. It was time for a player to pick up the torch first lit by the ultimate Big Man,

Bill Russell, and to carry it forward into this new era. I was starting to feel ready for what would come next in my life.

Organizations around the league already knew I was a great locker room guy and had the leadership skills to be an NBA coach at some level. I wanted to let everyone know I also had the knowledge of the game to do the job. I took to my social media accounts in a serious way and started to post responses to what I was seeing in games. I was breaking down plays and situations, just generally giving my takes on issues that were showing up on the court. It felt good to share the perspective I'd developed over a long NBA career.

After some time, my phone started to ring again. The calls weren't from teams looking to bring me in to play on the low block. In the past, there had been calls about playing overseas, but I'd made it clear I wasn't interested, and so they had stopped. Now when I picked up the phone, I was surprised to find producers from ESPN, FOX Sports, and other media outlets on the line. "Hey, Perk," they were telling me, "we're loving what you're doing on social media. Do you want to come in and give some takes on television or radio?"

"Hell, yeah, I do."

And with that response, hardly realizing what I was stepping into, a media career was born.

Just a Country Boy from the 409: The Making of a Media Career

FINDING A VOICE

ON APRIL 19, 2019, I JOINED ADRIAN WOJNAROWSKI ON *THE WOJ POD*, **ONE OF THE BEST** NBA podcasts in the industry. It was the perfect place, with a journalist I respected, to make an announcement that was deeply personal and meaningful to me but hardly noticed by anyone else at the time: I was retiring from the game of basketball.

Whether we admit it or not, every player wants a final moment with fans showing their appreciation of what we brought to the game. Few get such a dream farewell. These ceremonies and retirement tours are reserved for greats like Kobe Bryant, Dr. J, Larry Bird, and Kareem Abdul-Jabbar.

As I was making my final push to join an organization for one last playoff run, one final opportunity to impact the locker room of a team that needed leadership, one last chance to go out on my terms, I turned to the Boston Celtics. I got in touch with Danny Ainge, and it seemed like something might be available for me to join the team. In late March 2019, Danny reached out and informed me that though he loved me, I wasn't the right fit.

My emotions were mixed. I knew the value I'd bring as a veteran presence to that squad. At the same time, I felt like I had left it all on the table, knocked on every door, and that Danny, who gave me my first shot and had changed my life, had now let me know that it was time to move on. This calmed me and gave me a sense of closure.

The Woj Pod was both my curtain call and, unknowingly, the beginning of the next phase in my life. I turned my focus to building up my profile as a potential NBA coaching candidate, hoping to find myself a good role as an assistant coach as a stepping-stone to a future head coaching opportunity. My thought process was straightforward: I would get my name out there by using my social media and by doing shows like Woj's podcast.

What I didn't expect going into my session with Woj was how much I'd enjoy talking publicly about my experiences and about the state of basketball. I'd been living and breathing the game for decades by then, and I was talking so much basketball at home at the time that I could sense Vanity was about to lose it and throw me out of the house. But the time with Woj was different. It made me realize something that's so obvious and yet hard for many of us to grasp: *I had a voice.* For a shy boy from the Pear Orchard, this was a major discovery.

After my appearance on *The Woj Pod*, as I was trying to get my name out there, the media kept on calling. I agreed with Rich Gray that he should book me with anyone who offered to have me on. He did just that.

It began with a spot here or there, on television or radio, but it wasn't long before Rich was building packed schedules for me, at times up to twenty shows per day. If one radio station wanted me from 3:15 to 3:30, Rich would have another one lined up from 3:45 to 4, and so on throughout the morning and afternoon.

Then the bigger shows started dialing up Rich—*The Jump* with Rachel Nichols, *First Take* with Steven A., *The Undisputed* with Skip Bayless and Shannon Sharpe. On some days, I'd move from doing a segment on

ESPN's *First Take* with its millions of viewers to joining an independent podcast with a couple hundred listeners. It was a whirlwind, a kind of trial by fire, and I was soaking it in, learning, testing things out, and unwittingly moving toward a new life.

In the meantime, I kept my fingers busy typing out tweets. Twitter became more than a platform for me—it was a pulse. I read every reply to my bold but honest takes, and if people disagreed, I would address them like the numbers on a house. As KG would say, whether the news was full of love or hate, as players we had to absorb it. The difference now was that my naysayers and critics got to feel me live and direct.

I looked at it like practice. Rebutting random people in my Twitter comments got me the reps I needed to deal with the likes of Stephen A. Smith and Max Kellerman, two formidable, if very different, debating opponents. By the time I made it on *First Take*, there wasn't an argument or point of view I wasn't prepared to handle. Like in my playing days, if I went hard enough in practice, on game day I'd be ready.

My followers know the deal. My tweets, like a wing dinner, come in many sizes and flavors—from sweet and savory to *extra spicy*. Welcome to *MasterPerk Theater*:

When it's all said and done, when Giannis' career is over I strongly believe he will be the No. 2 power forward of all time, behind Tim Duncan! Carry the hell on . . .

Don't feed every dog that you see suffering—some just need strength to bite you! Carry on . . .

Just took me 47 minutes to put a damn visor on my son's football helmet. That can't be normal, right?! God Bless America.

What Jayson Tatum did tonight is what SUPERSTARS are supposed to do when other greats come into your house!!! He went toe-to-toe with Steph and protected his crib in great fashion with a 44-piece spicy and 10 biscuits with the W! Carry the hell on . . .

Like I said, Julius Randle is on the MVP CONVERSATION. He put a casual 40-piece wing dinner Lemon Pepper style with 11 rebounds and 6 assists with W! Btw the Knicks are currently on an 8-game winning streak! Carry the hell on . . .

If you know how quickly people forget the Dead . . . you will stop living to impress people!

Steph Curry will hit 100s by the end of this month! One thing I've learned is to never go against that Sniper. Carry on . . .

LaMelo Ball just threw the best full-court pass I've seen in the last 10 years!

No disrespect to the NFL but it's way harder to win an NBA Championship than it is to win an NFL Super Bowl!!! IMHO and don't @ me.

You are not required to set yourself on fire to keep other people warm.

Don't let nothing slide . . . that's how a leak turns into a flood! Carry on . . .

New York Stand Up, Spike Lee and @stephenASmith drinking Moonshine together chanting Orange and Blue Skies but it's about to get Cloudy for the Knicks in the first round! Hawks in 6 carry the hell on . . .

Can anybody explain to me what the hell is going on with Porzingis?

Just know when you're thriving upwards it's going to be the ones you least expect that's going to be praying on your downfall! I came into the media world and did it my way with no handout or favors just straight grind. I'm going to keep SHINING for you HATERS! Carry on . . .

After more than a year of being a guest on every media outlet imaginable—without once being paid anything beyond travel and accommodation costs—Fox Sports and ESPN came to the table with nonexclusive contracts for my services. I have to be honest: I was feeling myself a little and thought I deserved more. For the first time, I even went against my own philosophy: *Never turn down some fasho to get some mo.* In other words, I'm a firm believer in taking what's available, especially if the offer is reasonable.

But this time around, the situation felt different. Like one does in the NBA, I started looking at my peers in the media and what they were being paid and what they brought to the table as a measuring stick for myself. After our title run in 2007–2008, I needed to ask myself what a starting center and a defensive anchor for a championship team deserves in his next contract. It meant I had to turn down Danny's offer and accept the consequences: a trade to OKC. In the media world, I was being slotted as a young star with superstar potential. My Beaumont roots made me a humble grinder, but once that grind creates results, you want the lettuce that comes with it. I turned down both offers.

When it rains, it pours. At the same time the offers came in from ESPN and Fox Sports, my strategy of using the media to promote my coaching profile began to bear fruit. Murmurs were reaching me that Danny wanted to bring me onto the Celtics' staff. An offer came from Minnesota head coach Ryan Saunders to be an assistant coach for the Timberwolves.

It was a lot to process. Would I go back into the NBA lifestyle, which would take me away from my wife and kids for long stretches? Would I return to the safe, familiar environment of an NBA franchise and locker room—a space I knew inside and out? Or would I move into unknown territory, taking the big risk of starting an entirely new career?

It was a hard decision, and I had to lean on instinct and my gut feeling. My instinct was telling me that I had only scratched the surface of my potential in the media. And I was absolutely loving it. I didn't want to stop. It was the riskier direction, but I had to try. Again, as I did when I went to the league directly out of high school, I was betting that I'd be able to overcome obstacles to make it and thrive in a new professional environment.

Rich and I went to work, and the result of our negotiations was that ESPN offered me my first full-time, exclusive media contract. ESPN is the big stage—lights, camera, action. After I added my Southern flavor and charisma to a little-known Twitter show called *Hoop Streams*, we attracted massive streaming numbers, which led to major sponsorship dollars. I knew I was a big part of that. ESPN's initial offer didn't match this new profile, but one thing I learned early in this business is that you don't get what you deserve, you get what you have the leverage to negotiate. And suddenly, I had a lot of leverage. We inked the deal.

Doc Rivers had told me that if I worked hard and became a star in my role, I would have a long NBA career. I reflected on this advice again as I started my job as a full-time NBA analyst at ESPN. I had a thought: what if my role this time around wasn't to be a "screen-setting" and defensive enforcer? What if my role now, in my second act, was to take the big shot, to be a star?

Despite the confidence boost that came with ESPN's offer, I knew I had a lot to learn if I wanted to succeed at the highest level. Thankfully, other analysts were there to help me, especially Marcus "Big Swagu" Spears and Jay Williams. The professional journalists and show producers at ESPN were a huge help as I worked to improve and refine my on-air approach. Producers Steve Martinez, Antoine Lewis, Hilary Guy, Max Brodsky, and Mike Goldfarb were instrumental in my growth.

It was important to me to stay true to who I was, to my voice, but at the same time to always strive to be better. There are people who get into the media space, look around, and try to imitate what others are doing—to be the next Stephen A. or something like that. They might look and sound "normal," but there are intangible things lost in this desire to conform. That wasn't my approach. My idea was to do every-thing I could to allow my perspective and character to come through—to continue to be Big Perk no matter what was going on around me.

BUILDING A PROCESS

There's one thing I knew for sure. I wanted what I said in the media about the game of basketball or anything else to be based on a solid founda-tion of facts or well-considered opinion. As when I was an NBA player, I needed to build a process to get myself ready day in and day out, to be in "game shape" for my work in the media.

My media "day" began the night before. I would be up late watch-ing games and sharing some quick takes on social media. After the games ended, I'd review the questions and issues the producers had sent around and would start building what I wanted to talk about the next day. Around midnight, I'd get on the phone with Rich to let him know what I was thinking. He'd point out things to think about, or he'd offer a different perspective on an issue for me to consider.

In the morning, after I'd slept on it, Rich and I would talk again around 6:30. I'd run through the takes I was preparing, and he'd give me a last round of suggestions. I'd make final adjustments, and then it was showtime. I'd move from *Get Up!* with Mike Greenberg to the spectacle of verbal combat that is *First Take* with Stephen A. Smith to the more basketball-focused *The Jump*, where I joined some of the best people in the industry, including the Robin to my Batman, Richard Jefferson.

When the topics were centered on basketball, I was in my comfort zone. As Vanity knows better than anyone, I can talk the game of bas-ketball all day and night. But this was 2020, and issues in sports media that year traveled far from the court and into social, political, and cul-ture territory. This was a challenge, one I embraced. As with my takes on the game, I wanted to speak from the heart, with my voice, and at the same time to learn and grow, to educate myself, so that to the best of my ability I was speaking truth.

Some former NBA guys think they can walk into the media space and get by on their deep knowledge of the game without doing the preparation necessary to successfully bring that expertise into that space. It doesn't work like that, and the people who aren't putting in the work usually don't last long. Just like basketball, the media at its highest level isn't a world of amateurs. Professional sports journalists are driven, competitive, and know their stuff. They've spent decades around the game, honing their craft. I'm thinking about people like Michael Wilbon, Jackie MacMullan, Zach Lowe, and Brian Windhorst. It's true, they don't know the nuances of NBA basketball as well as former players, but they come into the studio every day prepared to give their take and armed with the necessary information to back up their points of view.

I know that many of the media folks on that side of the line didn't respect me at first, or they thought I was in above my head. They looked down on my command of the English language, with their broadcasting and English degrees from some of the top colleges and universities in the country. They laughed at my country wisdoms. That's okay—I had to earn my place. I had to show them that I could be me, Big Perk, and at the same time be successful with my approach. Again, as had been the case so often in my basketball career, I was able to listen to the right people, learn, and adapt quickly to shifting circumstances.

MEDIA AND THE NBA BROTHERHOOD

The pressure put on former players by the media establishment is nothing compared to the counterpressure we face from our loyalty to members of our NBA brotherhood. As NBA guys, we adhere to a certain code.

We watch each other's back. We don't rat each other out to the media. We don't do anything to undermine someone else's career or success. However much we go after each other on the court, off the court we stick together.

The role of sports analysts and media personalities is much different. Their role is to entertain an audience and to provide analysis and commentary on the sport of basketball. It can be tough, emotionally and psychologically, to switch from one mentality to the other. If a former player shifts too far, too fast, he can end up betraying confidences and abusing his platform. The key is to find the sweet spot where you can speak the truth about basketball but not use personal relationships and friendships to score cheap points in the daily battle for the best or "hottest" take.

When I first started out, I wanted to address these issues directly and would reach out to players and give them a heads-up if there were topics concerning them. I would be sure to ask if they had additional perspective or context. Eventually, though, I had to go away from that method because it was limiting my ability to speak out on important issues. I had to put my new occupation first. I had to be, first and foremost, an NBA analyst—albeit one with deep loyalties to the guys in the league. In this respect, I think I've mostly found the right balance. That's not to say I haven't had difficult moments when I've drawn fire from players in the league. I welcome it, and it's great to see that players have the power and the means to push back against the media to define and narrate their stories. Giannis Antetokounmpo did just that through his play on the court in the 2021 playoffs. After game six of the finals, with his team victorious, Giannis seemed to relish the moment as he took the microphone. For the first time in years, his critics in the media, including, or *especially*, Big Perk, had to shut the hell up and listen to what this man had to say. It was inspiring.

The hardest moment for me in the first days of my media career was when Kevin Durant, my former teammate and good friend, my brother, called me a "sellout." KD made the statement in response to my criticism of his Brooklyn Nets teammate Kyrie Irving. The broader issue surrounding my comments had to do with whether NBA players would agree to the league's plan to restart the 2020 season in the Bubble in Orlando, Florida. The players met, discussed, and decided as a body that they would support the restart under the conditions outlined in the commissioner's plan. Kyrie, at that point, had also agreed to the terms.

If the players had rejected the deal for whatever reason, I would have had their backs. Later on, Kyrie came out against the players' decision and tried to rally others to his side, outside of the normal channels of the players' collective decision-making. For me, as a former player, I had no problem with Kyrie's individual or personal stance against the restart, but I didn't think it was right to go against the process in place that was meant to give the players voice and power in negotiations with the league. Undermining the unity of the players' association, in my opinion, was a bad move in both the short and long term. I said so publicly.

"Sellout"—this was a harsh word, especially in the context of the escalation of protests and racial tensions in the spring and summer of 2020. At a time when Black Americans needed to come together like never before to unite in the fight for social justice and to hold back the wave of white supremacy that threatened our communities, I found any implication that I was somehow working against the interests of my people to be out of bounds. I've always lived my life close to my community, close to my people. This has been true from my childhood in Beaumont to my days in Boston and Oklahoma City. It is true today.

Still, it wasn't really the message that bothered me. Ignorant people say ignorant and stupid things all the time, and if a person wants to be in the media business, that person needs a damn thick skin. The issue here was that the messenger wasn't ignorant or stupid—he was a close friend and brother, a brother I'd gone to battle with for four years in OKC. Whatever he meant by calling me a "sellout," KD should have known better.

I reacted to KD's words the following day on *First Take*. I felt like I needed to speak from the heart. My words were no longer about the original issue: Kyrie's decision to oppose the restart. This was now about me and KD and the meaning of our relationship. I made a public appeal for KD to remember the depth of our friendship, hoping that the weight of what we had in the past would be enough for us to carry on as friends, even if we disagreed about what Kyrie Irving was doing.

The appeal failed. The result was a prolonged and painfully public social media battle that didn't do either of us any good. It was a stark lesson that words—my words and KD's words—matter, especially when those words come from members of the media with big platforms or from celebrities whose social media accounts reach millions or even tens of millions of people.

If I had it to do over again, I would do it differently—stay true to my opinion about what Kyrie was doing without jeopardizing my brotherhood with KD. This bond was the deeper truth for me, one that got clouded by the pressures of the moment and the demands of instant culture. For myself, I know that staying true to myself in the world of the fast-paced corporate media requires constant work and focus, constant recentering, especially since various temptations—fame, ambition, pride, money—are always there to entice us down sinful paths.

FACING THE CAMERA

I write this at the beginning of my time in the media. I came into the media after a long career as an NBA role player. I will never be a Hall of Famer. I wasn't an All-Star a single time—and got close only once, in

THE EDUCATION OF KENDRICK PERKINS

2008, when I fell one vote short. The star power of guys like Shaquille O'Neal, Dwyane Wade, and Charles Barkley is not available to me.

That's not to say I haven't learned a lot from them, especially from Barkley. Charles has done a masterful job developing his unique blend of authenticity, charisma, personality, and delivery. His voice and style seem to come naturally. He might often be wrong in the substance of what he's saying, but he is never boring—and I don't know a single person who tunes into *Inside the NBA* on TNT with Chuck, Shaq, Ernie, and Kenny Smith and ends up changing the channel. Those guys are at the summit of the NBA media mountain. I'm climbing my way up, following Barkley's path. I hope that by doing so, I will contribute to making the path wider for other role players and non–All-Stars to make the same transition.

The longer I work in the media, the more important it is to me to remain true to who I am. It is important for the quality of the entertainment. It's what makes us want to listen to Marcus Spears talk football or Barkley, Shaq, Ernie, and Kenny break down the NBA. At the same time, staying true to oneself has an important social function that goes far beyond sports. Former players who are staying true to themselves aren't getting caught up in the game of chasing ratings and profit if it means they would have to mimic the ways certain politicians and talk show hosts pander to the worst instincts in our society.

As former athletes, as Black men and women, we know better than that. We know better because we grew up in our Black communities throughout this country and have a deep and personal understanding of what's happening there. We see this reality every single day, no matter how rich and famous many of us have become. The reality stares back at us from the eyes of family and friends. The truth glimmers in my grandmother's eyes, just as it does in the eyes of my young twins, Zoey and Karter.

We know better than to appeal to hate and intolerance, because we spent our careers in locker rooms with guys of all different backgrounds, some of whom came from distant parts of the world, many, like Serge Ibaka and Giannis Antetokounmpo, who've overcome incredible hardships. Our teams depended on our ability and willingness to break down boundaries and build bridges.

We know better, finally, because we understand there are better ways of getting attention and drawing an audience. On the basketball court, we earn attention through the quality of our play. The better the team, the more precise and artistic the basketball, the more fans will flock to arenas and television sets around the country and the world. The same lesson applies to the media. The truth of our voice, the authenticity of our character, and our willingness to break down barriers and build bridges will prove to be the better way. I have no doubt about it.

As it says in Psalms 15, he who "in his heart acknowledges the truth," that man "shall never be shaken."

You know what's coming . . . Carry on!

Acknowledgments

To my friends, teammates, coaches, and colleagues, thank you for blessing me with your wisdom, without which this book could not have been written. This book would not have come together without the tireless efforts of my coauthor, Seth Rogoff. Seth and I were lucky to collaborate with the fantastic editor George Witte at St. Martin's Press. From the beginning, George worked to support and enhance our vision of a new type of sports book. Huge thanks to the team at St. Martin's: Joseph Rinaldi, Martin Quinn, Mac Nicholas, Tom Thompson, Laura Clark, and Brigitte Dale. Special thanks to Tom Cherwin for his excellent copyediting.

Seth and I would like to extend our gratitude to Hasan Kwame Jeffries for talking through many key historical issues. Hasan is one of the best scholars of Black history working today. Professor Judith Linsley is a specialist in the history of Beaumont, Texas, at Lamar University. Thank you, Judy. Your knowledge helped us discover the deeper history of my hometown. We would like to thank Duncan Whitmire for his feedback on early drafts of our chapters.

Rich Gray. Rich has been my advisor in countless ways over the past few years, since I retired from the NBA and embarked on a new career in the media. Rich was especially dedicated to this book. He worked closely with me and Seth at all stages. We cannot thank Rich enough for his work.

Special thanks to our literary agent, Tim Wojcik. His support from proposal to publication was unwavering.